William Jones

Memoirs of the life, studies, and writings of the Right Reverend George Horne, D.D. late Lord Bishop of Norwich.

With I. A new Preface, on certain interesting points in theology and philosophy; II. Dr. Horne's own collection of his thoughts on a vari

William Jones

Memoirs of the life, studies, and writings of the Right Reverend George Horne, D.D. late Lord Bishop of Norwich.

With I. A new Preface, on certain interesting points in theology and philosophy; II. Dr. Horne's own collection of his thoughts on a vari

ISBN/EAN: 9783337724450

Printed in Europe, USA, Canada, Australia, Japan

Cover: Foto ©ninafisch / pixelio.de

More available books at **www.hansebooks.com**

MEMOIRS

OF THE

LIFE, STUDIES, AND WRITINGS

OF

THE RIGHT REVEREND

GEORGE HORNE, D. D.

LATE LORD BISHOP OF NORWICH.

WITH

I. A NEW PREFACE, on certain interesting Points in THEOLOGY and PHILOSOPHY;

II. DR. HORNE's own COLLECTION of his THOUGHTS on a Variety of great and interesting SUBJECTS; and

III. A LETTER to the Hon. L. K. on the Use of the HEBREW LANGUAGE.

BY

WILLIAM JONES, M.A. F.R.S.

ONE OF HIS LORDSHIP'S CHAPLAINS.

THE SECOND EDITION.

LONDON:

PRINTED BY J. DAVIS, CHANCERY-LANE;

FOR G. G. AND J. ROBINSON, F. AND C. RIVINGTON, T. CADELL jun. W. DAVIS, AND J. HATCHARD; J. COOKE, OXFORD; AND W. KEYMER jun. COLCHESTER.

1799.

CONTENTS.

Dean

CONTENTS.

PREFACE

TO THE

SECOND EDITION *of* MEMOIRS *of the* LIFE *of* BISHOP HORNE, &c.

1799.

[*N. B. To be sold separately to the Purchasers of the First Edition.*]

IN publishing the Memoirs of the Life of Bishop Horne, my intention was only to give a true idea of that good man, as it presented itself to my memory and affections; and to produce an edifying book, rather than a formal history. I flatter myself it has done some good; and I hope it may do more. If any offence has been given, I can only say it was no part of my plan: but it is a common fault with plain Christians, who know little of the world, to tell more truth than is wanted; and they have nothing left but a good conscience, to support them under the mistake.

Some few exceptions have been made to the performance by little cavillers, which are not worth mentioning: but I brought myself into the most serious difficulty of all, by representing Bishop Horne as an *Hutchinsonian*; which thing (it seems) ought not to have been done; as it was strongly suggested to me, from the late learned *Doctor Farmer*, while my work was in hand. On this matter I beg leave to explain myself a little. I never said, nor did I ever think, that Bishop Horne owed every thing to *Hutchinson*, or was his implicit follower. I knew the contrary: but this I will say, because I know it to be true, that he owed to him the *beginning* of his extensive knowlege; for such a beginning as he made placed him on a new spot of high ground; from which he took all his prospects of religion and learning; and saw that whole road lying before him, which he afterwards pursued, with so much pleasure to himself, and benefit to the world. This declaration, however clear it may be to me, is more than some of my readers will be willing to admit, or able to bear. I perceive, by what has been written, that, if it can be effected, Bishop Horne must be taken away from the Hutchinsonians: or, if that cannot be done, his character must not be *set too high*; we must beware of *exaggeration*; he must be represented as *good* and *pious*, rather than *wise*

or

or *great.* This comes not from the *truth*, but from the *times*: and it is what we muſt expect to hear, till the times ſhall alter, and a few ſtumbling-blocks ſhall be removed out of the way. After what I had related, with ſo little diſguiſe, concerning the early ſtudies of Doctor Horne, I could foreſee that his character, excellent as it is, had a fiery trial to paſs: I therefore prepared myſelf to ſee—what I have ſeen.

But, while I heard ſome things which were unpleaſant, I heard others, which gave me encouragement. For, though it was commonly reported, that I had beſtowed too many words upon a cauſe, which neither required nor deſerved them, one of the wiſeſt men of this age, who is an hoſt of himſelf, wiſhed I had ſaid more; it being a cauſe of which the world *heard* much, but *knew* little, and *wanted* to know more. I ſhall take this opportunity of ſatisfying their curioſity as faithfully as I can.

But I find myſelf called upon, by the way, to juſtify the Biſhop againſt an unexpected accuſation of a late author; who charges him with *fancifulneſs* and *preſumption*: for what reaſon, and with how much juſtice, learning, and judgment, we ſhall ſee preſently: and I am glad this ſecond edition was deferred, becauſe the delay has given me an opportunity of ſeeing ſome things, of which I ought not to be ignorant.

In a *New Biographical Dictionary*, a life of Doctor Horne is inſerted; the author of which ſpeaks of him with as much caution, as a man would handle hot coals. For what he is pleaſed to ſay of *me*, as a writer of Doctor Horne's life, I am much obliged to him; and I think it more than I deſerve or deſire: but, I ſhould be falſe to the Biſhop's memory, were I to allow his account of *him* to be either juſt or true. He gives him the praiſe of being a *blameleſs* man! (cold enough!) when they, that have eyes to ſee, and judgment to diſcern, muſt diſcover him to be, both for matter and manner, one of the firſt orators and teachers this church can boaſt; and that he often diſplays a rich vein of wit, rarely indeed to be found in a man of ſo much ſweetneſs and good temper. What a poor figure does *Prieſtley* make in the hands of the *Undergraduate!* And the great philoſopher, *Hume*, in the letter to Doctor Adam Smith! Where the Biſhop is reflected upon, for being an *Hutchinſonian*, it is allowed, nevertheleſs, that he might be partly right in his natural philo-

ſophy;

ſophy; though I do not underſtand the biographer's method of making it out; and I queſtion whether he underſtood it himſelf. But then it is added, that "if he proceeded to "a ſuppoſed analogy between material and "immaterial things, and compared the agency "of the Son and Holy Ghoſt to that of light "and air in the natural world; it will ſurely "be thought, that he went upon very uncer-"tain and fanciful, not to ſay, preſumptuous "grounds." I thank him for ſpeaking out. But is this true divinity? Is there then no analogy between things natural and divine? And have I been beating the air, and writing a volume, to prove and explain it, and demonſtrate the great uſe and value of it; and has this author diſcovered at laſt, that there is no ſuch thing? How mortifying is it to me to hear, that ſo much of the labour of my life has been thrown away! This analogy, which he will not ſuffer Biſhop Horne to *ſuppoſe*, without being *fanciful* and *preſumptuous*, has been admitted and inſiſted upon, as plain and certain, by the beſt Divines of the Chriſtian Church; who uſed it, and admired it, becauſe they found it in the word of God: and it holds particularly in the two great objects of

 nature,

nature, *air* and *light*, where this *modern* divine, (for ſuch I ſuppoſe him) cannot ſee it himſelf, and will not permit us to ſee it without him. Was not the preſence of the Divine Spirit, on the day of Pentecoſt, announced to the ſenſes of men by the *ſound of a ruſhing, mighty wind?* Did not our Saviour, in his diſcourſe with Nicodemus, illuſtrate the agency of the Divine Spirit by that of the natural? *The wind bloweth where it liſteth, and thou heareſt the ſound thereof, but canſt not tell whence it cometh and whither it goeth: ſo is every one that is born of the Spirit.* Why did he communicate the Holy Ghoſt under the outward ſign of *breathing* upon them, if no compariſon is to be made between the ſign and the thing ſignified? The word *inſpiration*, which is the act of the Holy Ghoſt, denotes a blowing or breathing as of the air; and the name *Spirit* is common to the natural air and to the Holy Ghoſt. What is the meaning of all this? Does the word of God make compariſons, and put one thing for another; and ſhall we ſay, there is no analogy or likeneſs; that is, no ſenſe nor propriety in the ſubſtitution? That would indeed be preſumptuous, if not blaſphemous: and the author would not have entangled himſelf in this

manner,

manner, if he had not been frightened out of his wits at *Hutchinsonianism!* But, after all, to those who search for it, the analogy must instantly discover itself; and it hath been pointed out to us without reserve by a Divine of the *old* school, Bishop *Andrews*; who was in no fear of being called to an account for it by the learned of that age. In his first discourse, on the descent of the Holy Ghost, he has these words: "The wind, which is here "the type of the Holy Ghost, doth of all "creatures best express it: for, of all bodily "things, it is the least bodily, and even invi-"sible, as a Spirit is. It is *mighty* or violent; "seemingly of little force, and yet of the "greatest: but never so vehement as the Spirit "is in its proceedings. As the wind serveth "for breath, so doth the Spirit give life, and "is called the Spirit of life. As it serveth for "speech, so doth the Spirit give utterance: and, "as the one serveth for sound, so by the other "the sound of the Apostles went out into all "lands." This, and more to the same purpose, saith Bishop *Andrews*; and I call this true Divinity: he was in no fear about types and analogies; he finds the analogy as strict, as if the air had been created for this use.

And what Chriſtian, who reads his Bible, will find fault with Biſhop *Horne*, if he thought, and preached, as Biſhop *Andrews* did before him? The one was the delight of his times; and the other may continue to be the delight of our times; notwithſtanding the cenſures which have been thrown out againſt him, with ſo little experience, that I am aſhamed for the author of them.

The other great object of nature, where the analogy is not permitted to us, is that of the *light*: but it holds in this caſe as ſtrictly as in the other: for our Saviour calls himſelf the *true light, which lighteth every man that cometh into the world*; and a Prophet calls him *the Sun of righteouſneſs*. All the men of this world, who have light, have it from the ſame Sun; and all, that have the light of life, have it from the ſame Saviour. And the operations and attributes of the true light in the kingdom of Grace are the ſame as thoſe of the light in the natural world. We took the authority of Biſhop *Andrews* in the former example; we may now take that of Archbiſhop *Leighton* *; who ſees the analogy between the natural and divine

* See Sermon fifth of Archbiſhop Leighton's eighteen.

light:—

light:—firſt, in their *purity*; both are incapable of pollution: ſecondly, in their *univerſality*; both are imparted to all, without being diminiſhed: thirdly, in their *vivifying power*; the one raiſes plants and vegetables from the earth, the other raiſes men from the dead: fourthly, in their *diſpelling darkneſs*; all ſhadows fly before the Sun; all the types and ſhadows of the law, all the miſts of darkneſs and idolatry, at the appearance of the other, who is the light of the Gentiles, and the glory of Iſrael; even that glory, which had been ſo often foreſhewed to them: for, as the glory was in their tabernacle and filled it, ſo the *fulneſs of the Godhead dwelt bodily in Chriſt*: εσκηνωσεν εν ἡμιν,—he *dwelt in a tabernacle* amongſt us. Is not this a juſt and beautiful analogy? And can there be any man of taſte, who will not ſee and admire it? Is the Scripture *fanciful* in teaching it? And is this good Biſhop *preſumptuous* in following it? It is a grief to me to be urging ſo many queſtions in ſo plain a caſe: but wiſe men lay us under a cruel neceſſity, when they are in ſuch a hurry to run away from doctrines, which they call *Hutchinſonian*, without knowing, that they have been common to the Chriſtian world; and that every *maſter*

in

in Iſraël (ſuppoſing this gentleman to be of that character) is expected to have acquired, from a proper ſtudy of the Scripture, that experience which makes all theſe things plain, and enables us to ſee the ſpiritual in the natural world; the glaſs in which (δια, by means of which *) God hath been pleaſed to ſhew us *that* and *Himſelf*, till we ſhall ſee him face to face; and not, as we do now, by reflection from the objects of nature. All, who do not know the uſe of this grand *ſpeculum*, are under the poverty of ignorance; they loſe a great help to their faith, together with a great inſtrument for the improving of their underſtanding; at leaſt in ſpiritual things. What would Divinity be, and what can a teacher of it be, without the uſe of analogies, and the power we acquire, when we argue from them? They are ſo univerſal in the Scripture, that a man may as well read Engliſh without the alphabet, as read the Bible without underſtanding its analogies. They are, therefore, never to be given up, but to be inſiſted upon,

* δι' εσοπτρου εν αινιγματι—Though the prepoſition δια is here uſed, we do not ſuppoſe with our Engliſh verſion that the alluſion is to dioptrics, but catoptrics: ſo εισοπτρον is a *ſpeculum*, wherein things are ſeen by reflection.

and

and recommended to others, as the very life and ſoul of Chriſtian wiſdom *.

I would willingly have avoided a party *name*, being conſcious that I am not a party *man*; but diſpoſed to exerciſe an independent judgment, and take what is good and uſeful from every quarter where I can find it; either for my own benefit, or that of the public. If I can do good, I am willing to do it under any character which an honeſt man may wear. But my adverſaries (who are not a few) have found ſuch an advantage, for many years paſt, in giving me the name of an *Hutchinſonian*, that they will never part with it. So, as I am ſtamped with that name, I may ſpeak freely, without loſing any ground. Too many of the learned have ſhewn an unuſual propenſity, for many years, to cenſure and reject every principle reported to be *Hutchinſonian*, without firſt knowing what it is, and what is to be ſaid for it. The Biographer, againſt whom I have defended Biſhop *Horne*, attacks him as an Hutchinſonian, without knowing, that he was making his attack on that quarter where the Hutchinſonians are ſtrongeſt: and this, not

* For the Biſhop's ſentiments on this ſubject, ſee the Life, p. 182, 183, 184.

with weak arguments, but with no arguments at all; unless we can find one in the words—*it will surely be thought*—which is not an argument, but an appeal to the judgment of others, who are under the same prejudice with himself. To prevent which for the time to come, and to satisfy those, who, having heard some things to perplex them, would be glad of better information; I shall tell them, as well as I can, what the principles really are, by which an Hutchinsonian is distinguished from other men. But when I consider, that this inquiry will lead us into some great, deep and difficult subjects—of which no man can speak worthily—and of which so many have spoken rashly—I tremble at my undertaking; and intreat every wise and good man to make allowances for me, at a stage of life, when forces fail, and memory is weak; and to give me a fair and charitable hearing.

1. In the first place, the followers of Mr. Hutchinson give to *God* the pre-eminence in every thing. *His* authority with them is above all authority: His wisdom above all wisdom: His truth above all truth. They judge every thing to be good or bad, wise or foolish, as it promotes or hinders the belief of Christianity,

On which account, their firſt enemies are to be found among ſceptics, infidels and atheiſts. Their next enemies are thoſe who are afraid of believing too much: ſuch as our Socinians and their confederates, who admit Chriſtianity as a *fact*, but deny it as a *doctrine*.

2. They hold, that only one way of ſalvation has been revealed to man from the beginning of the world; viz. the way of faith in God, redemption by Jeſus Chriſt, and a detachment from the world: and that this way is revealed in both Teſtaments.

3. That in both Teſtaments divine things are explained and confirmed to the underſtandings of men, by alluſions to the natural creation. I ſay *confirmed*; becauſe the Scripture is ſo conſtant and uniform in the uſe it makes of natural objects, that ſuch an analogy appears between the ſenſible and ſpiritual world, as carries with it *ſenſible evidence* to the truth of revelation; and they think, that, where *this* evidence is once apprehended by the mind, no other will be wanted. They are therefore perſuaded, it may have great effect towards making men Chriſtians, in this laſt age of the world; now the original evidence of miracles is remote, and almoſt forgotten.

4. They

4. They are confirmed *Trinitarians.* They became ſuch at their baptiſm in common with other Chriſtians: and they are kept ſuch, by their principles; eſpecially by what is called the *Hutchinſonian philoſophy of fire, light, and air.* Nature ſhews us theſe three agents in the world, on which all natural life and motion depend: and theſe three are uſed in the Scripture to ſignify to us the three ſupreme *powers* of the Godhead, in the adminiſtration of the ſpiritual world; notwithſtanding the judgment which our new biographer hath paſſed againſt them. Let any philoſopher ſhew us one ſingle effect, of which it may be proved, that neither fire, light nor air contribute to it in any of their various forms*.

5. On

* To ſhew how differently the ſame things will appear to different men, and how men of learning, through habits of thinking, may be unprepared to judge of common things, I will mention the example of my own Tutor of Univerſity College in Oxford; who, having been perſuaded to read a little piece of Duncan Forbes on the ſyſtem of Hutchinſon, (which by the way I would recommend to the reader) was heard to ſay "there were ſome good things and ſome curi-"ous things in it; but *the man raves* when he talks of his "*fire, light* and *ſpirit.*" Now herein is to me a marvellous thing; that Learning, ſeated in the chair of *Alfred*, ſhould take this doctrine of fire, light and air to be *raving*; when

Ignorance,

5. On the authority of the Scriptures, they entertain ſo low an opinion of human nature, under the conſequences of the fall, that they derive every thing in religion from revelation or tradition. A ſyſtem may be fabricated, and called *natural*; but a *religion* it cannot be; for there never was a religion, among Jews or Gentiles, Greeks, Romans, or Barbarians, ſince the beginning of the world, without ſacrifice and prieſthood: of which natural religion, having neither, is conſequently no religion. The

Ignorance, with a tallow candle in its hand, need only light it, to ſee them all at work together. Air enters at the bottom, where the flame looks blue: fire and ſmoke from the ſnuff are at the top, and the brighteſt light is about the middle. No man can draw a line between them, or ſay where one ends and another begins. But here they are certainly; for, without air, the candle goes out: without fire, it will not burn us: and, without light, we ſhall not ſee by it. And all this is no theory, but a plain, undeniable matter of fact. How wonderful, that a philoſopher cannot ſee this; when a child or a ploughman may be made to underſtand it! Two ſtrange events of the ſame kind are more credible than one. The people among the Jews, who *knew* moſt, were thoſe who could *ſee* leaſt.

When the good Lord Preſident Forbes wrote his letter from Scotland, there were rocks and mountains in his way; and he had the mortification to ſee that he prevailed but little. Theſe are now not nearly ſo formidable as they were then: great

The imagination of man, by ſuppoſing a religion without theſe, has done infinite diſ-ſervice to the only religion by which man can be ſaved. It has produced the deiſtical ſubſtitution of naked morality, or Turkiſh honeſty, for the doctrines of interceſſion, redemption and divine grace. It has no *gift* from God, but that nature, which came poor, and blind, and naked out of Paradiſe; ſubject only to farther miſery, from its own luſts, and the temptations of the Devil. A religion, more flattering to the pride of man, pleaſes his fancy better than this; but it will never do him any good.

great and unexpected events have intervened. Infidelity, the grand adverſary, hath now overſhot its mark; and is found to have in it ſo much more of the felon, than the philoſopher, that gentlemen begin to be aſhamed of its company. Its opponents are inſpired with new zeal, and act with new vigour; as may be ſeen in two periodical publications of modern date. Attraction is going down; and the demonſtration of a *vacuum* is not to be ſupported; as I ſhall ſhew in another place. Electricity hath riſen up, and given us the knowlege of a new power in nature, which is an object of ſenſe, and may be extended to the whole ſyſtem of the world. Lord Forbes's letter to a Biſhop was written with the beſt intention in the world; but, when a ſcheme is *new*, and admitted in all its parts, more weight is laid upon ſome things, than they will bear. He tells his reader many curious things, for which I have not room; neither would I chooſe to introduce them, becauſe they depend on *Hebrew* evidence.

Hutchinſon

Hutchinson himſelf had ſo ſtrong a ſenſe of this, that he looked upon natural religion as Deiſm in diſguiſe; an engine of the Devil, in theſe latter days, for the overthrow of the Goſpel; and therefore boldly called it *the religion of Satan or Anti-chriſt*. Let the well-informed Chriſtian look about him and conſider, whether his words, extravagant as they might ſeem at firſt, have not been fully verified. I myſelf, for one, am ſo thoroughly perſuaded of this, that I determine never to give quarter to natural religion, when it falls in my way to ſpeak of the all-ſufficiency of the Goſpel of Jeſus Chriſt. We know very well how the Scripture is brought in, to give its countenance to the notion of a natural religion: but we know alſo that dark texts are drawn to ſuch a ſenſe, as to render all the reſt of the Scripture of no effect; as hath happened in the doctrines of pre-deſtination and natural religion; by the former of which we loſe the *Church*, by the latter its *Faith*. Facts bring a diſpute to a ſhort iſſue. If *Voltaire* were alive, I would be judged by him, whether Chriſtianity hath not been going down ever ſince natural religion came up. And we know, by what his diſciples, the French, have done, that natural religion comes up, when Chriſtianity is put down.

 Theſe

These facts teach us, that they will not stand long together. Whether they possibly *might* or not is not worth an inquiry; because he, that has got Christianity, may leave natural religion to shift for itself.

6. Few writers for natural religion have shewn any regard to the types and figures of the Scripture, or known much about them. But the Hutchinsonians, with the old Christian Fathers, and the Divines of the Reformation, are very attentive to them, and take great delight in them. They differ in their nature from all the learning of the world; and so much of the wisdom of revelation is contained in them, that no Christian should neglect the knowlege of them. All infidels abominate them. *Lord Bolingbroke* calls St. Paul a *Cabbalist* for arguing from them; but the Hutchinsonians are ambitious of being such Cabbalists as St. Paul was.

7. In natural philosophy, they have great regard to the name of *Newton*, as the most wonderful genius of his kind. But they are sure, his method of proving a *vacuum* is not agreeable to nature. A vacuum cannot be deduced from the theory of resistances: for, if motion be from impulsion, as Newton himself, and some

of

of the wiſeſt of his followers have ſuſpected; then the cauſe of motion will never reſiſt the motion which it cauſes. The rule, which is true when applied to *communicated motion*, does not hold when applied to the *motions of nature*. For the motions of nature change from leſs to more; as when a ſpark turns to a conflagration: but communicated motion always changes from more to leſs: ſo that there is an eſſential difference between them, and we cannot argue from the one to the other. Mr. *Cotes*'s demonſtration, it is well known, is applicable only to communicated motion: I mean, ſuch only as is *violent* or *artificial*. There is no need of a vacuum in the heavens: it is more reaſonable and more agreeable to nature that they ſhould be filled with a circulating fluid, which does not hinder motion, but begins it and preſerves it.

They cannot allow *inert* matter to be capable (as mind is) of *active* qualities; but aſcribe attraction, repulſion &c. to ſubtle cauſes, not immaterial. There may be caſes very intricate and difficult; but they take the rule from plain caſes, and, ſuppoſing nature to be uniform and conſiſtent, they apply it to the reſt.

8. In natural hiſtory, they maintain, againſt

all the wild theories of Infidels, which come up, one after another, like muſhrooms, and ſoon turn rotten, that the preſent condition of the earth bears evident marks of an univerſal flood; and that extraneous foſſils are to be accounted for from the ſame cataſtrophe. Many of them are therefore diligent collectors of foſſil bodies, which are valuable to the curious in conſideration of their origin.

9. What commonly paſſes under the name of *learning*, is a knowlege of *Heathen* books; but it ſhould always be admitted with great precaution. For they think of all Heathens, that, from the time when they commenced Heathens, they never worſhiped the *true* God, the Maker of heaven and earth; but, inſtead of him, the elements of the world, the powers of nature, and the lights of heaven: that the love of vice and vanity was the real cauſe of their ignorance: they did not *know* the true God, becauſe they did not *like* to know him: and that the ſame paſſions will give us an inclination to the principles of Heathens, rather than to the principles of Chriſtians; and that moſt of the ill principles of this age come out of the Heathen School. The favourers of Mr. Hutchinſon's ſcheme are therefore reputed to be the enemies of learning.

But

But they are not ſo. They are enemies only to the *abuſes* of it, and to the corruptions derived from it. To all falſe learning, that is, to human folly, affecting to be wiſdom, they have indeed a mortal averſion in their hearts, and can hardly be civil to it in their words; as knowing, that the more a man has of falſe wiſdom, the leſs room there will be for the true. Metaphyſics, which conſiſt of words without ideas; illuſtrations of Chriſtian ſubjects from Heathen parallels; theories founded only on imagination; ſpeculations on the mind of man, which yield no ſolid matter to it, but lead it into dangerous opinions about itſelf: theſe and other things of the kind, with which modern learning abounds, they regard as they would the painting of a ghoſt, or the ſplitting of an atom*.

10. Of *Jews* they think, that they are the inveterate enemies of Chriſtianity; never to be truſted as our aſſociates either in Hebrew or Divinity. No *Philo*, no *Joſephus*, no *Talmudiſt*, is to be depended upon; but ſuſpected and ſifted, as dangerous Apoſtates from *true Judaiſm*. It is plauſibly argued, that Jews, as native *Hebrews*, muſt, like other natives, be beſt acquainted

* See more on this ſubject, page 94 of the Life.

with their own language. But the caſe of the Jews is without a parallel upon earth. They are out of their native ſtate; and have an intereſt in deceiving Chriſtians by every poſſible means, and depriving them of the evidence of the Old Teſtament.

11. They are of opinion, that the *Hebrew* is the primæval and original language; that its ſtructure ſhews it to be divine; and that a compariſon with other languages ſhews its priority.

12. *The Cherubim* of the Scriptures were myſtical figures, of high antiquity and great ſignification. Thoſe of Eden, and of the Tabernacle, and of Ezekiel's viſion, all belong to the ſame original. *Irenæus* has enough upon them to juſtify the Hutchinſonian acceptation of them. The place they had in the Holy of Holies, and their uſe in the Sacred Ritual, ſets them very high. Their appellation, as * *Cherubim of glory*, does the ſame; and the reaſoning of Saint *Paul*, from the ſhadows of the law to the prieſthood of Chriſt, ſets them higheſt of all; obliging us to infer, that they were ſymbolical of the Divine Preſence. The τεσσαρα ζωα in the Revelation of Saint John (improperly called *beaſts*; for one of them was a *man*, and another a *bird*)

* Compare Acts vii. 2. Ὁ Θεὸς τῆς δόξης.

must

muſt be taken for the ſame: where the figures of the old law bow down and ſurrender all power and glory to the evangelical figure of the Lamb that was ſlain. Here the doctrine is thought to labour a little: but, if the ζωα are conſidered only as figures, the caſe alters. And, if this great ſubject ſhould have parts and circumſtances not to be underſtood, we muſt argue from what *is* underſtood. They ſeem to have been known in the Chriſtian Church of the firſt centuries; but not with the help of the *Jews*. So alſo was the analogy of the three agents (φως, πυρ, πνευμα,) theſe being expreſsly mentioned by Epiphanius, as ſimilitudes of the Divine Trinity.

In their phyſiological capacity, ſo far as we can find, the Cherubim ſeem never to have been conſidered before Mr. Hutchinſon; who very properly derives from them all *animal-worſhip* among the Heathens. This ſubject is of great extent and depth; comprehending a maſs of Mythological learning, well worthy of a diligent examination.

Theſe things come down to us under the name of *John Hutchinſon*; a character *ſui generis*, ſuch as the common forms of education could never have produced: and it ſeems to me not to have been well explained, how and by what means he fell upon things, seemingly so new and uncommon: but we do not enquire *whose* they are, but *what* they are, and what they are good for. If the tide had brought them to shore in a trunk, marked with the initials J. H. while I was walking by the sea-side, I would have taken them up, and kept them for use; without being solicitous to know, what ship they came out off, or how far, and how long, they had been floating at the mercy of the wind and waves. If they should get from my hands into better hands, I should rejoice; being persuaded they would revive in others the dying flame of Christian faith, as they did in Bishop Horne and myself. And why should any good men be afraid of them? There is nothing here, that tends to make men troublesome, as Heretics, Fanatics, Sectaries, Rebels, or Corrupters of any kind of useful learning. All these things a man may believe, and still be a good subject, a devout Christian, and a sound member of the Church of England: perhaps more sound, and more useful, than he would have been without them. For myself I may say, (as I do in great humility) that, by following them through the course of a long life, I

have

have found myself much enlightened, much assisted in evidence and argument, and never corrupted; as I hope my writings, if they should last, will long bear me witness. If these principles should come into use with other people, I am confident they would turn Christians into Scholars, and Scholars into Christians; enabling them to demonstrate, how shallow Infidels are in their learning, and how greatly every man is a loser by his ignorance of Revelation.

When we are describing Hutchinsonians, it would be unjust to forget, that they are *true Churchmen* and *Loyalists*; steady in the fellowship of the Apostles, and faithful to the Monarchy under which they live. This, however, is not from what they find in Hutchinson, though it *is* to be found in him *; but from what he has taught them to find, by taking their principles from the Scripture. Had this man been a splendid character, and a great favourite with the world, we might have received his doctrines

* No being whatever can have any power over man, but the God that made him: therefore no man can have any power over any other man, unless he has it from God. Parents have it over their children by Creation; therefore from the Creator: and Rulers have it, by being God's Ministers. This is Mr. Hutchinson's argument; and it is as close as a demonstration.

with

with our mouths open, and our eyes ſhut: but our dangers are quite of another kind. From *him* nothing is to be taken upon truſt: every thing muſt be ſifted and examined to the uttermoſt. And ſo let it: for thus it will be better underſtood. Prove it well, and hold it faſt. Of leaders and guides in learning beware; for, as wiſely ſpeaks the author of the *Purſuits of Literature*, they ought, in this age, to be *well watched*: if they fall into dangerous miſtakes, many fall with them: and, if evil once creeps in, and finds public entertainment, no man can ſay how or when we ſhall get rid of it. Such leaders are as watchful againſt *us*, as we ought to be againſt *them*. They neither *enter in themſelves*, nor ſuffer other people, if they can prevent it. Many young men would find employment and amuſement for their lives, if the way were open, and they were permitted to enquire for themſelves. Here, *free inquiry* would be honourable, ſafe and laudable: but diſcouragements are often thrown in their way; and I have met with ſome examples of it; one in particular, which made a great impreſſion upon me.

Some years ago I became acquainted with a young man, of bright parts, a ſtudious diſ-

poſition,

position, and a pious turn of mind; in whose conversation I found comfort and pleasure. To such advice as I gave him, in regard to his future studies, he was remarkably attentive. He saw a new field of learning opening to his view, which promised him much profitable employment; and he seemed in haste to enter upon it. As he was intended for the Church, I flattered myself he would take some active part in the defence of Christian truth as a writer; together with the advancement of Christian piety as a preacher. With this prospect upon my mind, he left me for many months. But, at his return, I found him totally changed; and I rarely conversed with him but to my disappointment. His mind, which used to be undisguised and open, was now guarded at every pass: and, whatever I proposed, as formerly, he had now an evasion ready. It seemed as if somebody had hung a bell about my neck, so that I could not stir without raising an alarm. To a man, rather shy of making proselytes, but always pleased to meet with volunteers, fit for the service of God and his Church, my situation was distressing. I discovered, that my friend was no longer his own man: I guessed at the

cause;

caufe; and gave little trouble afterwards to him or myfelf. But I lamented, that he had loft a view of things, which would have animated him; and, while it found exercife for the beft of his talents, would have given ftrength and effect to all his labours. His purfuits in literature will now moft probably be frivolous in themfelves, and foreign to his profeffion as a clergyman. No man will do great things, when he yields to fecular influence, where literary and religious ought to prevail. The vineyard is a better fpot to cultivate than the high-way; and, when labourers are wanted, 'tis pity any one fhould be led away upon other fervice, lefs pleafant and lefs profitable. *Why even of your ownfelves judge ye not what is right?* faid our Saviour to thofe, who could judge of the weather from the face of the fky, without going to afk the *Pharifees*: and who ought, after the fame manner, to have judged for themfelves, in matters of much greater moment, from the figns of the times and the ftate of the church. I hazarded a great, and, as it may be thought, a rafh, affertion, at page 77 of the following Life: I faid, "that, if we were ever to fee fuch ano-"ther man as Bifhop *Horne*, he muft *come out* "*of the ſame ſchool.*" I am ſtill of the ſame mind; for I think no other ſchool will form ſuch a man. I will now hazard a farther opinion to the ſame effect: for I think it not improbable, that if ſome man were to ariſe, with abilities for the purpoſe, well prepared in his learning, and able to guide his words with diſcretion; and ſuch a man were to take up the principles called Hutchinſonian, and do them juſtice; the world would find it much harder to ſtand againſt him than they are aware of, even with all the *new biographers* of the age, to encourage and aſſiſt them. I may be called a *viſionary*, when I ſay this: that I cannot help: but how many ſtranger viſions have been realized of late, which, twenty years ago, would have been pronounced utterly incredible! When ſtrange things are to be done, ſtrange men ariſe to do them. One man, as powerful in truth, as *Voltaire* was in error, might produce very unexpected alterations, and in leſs time than he did. Then might a new æra of learning ſucceed; as friendly to the Chriſtian cauſe, as the learning, which has been growing up amongſt us for the laſt hundred years, has been hoſtile and deſtructive. As to confirmed infidelity, it is a deaf adder, never to be charmed. Yet even here the caſe is not always to be given up in deſpair. Many forſake truth, becauſe they hate it: of ſuch there is no hope: but ſome believe wrong, only becauſe they never were taught right.

Nayland, July 30, 1799.

A

PREFATORY EPISTLE

TO

WILLIAM STEVENS, ESQ.

A

PREFATORY EPISTLE

TO

WILLIAM STEVENS, Esq.

MY DEAR FRIEND,

THE works of the late Bishop Horne are in many hands, and will be in many more. No reader of any judgment can proceed far into them, without discovering, that the author was a person of eminence for his learning, eloquence, and piety; with as much wit, and force of expression, as were consistent with a temper so much corrected and sweetened by devotion.

To all those who are pleased and edified by his writings, some account of his life and conversation will be interesting. They will naturally wish to hear what passed between such a man and the world in which he lived. You and I, who knew him so well and loved him so much, may be suspected of partiality to his me-

 mory:

mory: but we have unexceptionable teſtimony to the greatneſs and importance of his character. While we were under the firſt impreſſions of our grief for the loſs of him, a perſon of high diſtinction, who was intimate with him for many years, declared to you and to me, that he verily believed him to have been *the beſt man he ever knew.* Soon after the late Earl of Guilford was made Chancellor of the Univerſity of Oxford, another great man, who was allowed to be an excellent judge of the weight and wit of converſation, recommended Dr. Horne, who was then vice-chancellor, to him in the following terms: "My Lord, I queſ-" tion whether you know your vice-chancellor "ſo well as you ought. When you are next at "Oxford, go and dine with him; and, when "you have done this once, I need not aſk you "to do it again; you will find him the pleaſant-" eſt man you ever met with." And ſo his lordſhip ſeemed to think (who was himſelf as pleaſant a man as moſt in the kingdom) from the attention he paid to him ever after. I have heard it obſerved of him by another gentleman, who never was ſuſpected of a want of judgment, that, if ſome friend had followed him about with a pen and ink, to note down his ſayings and

ob-

obſervations, they might have furniſhed out a collection like that which Mr. Boſwell has given to the public; but frequently of a ſuperior quality; becauſe the ſubjects which fell in his way were occaſionally of an higher nature, out of which more improvement would ariſe to thoſe that heard him: and it is now much to be lamented, that ſo many of them have run to waſte *.

An alluſion to the life of Dr. Johnſon, reminds me how much it was wiſhed, and by Dr. Horne in particular, who well knew and highly valued him, that Johnſon would have directed the force of his underſtanding againſt that modern paper-building of philoſophical infidelity, which is founded in pride and ignorance, and ſupported by ſenſuality and ridicule. A great perſonage was of opinion, that Johnſon, ſo employed, would have borne them down with the weight of his language: and he is reported to have expreſſed the ſentiment with ſingular felicity to a certain perſon, when the miſchievous writings of Voltaire were brought into queſtion: "I wiſh Johnſon would mount his dray-"horſe, and ride over ſome of thoſe fellows." Againſt *thoſe fellows* Dr. Horne employed

* A collection of his thoughts on various ſubjects is preſerved in a manuſcript, written with his own hand.

much of his time, and ſome of the moſt uſeful of his talents: not mounted upon a dray-horſe, to overbear them; but upon a light courſer, to hunt them fairly down; with ſuch eaſy arguments, and pleaſant reflections, as render them completely abſurd and ridiculous: an account of which will come before us in the proper place. His *Conſiderations on the Life and Death of St. John the Baptiſt*, and his Sermon preached in St. Sepulchre's church at London, for the benefit of a Charity-ſchool for girls, on the *Female Character*, ſeem to me, above all the reſt of his compoſitions, to mark the peculiar temper of his mind, and the direction of his thoughts. When I read his book on *John the Baptiſt*, I am perſuaded, there was no other man of his time, whoſe fancy, as a writer, was bright enough, whoſe ſkill, as an interpreter, was deep enough, and whoſe heart, as a moraliſt, was pure enough to have made him the author of that little work. His *Female Character*, as it ſtands in the ſermon above-mentioned, now printed in his fourth volume, diſplays ſo much judgment in diſcriminating, ſuch gentle benevolence of heart, and ſo much of the elegance of a poliſhed underſtanding, in deſcribing and doing juſtice to the ſex; that every ſenſible and virtuous woman,

who

who ſhall read and conſider that ſingular diſcourſe, will bleſs his memory to the end of the world.

While we ſpeak of thoſe writings which are known to the public, you and I cannot forget his readineſs and excellence in writing letters; in which employment he always took delight from his earlieſt youth; and never failed to entertain or inſtruct his correſpondents. His mind had ſo much to communicate, and his words were ſo natural and lively, that I rank ſome of his letters among the moſt valuable productions of the kind. I have therefore reaſon to rejoice, that, amidſt all my interruptions and removals, I have preſerved more than a hundred of them; in reviewing of which, I find many obſervations on the ſubjects of Religion, Learning, Politics, Manners, &c. which are equally inſtructive and entertaining; and would certainly be ſo eſteemed, if they were communicated to the world; at leaſt, to the better part of it: for there were very few occurrences or tranſactions of any importance, either in the church, or the ſtate, or the literary world, that eſcaped his obſervation; and in ſeveral of them he took an active part. But in familiar letters, not intended for the public eye (as none of his ever were) and ſuggeſted by

 the

the incidents of the time, ſome of them trivial and domeſtic, there will be of courſe many paſſages of leſs dignity than will entitle them to publication: yet, upon the whole, I am ſatiſfied that a very uſeful ſelection might be made out of them; and I will not deſpair of making it myſelf at ſome future opportunity*.

From an early acquaintance with Greek and Latin authors, and the gift of a lively imagination, he addicted himſelf to poetry; and ſome of his productions have been deſervedly admired. But his ſtudies were ſo ſoon turned from the treaſures of claſſical wit to the ſources of chriſtian wiſdom, that all his poetry is either upon ſacred ſubjects, or upon a common ſubject applied to ſome ſacred uſe; ſo that a pious reader will be ſure to gain ſomething by every poetical effort of his mind. And let me not omit another remarkable trait of his character. You can be a witneſs with me, and ſo could many others who were uſed to his company, that few

* In the Gentleman's Magazine for Auguſt 1793, p. 688, I threw out a letter of Biſhop Horne, as a ſpecimen both of the ſtyle and of the uſual ſubjects of his epiſtolary writings. It was the firſt that came to hand on opening a large parcel of them: and I may leave every reader to judge whether that letter be not curious and important. Compared with the preſent times, it ſeems prophetical.

ſouls

ſouls were ever more ſuſceptible than his of the charms of muſic, eſpecially the ſacred muſic of the church: at the hearing of which, his countenance was illuminated; as if he had been favoured with impreſſions beyond thoſe of other men; as if heavenly viſion had been ſuperadded to earthly devotion. He therefore accounted it a peculiar happineſs of his life, that, from the age of twenty years, he was conſtantly gratified with the ſervice of a choir; at Magdalen College, at Canterbury, and at Norwich. His lot was caſt by providence amidſt the ſweets of cloyſtered retirement, and the daily uſe of divine harmony; for the enjoyment of both which he was framed by nature, and formed by a religious education. Upon the whole, I never knew a perſon, in whom thoſe beautiful lines of Milton*, of which he was a great admirer, were more exactly verified:

But let my due feet never fail
To walk the ſtudious cloyſter's pale;
And love the high embower'd roof
With antique pillars maſſy proof;
And ſtoried windows richly dight,
Caſting a dim religious light.
There let the pealing organ blow,
To the full voic'd quire below;

* In the *Il Penſeroſo.*

 In

In ſervice high, and anthems clear,
As may, with ſweetneſs through mine ear,
Diſſolve me into ecſtaſies,
And bring all heav'n before my eyes.

You, who are ſo perfectly acquainted with the diſcourſe delivered at Canterbury, 1784, when the new organ was opened in the great church, may gueſs how refined his raptures were: by what he has there ſaid, it may be known what he felt. And I can aſſure you farther, he was ſo earneſt in this ſubject, that he took the pains to extract, in his own hand writing, all the matter that is moſt obſervable and uſeful in the five quarto volumes of Sir John Hawkins upon muſic. I find among his papers this curious abridgment, which is made with critical taſte and diſcernment.

But his greateſt affection being to the ſcience of divinity, he would there of conſequence make the greateſt improvements; and there the world will find themſelves moſt obliged to him. No conſiderable progreſs, no improvement in any ſcience, can be expected, unleſs it be beloved for its own ſake. How this can happen in divinity, all men may not be able to ſee; but it is poſſible for the eye of the underſtanding to be as truly delighted with a ſight of the divine wiſdom in the great œconomy of redemption and revelation, as for the eye of the aſtronomer to take pleaſure in obſerving the lights of heaven, or the naturaliſt in exploring and collecting, perhaps at the hazard of his life, the treaſures of the natural creation. What I here ſay will be beſt underſtood by thoſe, who know what affection, what animation, is found in the firſt writers of the chriſtian church; with what delight they dwell upon the wonders of the chriſtian plan, and comment upon the peculiar wiſdom of the word of God. To the beſt writers of the beſt ages he put himſelf to ſchool very early, and profited by them ſo much, that I hope no injuſtice will be done to their memory, if I think he has in ſome reſpects improved upon his teachers.

A man with ſuch talents, and ſuch a temper, muſt have been generally beloved and admired; which he was almoſt univerſally; the exceptions being ſo few, as would barely ſuffice to exempt him from that *woe* of the Goſpel, which is pronounced againſt the favourites of the world. But his undiſguiſed attachment to the doctrines of the Church of England, which are ſtill, and, we hope, ever will be, of the *old faſhion*, would neceſſarily

ceſſarily expoſe him to the unmannerly cenſures of ſome, and the frigid commendations of others, which are ſometimes of worſe effect than open ſcandal. But he never appeared to be hurt by any thing of this ſort that happened to him. An anonymous pamphlet, which the public gave to the late Dr. Kennicott, attacked him very ſeverely; and ſoon received an anſwer from him; which, though very cloſe and ſtrong, was the anſwer of a wiſe and temperate man. He alſo, in his turn, not foreſeeing ſo much benefit to the Scriptures, as ſome others did, from Dr. Kennicott's plan for collating Hebrew manuſcripts, and correcting the Hebrew text, wrote againſt that undertaking; expreſſing his objections and ſuſpicions, and giving his name to the world, without any fear or reſerve. But ſo it came to paſs, from the moderation and farther experience of both the parties, that, though their acquaintance began in hoſtility, they at length contracted a friendſhip for each other, which brought on an interchange of every kind office between them, and laſted to the end of their lives, and is now ſubſiſting between their families. To all men of learning, who mean well to the cauſe of truth and piety, while they are warmly oppoſing one

another,

another, may their example be a lafting admonition! But let not this obfervation be carried farther than it will go:

> ——————Non ut
> Serpentes avibus geminentur, tigribus agni.

In his intercourfe with his own family, while the treafures of his mind afforded them fome daily opportunities of improvement, the fweetnefs of his humour was to them a perennial fountain of entertainment. He had the rare and happy talent of difarming all the little vexatious incidents of life of their power to moleft, by giving them fome unexpected turn. And occurrences of a more ferious nature, even fome of a frightful afpect, were treated by him with the like eafe and pleafantry; of which I could give fome remarkable inftances.

Surely, the life of fuch a man as this ought not to be forgotten! You and I, who faw and heard fo much of it, fhall, I truft, never recollect it without being the better for it: and, if we can fucceed in fhewing it fo truly to the world, that they alfo may be the better for it, we fhall do them an acceptable fervice. I have heard it faid, and I was a little difcouraged by it, that

Dr.

Dr. Horne was a perſon, whoſe life was not productive of *events* conſiderable enough to furniſh matter for a hiſtory. But they, who judge thus, have taken but a ſuperficial view of human life; and do not rightly meaſure the importance of the different events which happen to different ſorts of men. Dr. Horne, I muſt allow, was no circumnavigator: he neither ſailed with Drake, Anſon, nor Cooke; but he was a man, whoſe mind ſurveyed the intellectual world, and brought home from thence many excellent obſervations for the benefit of his native country. He was no military commander; he took no cities; he conquered no countries; but he ſpent his life in ſubduing his paſſions, and in teaching us how to do the ſame. He fought no battles by land or by ſea; but he oppoſed the enemies of God and his truth, and obtained ſome victories which are worthy to be recorded. He was no prime miniſter to any earthly potentate; but he was a miniſter to the King of Heaven and Earth: an office at leaſt as uſeful to mankind, and in the adminiſtration of which no miniſter to any earthly king ever exceeded him in zeal and fidelity. He made no ſplendid diſcoveries in natural hiſtory; but he did what was better: he applied universal nature to the improvement of the mind, and the illustration of heavenly doctrines. I call these *events:* not such as make a great noise and signify little; but such as are little celebrated, and of great signification. The same difference is found between Dr. Horne and some other men who have been the subject of history, as between the life of the bee, and that of the wasp or hornet. The latter may boast of their encroachments and depredations, and value themselves on being a plague and a terror to mankind. But let it rather be my amusement to follow and observe the motions of the bee. Her journies are always pleasant; the objects of her attention are beautiful to the eye, and she passes none of them over without examining what is to be extracted from them: her workmanship is admirable; her œconomy is a lesson of wisdom to the world: she may be accounted *little among them that fly*, but the fruit of her labour is the *chief of sweet things*.

You know, sir, to what interruptions my life has been subject for thirty years past, and there is some tender ground before us, on which I am to tread as lightly as truth will permit; you

you will pardon me therefore if my progreſs hath not been ſo quick as you could have wiſhed; and believe me to be, as I have long been,

Dear Sir,

Your moſt affectionate and

obliged, humble ſervant,

WILLIAM JONES.

THE LIFE AND WRITINGS OF *Dr. HORNE, &c.*

DOCTOR George Horne, late Bishop of Norwich, and for several years President of Magdalen College in Oxford, and Dean of Canterbury, was born at Otham, a small village near Maidstone in Kent, on the first of November, in the year 1730. His father was the Reverend * Samuel Horne, M. A. rector of Otham, a very learned and respectable clergyman, who for some years had been a tutor at Oxford. This gentleman had so determined with himself, to preserve the integrity of his mind against all temptations from worldly advantage, that he was heard to say, and used often to repeat it, he had rather be a toad-eater to a mountebank, than flatter any great man against his conscience. To this he

* He died in 1768, aged 75.

adhered

adhered through the whole courſe of his life; a conſiderable part of which was ſpent in the education of his children, and in a regular performance of all the duties of his pariſh. He married a daughter of Bowyer Hendley, Eſq. by whom he had ſeven children, four ſons and three daughters. The eldeſt ſon died very young. The late Biſhop was the next. His younger brother, Samuel, was a Fellow of Univerſity College; where he died, greatly reſpected and lamented. He inherited the integrity of his father, and was an *Iſraelite indeed*, who never did or wiſhed harm to any mortal. Yet his character was by no means of the inſipid kind: he had much of the humour and ſpirit of his elder brother; had a like talent for preaching; and was well attended to as often as he appeared in the Univerſity pulpit. His death was announced to an intimate friend by his elder brother in the following ſhort and pathetic letter:

My dear Friend, (No date.)

Laſt night, about half an hour paſt eight, it pleaſed God to take from us, by a violent fit of the ſtone in the gall-bladder, my dear brother Sam. He received the bleſſed ſacrament, with my mother and myſelf, from the hands of Dr. Wetherell*; and, full of faith, with the moſt perfect reſignation, departed in peace with God, the world, and himſelf. It is a heavy ſtroke to my poor mother; but ſhe and my ſiſters bear up

* The preſent Maſter of Univerſity College, and Dean of Hereford, &c.

with

with great fortitude. I have loſt a very dear friend, and pleaſant companion! Pray for us—All join in every affectionate wiſh for the happineſs of you and yours, with G. H.

The youngeſt brother, the Reverend William Horne, was educated at Magdalen College in Oxford, and is the preſent worthy rector of Otham, in which he ſucceeded his father, as alſo in the more valuable rectory of Brede in the county of Suſſex.

Mr. Horne, the father of the family, was of ſo mild and quiet a temper, that he ſtudiouſly avoided giving trouble on any occaſion. This he carried ſo far, that, when his ſon George was an infant, he uſed to wake him with playing upon a flute; that the change from ſleeping to waking might be gradual and pleaſant, and not produce an outcry; which frequently happens when children are awakened ſuddenly. What impreſſion this early cuſtom of his father might make upon his temper, we cannot ſay: but certainly, he was remarkable, as he grew up, for a tender feeling of muſic, eſpecially that of the church.

Under his father's tuition, he led a pleaſant life, and made a rapid progreſs in Greek and Latin. But ſome well meaning friend, fearing he might be ſpoiled by ſtaying ſo long at home, adviſed the ſending of him to ſchool. To this his good father, who never was given to make much reſiſtance, readily conſented: and he was accordingly placed in the ſchool at Maidſtone, under the care of the Reverend Deodatus Bye, a man of good principles, and well learned in Latin, Greek and Hebrew; who, when he had received his new ſcholar, and examined him at the age of thirteen, was ſo ſurpriſed at his proficiency, that he aſked him why he came to ſchool, when he was rather fit to go *from* ſchool? With this gentleman he continued two years; during which, he added much to his ſtock of learning, and among other things a little elementary knowlege of the Hebrew, on the plan of Buxtorf, which was of great advantage to him afterwards. I am a witneſs to the high reſpect with which he always ſpoke of his maſter; whom he had newly left, when my acquaintance with him firſt commenced at Univerſity College, to which he was ſent when he was little more than fifteen years of age. When ſervants ſpeak well of a maſter or miſtreſs, we are ſure they are good ſervants: and, when a ſcholar ſpeaks well of his teacher, we may be as certain he is, in every ſenſe of the word, a good ſcholar.

I cannot help recounting, on this occaſion, that there was under the ſaid Deodatus Bye another ſcholar, very nearly related to Mr. Horne, of whom the maſter was heard to ſay, that he never did any thing which he wiſhed him not to have done. But, when the lad was told of this, he very honeſtly obſerved upon it, that he had done many things which his maſter *never heard of*. He is now in an office of great reſponſibility. They, who placed him in it, ſuppoſed him ſtill to retain the honeſty he brought with him from

Maidſtone

Maidſtone ſchool; and I never heard that he had diſappointed them.

While Mr. Horne was at ſchool, a Maidſtone ſcholarſhip in Univerſity College became vacant; in his application for which he ſucceeded, and, young as he was, the maſter recommended his going directly to College.

Soon after he was ſettled at Univerſity College, (where he was admitted on the 15th of March 1745-6.) Mr. Hobſon, a good and learned tutor of the houſe, gave out an exerciſe, for a trial of ſkill, to Mr. Horne and the preſent writer of his life, who was alſo in his firſt year. They were ordered to take a favourite Latin ode of Boëtius, and preſent it to the tutor in a different Latin metre. This they both did as well as they could: and the conteſt, inſtead of dividing, united them ever after, and had alſo the effect of inſpiring them with a love of the Lyric Poetry of that author; which ſeems not to be ſufficiently known among ſcholars, though beautiful in its kind. The whole work was once in ſuch eſteem, that King Alfred, the founder of Univerſity College, and of the Engliſh Conſtitution, tranſlated it.

His ſtudies, for a time, were in general the ſame with thoſe of other ingenious young men; and the vivacity of his mind, which never was exceeded, and made his converſation very deſirable, introduced him to many gentlemen of his own ſtanding, who reſembled him in their learning and their manners, particularly to Mr. Jenkinſon, now Earl of Liverpool,

Mr. Moore, now Archbiſhop of Canterbury, Mr. Cracherode, Mr. Benſon, the Honourable Hamilton Boyle, ſon of Lord Orrery, the late Reverend Jaſper Selwin, and many others. Mr. Denny Martin, now Dr. Fairfax, of Leeds Caſtle, in Kent, was from the ſame ſchool with Mr. Horne; and has always been very nearly connected with him, as a companion of his ſtudies, a lover of his virtues, and an admirer of his writings.

To ſhow how high Mr. Horne's character ſtood with all the members of his College, old and young, I need only mention the following fact. It happened about the time when he took his Bachelor's degree, which was on the 27th of October 1749, that a Kentiſh fellowſhip became vacant at Magdalen College; and there was, at that time, no ſcholar of the houſe who was upon the county. The ſenior Fellow of Univerſity College, having heard of this, ſaid nothing of it to Mr. Horne, but went down to Magdalen College, told them what an extraordinary young man they might find in Univerſity College, and gave him ſuch a recommendation as diſpoſed the ſociety to accept of him. When the day of election came, they found him ſuch as he had been repreſented, and much more; and in 1750 he was accordingly choſen a Fellow of Magdalen College, and on the firſt of June 1752 he took the degree of Maſter of Arts.

If we look back upon our paſt lives, it will generally be found, that the leading events, which gave a direction to all that followed, were not according to our own choice or knowlege, but from the hand of an over-ruling providence, which acts without consulting us; putting us into situations, which are either best for ourselves, or best for the world, or best for both; and leading us, as it led the patriarch Abraham; of whom we are told, that he *knew not whither he was going*. This was plainly the case in Mr. Horne's election to Magdalen College. A person took up the matter, unsolicited and in secret: he succeeded. When Fellow, his character and conduct gave him favour with the society, and, when Dr. Jenner died, they elected him President: the headship of the College introduced him to the office of Vice-chancellor; which at length made him as well known to Lord North, as to the Earl of Liverpool: this led to the Deanry of Canterbury, and that to the Bishopric of Norwich.

If we return to the account of his studies, we shall there find something else falling in his way which he never sought after, and attended with a train of very important consequences. While he was deeply engaged in the pursuits of Oratory, Poetry, Philosophy, and History, and making himself well acquainted with the Greek Tragedians, of which he was become a great admirer, an accident, of which I shall relate the account as plainly and faithfully as I can, without disguising or diminishing, drew him into a new situation in respect of his mind, and gave a new turn to his studies, before he had arrived at his Bachelor's degree. I may indeed say of this, that it certainly gave much of the colour which his character assumed from that

 time,

time, and opened the way to most of his undertakings and publications; as he himself would witness if he were now alive.

It is known to the public, that he came very early upon the stage as an author, though an anonymous one, and brought himself into some difficulty under the denomination of an *Hutchinsonian*; for this was the name given to those gentlemen who studied Hebrew and examined the writings of John Hutchinson Esq. the famous Mosaic philosopher, and became inclined to favour his opinions in Theology and Philosophy.

About the time of which I am speaking, there were many good and learned men of both Universities, but chiefly in and of the University of Oxford, who, from the representation given to the public, some years before, by the Right Honourable Duncan Forbes, then Lord President of the Court of Session in Scotland, and from a new and more promising method of studying the Hebrew language, independently of Jewish error, and from a flattering prospect also of many other advantages to the general interests of religion and learning, were become zealous advocates in favour of the new scheme of Mr. Hutchinson. Mr. Horne was led into this enquiry, partly by an accident which had happened to myself.

An attachment to some friends, then well known in the University for their abilities in music, of whom the principal were, Mr. Phocion Henley of Wadham College, Mr. Pixel of Queen's, and Mr. Short of Worcester, drew me often to Wadham College; which society

ſociety has two Hebrew ſcholarſhips, on one of which there was a gentleman, a Mr. Catcott of Briſtol, whoſe father, as I afterwards underſtood, was one of thoſe authors who firſt diſtinguiſhed themſelves as writers on the ſide of Mr. Hutchinſon: he poſſeſſed a very curious collection of foſſils, ſome of which he had digged and ſcratched out of the earth with his own hands at the hazard of his life; a pit near Wadham College, which would have buried him, having fallen in very ſoon after he was out of it. This collection*

* It is now depoſited in the public library at Briſtol, to the corporation of which city he left that and his MSS. on a principle of gratitude for the preferment they had given him; and there I ſaw it in the year 1790, with many large and valuable additions.

Of the collector it may be truly ſaid, that he was not only an *Hebræan* in his learning, but an *Iſraelite* in life and manners. To his induſtry we owe a Treatiſe on the Deluge, which, when compared with many others, will be found to give the beſt and moſt curious information upon the ſubject. This good and innocent man, whoſe heart was well affected to all mankind, died before his time; and the manner of his death, if it has been truly reported, will raiſe the indignation of every ſenſible and charitable mind. He kept his bed with a bad fever; and, when reſt was neceſſary, he was diſturbed by the continual barking of a dog that was chained up near at hand. When his friends ſent a civil meſſage deſiring that the dog might be removed till the patient was better, it was refuſed; and, in the event, he was fairly barked to death. If this fact be true, how cheap are the lives and ſufferings of ſome men in the eſtimation of others!—*Hercule! homini plurima ex homine ſunt mala!*—for the dog intended no harm.—Of this gentleman himſelf, we are informed by one of his intimate friends, that, when he ſettled his account at the year's end, he conſidered all the money that remained after his own debts were paid as the property not of himſelf but of the poor, to whoſe uſe (being a ſingle man) he never failed to apply it.

I was invited to ſee, and readily accepted the invitation, out of a general curioſity, without any particular knowlege of the ſubject. This gentleman, perceiving my attention to be much engaged by the novelty and curioſity of what he exhibited, threw out ſo many hints about things of which I had never heard, that I requeſted the favour of ſome farther converſation with him on a future occaſion. One conference followed another, till I ſaw a new field of learning opened, particularly in the department of Natural Hiſtory, which promiſed me ſo much information and entertainment, that I fell very ſoon into the ſame way of reading. Dr. Woodward the phyſician, who had been a fellow-labourer with Hutchinſon, and followed very nearly the ſame principles, had made the Natural Hiſtory of the Earth, and the diluvian origination of extraneous foſſils, ſo agreeable and ſo intelligible, that I was captivated by his writings: and from them I went to others; taking what I found, with a taſte and appetite, which could not, at that time, make ſuch diſtinctions as I may have been able to make ſince. In the ſimplicity of my heart, I communicated ſome of the novelties, with which my mind was now filled, to my dear and conſtant companion, Mr. Horne, from whom I ſeldom concealed any thing; but found him very little inclined to conſider them; and I had the mortification to ſee, that I was rather loſing ground in his eſtimation. Our College-Lectures on Geometry and Natural Philoſophy (which were not very deep) we had gone through with ſome attention, and thought ourſelves

ourſelves qualified to ſpeak up for the Philoſophy of Newton. It was therefore ſhocking to hear, that *attraction* was *no phyſical principle*, and that a *vacuum* never had been, and never would be, *demonſtrated*. Here therefore Mr. Horne inſiſted, that if Sir I. Newton's Philoſophy ſhould be falſe in theſe principles, no Philoſophy would ever be true. How it was objected to, and how it was defended, I do not now exactly remember; I fear, not with any profound ſkill on either ſide; but this I well recollect, that our diſputes, which happened at a pleaſant ſeaſon of the year, kept us walking to and fro in the Quadrangle till paſt midnight. As I got more information for myſelf, I gained more upon my companion: but I have no title to the merit of forming him into what he afterwards proved to be.

In the ſame College with us, there lived a very extraordinary perſon. He was a claſſical ſcholar of the firſt rate, from a public ſchool, remarkable for an unuſual degree of taſte and judgment in poetry and oratory; his perſon was elegant and ſtriking, and his countenance expreſſed at once both the gentleneſs of his temper and the quickneſs of his underſtanding. His manners and addreſs were thoſe of a perfect gentleman: his common talk, though eaſy and fluent, had the correctneſs of ſtudied compoſition: his benevolence was ſo great, that all the beggars in Oxford knew the way to his chamber-door: upon the whole, his character was ſo ſpotleſs, and his conduct ſo exemplary, that, mild and gentle as he was in his car-

riage

riage toward them, no young man dared to be rude in his company. By many of the firſt people in the Univerſity he was known and admired: and it being my fortune to live in the ſame ſtaircaſe with him, he was very kind and attentive to me, though I was much his junior: he often allowed me the pleaſure of his converſation, and ſometimes gave me the benefit of his advice, of which I knew the meaning to be ſo good, that I always heard it with reſpect, and followed it as well as I could. This gentleman, with all his other qualifications, was a reader of Hebrew, and a favourer of Mr. Hutchinſon's Philoſophy; but had kept it to himſelf, in the ſpirit of Nicodemus; and, when I aſked him the reaſon of it afterwards, and complained of the reſerve with which he had ſo long treated me in this reſpect; "Why," ſaid he, "theſe "things are in no repute; the world does not receive "them; and you, being a young man, who muſt keep "what friends you have, and make your fortune in the "world, I thought it better to let you go on in your "own way, than bring you into that embarraſſment "which might be productive of more harm than good, "and embitter the future courſe of your life: beſides, "it was far from being clear to me, how you would re-"ceive them; and then I might have loſt your friend-"ſhip." It was now too late for ſuch a remonſtrance to have any effect; I therefore, on the contrary, prevailed upon him to become my maſter in Hebrew, which I was very deſirous to learn: and in this he acquitted himſelf with ſo much ſkill and kind attention,

writing

writing out for me with his own hand ſuch grammatical rules and directions as he judged neceſſary, that in a very ſhort time I could go on without my guide. I remember however, that I had nearly worked myſelf to death, by determining, like Duns Scotus in the Picture-Gallery, to go through a whole chapter in the Hebrew before night.

To this gentleman, whoſe name was George Watſon, I recommended Mr. Horne at my departure from Oxford; and they were ſo well pleaſed with each other, that Mr. Horne, inſtead of going home to his friends in the vacation, ſtayed for the advantage of following his ſtudies at Oxford, under the direction of his new teacher: and, in the autumn of the year 1749, he began a Series of Letters to his Father, which fill above thirty pages in large quarto, very cloſely written; from the whole tenor of which, it is pleaſant to ſee, how entire a friendſhip and confidence there was between a grave and learned father, and a ſon, not yet twenty years of age! Of theſe letters, though they are by no means correct enough, either for ſtyle or judgment, to ſtand the teſt of ſevere criticiſm, it is highly proper I ſhould give ſome account; to ſhew what thoſe opinions were, which had now got poſſeſſion of his mind; intermixing with my abſtract ſuch notes and explanations as ſhall ſeem requiſite for a better underſtanding of it.

Having firſt apologized to his father, for not viſiting him in the vacation, he gives him an account of his teacher. "I am obliged for the happineſs I have

"enjoyed

"enjoyed of late to a gentleman of this ſociety, and "ſhall always bleſs God that his providence ever "brought me acquainted with him. He is a Fellow "of our houſe; and, though but ſix-and-twenty, as "complete a ſcholar in the whole circle of learning, "as great a divine, as good a man, and as polite a "gentleman, as the preſent age can boaſt of." Theſe words of Mr. Horne I introduce with peculiar ſatiſfaction; becauſe they afford ſo ſtrong a concurring teſtimony to the truth of what I have already ventured to ſay of Mr. Watſon. This excellent man never publiſhed any large work, and will be known to poſterity only by ſome occaſional pieces which he printed in his life-time. His Sermon on the 19th Pſalm, which he preached before the Univerſity, and afterwards left the printing of to my care, ſo delighted Mr. Horne (as it appears from theſe letters to his father) that it probably raiſed in his mind the firſt deſire of undertaking that Commentary on the whole book of Pſalms, which he afterwards brought to ſuch perfection*. Mr. Watſon publiſhed another Sermon on the Divine Appearance in Gen. 18; which was furiouſly ſhot at by the buſh-fighters of that time in the *Monthly Review*; inſomuch that the author thought it might be of ſome ſervice to take up his pen and write them a letter; in which their inſolence is reproved with ſuch ſuperior dignity of mind and ſerenity of temper, and their

* This is the gentleman who is ſpoken of in a Note to the Comment on Pſ. 19.

ignorance and error so learnedly exposed, that, if I were desirous of shewing to any reader what Mr. Watson was, and what *they* were, I would by all means put that letter into his hand; of which I suppose no copies are now to be found, but in the possession of some of his surviving friends. It is however made mention of with due honour by Dr. Delany, the celebrated Dean of Down in Ireland, who was once the intimate friend of Swift, and has given us the best account of his life and character in his Observations in answer to Lord Orrery. In a Preface to the third volume of his Revelation examined with Candour, which he printed at London very late in life, he speaks of a malignant style of criticism, in practice at that time with the obscure and unknown authors of a Monthly Review; and observes upon the case, that "he must seem at first sight a rash "as well as a bold man, who would venture to wage "war at once with Billingsgate and Banditti. And "yet in truth," adds he, "such a war (defensive only) "hath been waged with them to great advantage, by a "gentleman, whose mind and manners are as remote "from illiberal scurrility and abuse, as his adversaries "appear to be from learning, from candour, and from "every character of true criticism. Mr. Watson, the "defendant here mentioned, hath, in return to their "scurrility, answered and exposed them with strong, "clear and irresistible reasoning, and such a meek, calm "and Christian spirit, as hath done honour to his own "character, and uncommon justice to the Christian "cause; such as were sufficient to silence any thing "but

"but effrontery, hardened in ignorance, to the end of "the world." Mr. Watſon alſo printed a Sermon, preached before the Univerſity on the 29th of May, which he calls an Admonition to the Church of England. In a long Preface to this Sermon, he has thrown out ſuch valuable obſervations, that an excellent Manual might be formed out of them, for preſerving the members of the Church of England ſteady in their profeſſion; by ſhewing to them, ſo plainly as is here done, the principal dangers to which they are now expoſed. Having ſaid thus much of his teacher (and I could with pleaſure have ſaid much more) I muſt now ſhew what he learned under him.

From the general account he gives of his ſtudies, he appears, in conſequence of his intercourſe with Mr. Watſon, to have been perſuaded, that the Syſtem of Divinity in the Holy Scripture is explained and atteſted by the ſcriptural account of created nature; and that this account, including the Moſaic Coſmogony, is true ſo far as it goes: and that the Bible, in virtue of its originality, is fitter to explain all the books in the world than they are to explain it: that much of the learning of the age was either unprofitable in itſelf, or dangerous in its effect; and that literature, ſo far as it was a faſhion, was in general unfavourable to Chriſtianity, and to a right underſtanding of the Scripture: that the Jews had done much hurt in the Hebrew; not to the text by corrupting it, but by leading us into their falſe way of interpreting and underſtanding it; and that their Rabbinical writers were therefore not to be taken as teachers by Chriſtian

ſtudents:

ſtudents: that a notion lately conceived of the Moſaic law, as an inſtitution merely civil or ſecular, without the doctrines of life and immortality in it, was of pernicious tendency; contrary to the ſenſe of all the primitive writers, and the avowed doctrine of the Church of England: that the ſciences of Metaphyſics and Ethics had a near alliance to Deiſm; and that, in conſequence of the authority they had obtained, the doctrine of our pulpits was in general fallen below the Chriſtian ſtandard; and that the Saviour and the Redemption, without which our religion is nothing, were in a manner forgotten; which had given too much occaſion to the irregular teaching of the Tabernacle: that the ſin of modern Deiſm is the ſame in kind with the ſin of Paradiſe, which brought death into the world; becauſe it aſpires to divine wiſdom, that is, to the knowlege of divine things, and the diſtinction between good and evil, independently of God.

He had learned farther, that the Hebrew language, and the Hebrew antiquities, lead to a ſuperior way of underſtanding the mythology and writings of the Heathen claſſical authors: and that the Hebrew is a language of ideas; whoſe terms for inviſible and ſpiritual things are taken with great advantage from the objects of nature; and that there can be no other way of conceiving ſuch things, becauſe all our ideas enter by the ſenſes: whereas in all other languages, there are arbitrary ſounds without ideas.

It appeared to him farther, that unbelief and blaſphemy

phemy were gaining ground upon us, in virtue of ſome popular miſtakes in Natural Philoſophy, and threatened to baniſh all religion out of the world. Voltaire began very early to make his uſe of philoſophy, and corrupt the world with it. He never was fit to mount it; but he walked by the ſide of it, and uſed it as a ſtalking-horſe. It is therefore of great conſequence to the learned to know, that, as the heavens and the elements of the world had been ſet up by the Heathens, as having power in themſelves; and that as the Heathens, building on this falſe foundation, had loſt the knowlege of God; the modern doctrine, which gives innate powers to matter, as the followers of Democritus and Epicurus did, would probably end in Atheiſm*: that the forces, which the modern Philoſophy uſes, are not the forces of nature; but that the world is carried on by the action of the elements on one another, and all under God: that it is no better than raving, to give active powers to matter, ſuppoſing it capable of acting where it is not; and to affirm, at the ſame time, that all matter is inert, that is inactive, and that even the Deity cannot act but where he is preſent, becauſe his *power* cannot be but where his *ſubſtance* is.

He was alſo convinced, that infinite miſchief had been done, not only by the tribe of Deiſts and Philoſophers, but by ſome of our moſt celebrated divines, in extolling the dignity of human nature and the wiſdom of human reaſon; both of which the ſcripture

* This hath now actually come to paſs.

delivers

delivers to us under a very different character; which the experience of the world is daily confirming. That infidels and profligates ſhould wiſh to eſtabliſh their own opinions upon the ruins of revelation was not to be wondered at; but that they, whoſe office it was to dreſs and defend the ſacred vineyard, ſhould fall in with them, and join with the wild boar out of the wood to root it up, was a matter of grief and ſurpriſe. A diſtemper muſt indeed be epidemical, when the phyſicians themſelves are ſeized with it. This malady, when traced to its fountain head, appears to have ariſen from a general neglect in ſchools and ſeminaries of the ſtudy of the Scriptures in their original languages; where they attend ſo much to the works of heathens, and ſo little to the book of light, life and immortality. While the heads of boys are filled with tales of Jupiter, Juno, Mars, Bacchus, and Venus, the Bible is little heard of; and ſo the heathen creed becomes not only the firſt but the whole ſtudy. Jews, miſtaken as they are, are ſtill diligent in teaching the Scripture to their children in their own way; while we are teaching what even Jews are wiſe enough to abominate. Poſſeſſed by this opinion, that all polite knowlege is in heathen authors, and the Bible but a dull heavy book, which, inſtead of promoting, rather ſtands in the way of improvement, a lad is ſent from ſchool to the Univerſity. Here is a very alarming criſis. If he happen to be of a ſprightly wit, he falls into looſe company, and, for want of religious principles, is led into all manner of wickedneſs. Should he ſtudy, he obtains Logic under the form of a ſcholaſtic jargon, which in its ſimplicity* is of excellent uſe. Then he learns a ſyſtem of Ethics, which teaches morals without religious data, as the heathens did. After which, he probably goes on to Wollaſton, Shaftſbury, and others; and is at length fixed in the opinion, that reaſon is ſufficient for man without revelation. Our young philoſopher, having proceeded thus far, wants nothing but Metaphyſics to complete him; by ſetting him to reaſon without principles, to judge without evidence, and to comprehend without ideas. He learns to deduce the being and attributes of God *à priori*; in conſequence of which he diſcovers, that God is not a Trinity, but a ſingle perſon. When a gentleman, thus equipped, takes the Bible into his hand and commences divine, what muſt become of *it*, and of *him!* Thus it appears, that, as things go now, a man may be a maſter of what is called human learning, and yet ignorant to the laſt degree of what only is worth knowing.

The foregoing abſtract, which I have taken as faithfully as I could, is ſufficient to ſhew upon what great and important ſubjects Mr. Horne's mind was employed at this early period of his life. In the courſe of this correſpondence, there are ſeveral ſtrokes of humour which ought not to be forgotten. The Hebrew

* The more *ſimple* the better: but the *old logic*, even with all its jargon, is a better guard to truth, than the new which has ſuperſeded it; and is found by many, who have conſidered the difference, ſo to be.

Concord-

Concordance of Marius de Calasio had lately been republished by the Rev. Mr. Romaine, and was an expensive work, so high as ten guineas at that time, though now at a price very much reduced. Mr. Horne had set his heart upon this work, thinking it necessary to his present studies; but knew not how to purchase it out of his allowance, or to ask his father in plain terms to make him a present of it; so he told him a story, and left the moral of it to speak for itself.

In the last age, when Bishop Walton's Polyglott was first published, there was at Cambridge a Mr. Edwards, passionately fond of Oriental learning; who afterwards went by the name of Rabbi Edwards: he was a good man, and a good scholar: but being then rather young in the University, and not very rich, Walton's great work was far above his pocket. Neverthelefs, not being able to sleep well without it, he sold his bed, and some of his furniture, and made the purchase: in consequence of which, he was obliged to sleep in a large chest, originally made to hold his clothes. But getting into his chest one night rather uncautiously, the lid of it, which had a bolt with a spring, fell down upon him and locked him in past recovery; and there he lay well nigh smothered to death. In the morning, Edwards, who was always an exact man, not appearing, it was wondered what was become of him: till at last his bed-maker, or the person who in better times *had been his bed-maker*, being alarmed, went to his chambers time enough to release him: and the accident, getting air, came to the ears of his friends, who soon redeemed his bed for him. This story Mr. Horne told his father; and it had the desired effect. His father immediately sent him the money; for which he returns him abundant thanks, promising to repay him in the only possible way, viz. that of using the books to the best advantage. They were without question diligently turned over while he worked at his Commentary on the Psalms, and yielded him no small assistance.

The use of Hebrew to divines was well understood by Bishop Bull, who did not content himself with a slight and superficial knowlege of it; and judged it so necessary in divinity, that it was usual with him to recommend the study of it to the candidates for orders, as a foundation for their future theological performances. Without this knowlege in Mr. Horne, we should never have seen his Commentary upon the Psalms.

When a student hath once persuaded himself that he sees truth in the principles of Mr. Hutchinson, a great revolution succeeds in his ideas of the natural world and its œconomy. Qualities in matter, with a vacuum for them to act in, are no longer venerable; and the authority of Newton's name, which goes with them, loses some of its influence. Nor is this in the present case so much to be wondered at: for Mr. Hutchinson had conceived an opinion, which possessed his mind very strongly, that Sir I. Newton and Dr. Clarke had formed a design, by introducing certain speculations founded on their new mode of philosophi-

zing,

zing, to undermine and overthrow the theology of the Scripture, and to bring in the Heathen Jupiter or Stoical *anima mundi* into the place of the true God, whom we Christians believe and worship. This will seem less extravagant, when it is known, that Mr. Boyle* had also expressed his suspicions, many years before, that Heathenism was about to rise again out of some new speculations, and reputedly grand discoveries, in Natural Philosophy. Yet I am not willing to believe, that the eminent persons above-mentioned had actually formed any such design. What advantage unbelievers have, since their time, taken of their speculations in divinity and philosophy, and of the high repute which has attended them, and of the exclusive honours given to mathematical learning and mathematical reasoning, is another question; and it calls for a serious examination at this time, when the moral world is in great disorder, from causes not well understood.

However these things may be, the prejudice so strongly infused by Mr. Hutchinson against an evil design in Clarke and Newton, took possession of Mr. Horne's mind at the age of nineteen; and was farther confirmed by reports which he had heard of a private good understanding betwixt them and the Sceptics of the day, such as Collins, Toland, Tindal, &c. more than the world generally knew of. It is an undoubted fact, that there was an attempt to in-

* This remarkable passage from Mr. Boyle is quoted in The Scholar Armed, lately published for the Rivingtons, vol. ii. p. 282.

troduce Atheism, or Materialism, which is the same thing, here in England, toward the beginning of this century; of which the *Pantheisticon* of *Janus Junius Eoganesius*, a technical name for John Toland, is a sufficient proof: and Hutchinson, who knew all the parties concerned, and the designs going forward, dropped such hints in his Treatise on Power* Essential and Mechanical, as gave a serious alarm to many persons well disposed. But our young scholar, viewing the whole matter at first on the ridiculous side, and considering it not only as a dangerous attempt upon religion, but a palpable offence against truth and reason, drew a parallel between the Heathen doctrines in the *Somnium Scipionis* of Cicero, and the Newtonian Philosophy; which he published, but without his name, in the year 1751; all the particulars of which parallel I shall not undertake to justify. I see its faulty flights and wanderings, from a want of more mature judgment and experience. It provoked several remarks, some in print, and some in manuscript; of which remarks the judgment was not greater, and the levity not less. The question was in reality too deep for those who attempted to fathom it at that time. Mr. Horne soon saw the impropriety of the style and manner, which as a young man he had assumed for merriment in that little piece: these were by no means agreeable to the constitution of his mind and temper. He therefore observed a very different manner after-

* See p. 243, &c. of the old edition; beginning with the account of Woodward's conduct.

wards;

wards; and, as ſoon as he had taken time to bethink himſelf, he reſumed and reconſidered the ſubject; publiſhing his ſentiments in 1753, (the year after that in which he had taken his degree of M. A.) in a mild and ſerious pamphlet, which he called A fair, candid, and impartial State of the Caſe between Sir I. Newton and Mr. Hutchinſon: allowing to Sir Iſaac the great merit of having ſettled laws and rules in Natural Philoſophy; but at the ſame time claiming for Mr. Hutchinſon the diſcovery of the true phyſiological cauſes, by which, under the power of the Creator, the natural world is moved and directed. The piece certainly is, what it calls itſelf, *fair*, *candid*, and *impartial*; and the merits of the cauſe are very judiciouſly ſtated between the two parties: in conſequence of which, a reader will diſtinguiſh, that Newton may be of ſovereign ſkill in meaſuring *forces* as a Mathematician; and yet, that Hutchinſon may be right in aſſigning *cauſes*, as a Phyſiologiſt. It would carry me out too far, if I were to ſhew by what arguments and evidence Mr. Horne has ſupported this diſtinction. For theſe I muſt refer to the pamphlet itſelf, which, having become very ſcarce*, hath been lately reprinted with ſome other of his works: and I will venture to ſay thus much in its behalf, that, whatever becomes of the argument, the manner in which it is handled ſhews Mr. Horne, who, when he wrote it, was only

* This Pamphlet, together with another entitled An Apology for certain Gentlemen in the Univerſity of Oxford, being reprinted, may be had of the Bookſellers by whom the Life is ſold.

in his twenty-third year, to have been a very extraordinary young man.

New ſtudies and new principles never fail to bring a man into new company; all mankind being naturally diſpoſed to aſſociate with thoſe who agree beſt with themſelves. Of theſe his new friends it will be juſt and proper to give ſome ſhort account. The chief of them was Mr. Watſon, whom I have already mentioned. Another of them was Dr. Hodges, the Provoſt of Oriel College; who compoſed a work to which he gave the title of Elihu; the chief ſubject of it being the character of Elihu in the Book of Job. The ſtyle of it has great dignity and ſtatelineſs, without being formal; and is at the ſame time clear, and eaſy to be underſtood. Dr. Hodges was undoubtedly a very great maſter of his pen; but, having declared himſelf without reſerve in favour of Mr. Hutchinſon's doctrines, his work was virulently aſſaulted and groſsly miſrepreſented. Of this he complained; as he might well do: and what did he get by it? He was told in return, that a writer upon the Book of *Job* ſhould take every thing with *patience!* His book, however, went into a ſecond edition. He was a man of a venerable appearance, with an addreſs and delivery which made him very popular as a preacher in the Univerſity.

The learned Provoſt of Oriel, ſo far as it occurs to me, was the firſt who with a ſtrong hand ſounded the alarm-bell againſt thoſe ſpeculations and their conſequences, which have now prevailed to the over-

throw

throw of the church and kingdom of France. A piece intitled *Les Mœurs (Manners)* was publiſhed there in the year 1748; the tendency of which was to eſtabliſh natural religion on the ruins of all external worſhip, and ſo to free the world from all laws human and divine; that man might be guided by nothing but the light of his own mind. This was burned by the hangman at Paris; the ſoil, as Dr. Hodges obſerved, being not *quite*, though *nearly*, prepared for the reception of theſe tares. The country and the climate choſen by the writer were certainly promiſing, on this conſideration, that ſuperſtition and irreligion are generally obſerved to be the reciprocal cauſes and effects of each other. Againſt the principles and ſpirit of this undertaking, the author of *Elihu* was ſo much in earneſt, that he gave an abridgment of the work from a French copy, which he procured for that purpoſe. I could here ſtop with great pleaſure, if it were proper, to extract ſome of the evidence ſo powerfully urged againſt all ſuch attempts by this learned gentleman: but I muſt refer the reader to his *Preliminary Diſcourſe*. It is, however, a fact never to be neglected, which he and others have aſcertained by abundant authority, that "all the religion of the heathen world was traditional "revelation corrupted:" which, if it can be made good, overthrows at once all the modern theories of infidelity.

The Rev. Mr. Holloway, Rector of Middleton-Stoney in Oxfordſhire, had been a private tutor to Lord

Lord Spencer, in the houſe of the Hon. John Spencer his father; who, with all his extravagances, never failed to preſerve due reſpect* to Mr. Holloway, and liſtened to him with attention, when he converſed freely with the company at his table. This gentleman had been perſonally acquainted with Mr. Hutchinſon, and had publiſhed an elementary piece in favour of his philoſophical principles. But he was better known in the Univerſity of Oxford by three excellent diſcourſes on the Doctrine of Repentance, with a Supplement in anſwer to the perverſe Gloſſes of Tindal the Freethinker. The Vice-chancellor of that time took a pique againſt him for dropping a hint, in his Supplement againſt Tindal, that the perſon of Melchizedec was an exhibition of Chriſt before his Incarnation. This was no novel opinion; it had been advanced by others, before and after the Reformation; and in *them* the doctrine had given no offence. But Mr. Holloway, being a man ſuſpected and proſcribed on ſome other accounts, met with ſome hard and unworthy treatment upon the occaſion: yet to avoid a miſunderſtanding with the whole Univerſity, when

* A military gentleman, who was ſometimes of the party, remarked to a friend, that the ſtricteſt decorum was always obſerved, whenever Mr. Holloway, who ſupported the dignity of his profeſſion, was preſent; while another clergyman, who thought to recommend himſelf by laying aſide the clerical character, was treated with little ceremony and held in ſovereign contempt; from which he naturally inferred, that the clergy would not fail to meet with proper reſpect, if it was not their own fault.

only

only ſome individuals were concerned, he ſuppreſſed what he had written in his own defence. His ſcheme for an Analyſis of the Hebrew Language, though it comprehends a vaſt compaſs of learning, is partly fanciful, and would bear a long diſpute, into which I ſhall not enter: but this muſt be ſaid in reſpect to Mr. Horne, that when he firſt commenced his theological ſtudies, he derived many real advantages from his acquaintance with this gentleman; and I could name one of his moſt ſhining and uſeful diſcourſes, which, in the main argument of it, was taken from ſome looſe papers of Remarks on Warburton's Divine Legation; to the principles of which this learned gentleman, for many good reaſons, which he ſpared not to give, was a zealous adverſary. To ſay the truth, there was little cordiality on either ſide between the renowned writer of the Divine Legation and the readers of Mr. Hutchinſon. On moſt ſubjects of religion and learning, their opinions were irreconcileable. He deſpiſed their doctrines and interpretations, and railed at them as *Cabbaliſtical*; and they deſpiſed his Empirical Divinity; while, at the ſame time, they dreaded the ill effect of it, from the boldneſs of the man, and the popularity of his books; which have a great flaſh of learning, but with little ſolidity, and leſs piety. To the purity of Chriſtian Literature they have certainly done, and are ſtill doing, much hurt. When the firſt volume of the Divine Legation was ſhewn to Dr. Bentley, (as his ſon-in-law the late Biſhop Cumberland told me) he looked it over, and then obſerved

of

of the author to his friend—*This man has a monſtrous appetite, with a very bad digeſtion**. In juſtice to Mr. Holloway, whatever might be ſaid againſt him, it muſt be ſaid for him, that he was a ſound claſſical ſcholar, who had gone farther than moſt men into the myſteries of the Greek Philoſophy; and to an attentive ſtudy of the Chriſtian Fathers had added great ſkill in the Hebrew and Arabic languages; ſuch as qualified him to take up and maintain the cauſe of the *Hebrew Primævity* againſt its opponents. Confined as he was to the ſolitude of a country pariſh, if he found himſelf out of practice in the writing of Latin, he uſed to renew it occaſionally by reading over the *Moriæ Encomium* of Eraſmus, which never failed to reinſtate him: and I am perſuaded the anecdote may

* This was written before I had a ſight of the learned Biſhop Hurd's Life of Dr. Warburton, lately publiſhed, in which ſuch ſublime praiſes are beſtowed on the Alliance, the Divine Legation, and other works of that fanciful but very ingenious projector of unfounded theories. Though I honour the character of Biſhop Hurd, and admire every thing he writes, my opinion of the *uſefulneſs* of the works of Dr. Warburton is very little changed by what I have ſeen. I am ſtill perſuaded, that neither religion nor learning will ever derive much benefit, nor the Chriſtian world any conſiderable *edification*, from the works of that famous writer: neither will they probably derive any great harm; becauſe it is apprehended, the reading of Biſhop Warburton's books will hereafter be much leſs than it hath been. The Methodiſts deſpiſed him for a part of his Chriſtian character, as much as he deſpiſed them for a part of their character; and both had equal reaſon. His learning is almoſt as much unlike to Chriſtianity, as their Chriſtianity is unlike to learning. I forbear to indulge any farther reflections on ſo critical a ſubject.

be

be of uſe to other ſcholars when in danger of loſing their Latinity.

Mr. Holloway was firſt induced to take notice of Mr. Horne, on occaſion of ſome verſes which he had addreſſed to his friend Mr. Watſon. They expreſſed the ardor of his gratitude, and diſcovered a poetical genius*.

The Rev. Mr. Welbourne of Wendelbury near Biceſter in Oxfordſhire, whom, from the monaſtic ſpirit of a ſingle life, and a remarkable attachment to the ſtudy of Antiquity, Mr. Horne delighted to call by the name of *Robertus Wendelburienſis*, was very much reſpected and beloved, and often viſited by Mr. Horne ſo long as he lived. Educated at Weſtminſter and Chriſt-church, he was a ſcholar of the politer claſs; and a deep and ſkilful ſtudent in the Scripture, of which he gave a ſpecimen in an interpretation of the laſt words of David from the Hebrew. He went farther in this, and with better ſucceſs, than the learned and ingenious Dr. Grey, the verſifier of the Book of Job, after the manner of Biſhop Hare's Pſalms, with whom he had been acquainted. He wrote well in Engliſh and Latin, and compoſed ſeveral learned works, which had their exceptionable paſſages, from a viſible inclination toward ſome of the peculiarities of the Church of Rome. He had lived ſeveral years in

* It was rather officious to give them to the world, as ſomebody hath done ſince Dr. Horne's death. Our opinion of a great and good man, who has finiſhed his courſe, ought not to be gathered from the haſty and ardent productions of his youth.

strict friendship with Dr. Frewen the physician, in whose house he always resided when he made a visit to Oxford; also with the Reverend Sir John Dolben, of Finedon in Northamptonshire, the learned, accomplished, devout, and charitable father of the present worthy Sir William Dolben, member for the University of Oxford; and also Mr. Counsellor Gilpin; to the last of whom he left his collection of Grecian and Roman coins; which, if I am rightly informed, is now in the new library at Christ-church*.

Another excellent friend of Mr. Horne was the late Dr. Patten, of Corpus Christi College; a gentleman of the purest manners and unquestionable erudition. On re-considering the state of the question between Christians and Infidels, and seeing how absolutely necessary it was to speak a plain language in a case of such importance to the world, he gave to the University of Oxford a discourse which he called the "Christian Apology;" and which the Vice-chancellor and Heads of Houses requested him to publish. It went upon true and indisputable principles; but it was not relished by the rash reasoners of the Warburtonian school; and a Mr. Heathcote, a very intemperate and unmannerly writer, who was at that time an assistant-preacher to Dr. Warburton at Lincoln's Inn, published a pamphlet against it; laying himself open,

* The complexion of this good man's character may be distinguished in the last letter I received from him, about two months before his death, of which I had an account from Dr. Horne. I shall give both the letters in the Appendix.

both

both in the matter and the manner of it, to the criticiſms of Dr. Patten; who will appear to any candid reader, who ſhall review that controverſy, to have been greatly his ſuperior as a ſcholar and a divine. Dr. Patten could not with any propriety be ſaid to have written on the Hutchinſonian plan; but Mr. Heathcote, in aid of his own arguments, found it convenient to charge him with it, and ſuggeſt to the public that he was an Hutchinſonian; which gave Dr. Patten an opportunity of ſpeaking his private ſentiments, and doing juſtice to thoſe gentlemen in the Univerſity of Oxford, who were then under the reproach of being followers of Mr. Hutchinſon*.

The Rev. Dr. Wetherell, now Dean of Hereford, was then a young man in the College of which he is now the worthy Maſter: and ſuch was his zeal at that time in favour of Hebrew literature, that Mr. Horne, Mr. Wetherell, and Mr. Martin (now Dr. Fairfax) and a fourth perſon intimately connected with them all, ſat down for one whole winter, to examine and ſettle, as far as they were able, all the *Themata* of the Hebrew language: writing down their remarks

* On occaſion of this paragraph, I have re-conſidered Dr. Patten's Diſcourſe and the Defence of it; and am perſuaded it might be of much ſervice, if every young man were to read them both, before he takes holy orders. His picture of faſhionable Chriſtianity is very alarming, and I fear it is not exaggerated. Another Diſcourſe preached before the Univerſity, and from the ſame pen, publiſhed alſo by requeſt, intitled "The oppoſition between the Goſ"pel of Jeſus Chriſt, and what is called the religion of Nature," deſerves to be noticed here.

 daily,

daily, and collecting from Marius, and Buxtorf, and Pagninus and others, what might be of use for compiling a new Lexicon. How much judgment they had, at this early period, to render their papers valuable, we dare not say: but, such as they were, the fruits of a faithful and laborious scrutiny, a copy of them was handed to the learned Mr. Parkhurst, late of the University of Cambridge, an eminent labourer in the same vineyard, to whom the public have since been greatly indebted for three editions of his Hebrew Lexicon; which contains such variety of curious and useful information, that, contrary to the nature of other Dictionaries (properly so called) it may be turned over for entertainment as a Commentary on the Scripture, and a magazine of Biblical Erudition. His two scriptural Lexicons, the one Greek, and the other Hebrew, are both so excellent in their way, that they will last as long as the world; unless the new Goths of infidelity should break in upon us and destroy, as they certainly wish to do, all the monuments of Christian learning*.

Doctor George Berkeley, of late years a Prebendary of the church of Canterbury and Chancellor of Brecknock, was then Mr. George Berkeley, a student of Christ-church, a son of that celebrated pattern of virtue, science, and apostolical zeal, Dr. Berkeley,

* The third edition of Mr. Parkhurst's Hebrew Lexicon was promoted by Bishop Horne, whose name stands first among the patrons to whom it is inscribed; though Bishop Horne did not live till it was published.

Bishop

Bishop of Cloyne in the kingdom of Ireland; who chose to spend the latter days of his life in retirement at Oxford, while his son was a member of the University. Between this gentleman and Mr. Horne a very early intimacy commenced, and much of their time was spent in each other's company. Under the training and with the example of so excellent a father, Mr. Berkeley grew up into a firm believer of the Christian religion, and discovered an affectionate regard to every man of letters, who was ready, like himself, to explain and defend it. He was consequently a very zealous admirer of Mr. Horne; and the one had the happiness of belonging to the Chapter, while the other for several years was Dean of Canterbury: and when his friend was removed to the See of Norwich, Dr. Berkeley preached his Consecration Sermon at Lambeth; an act of respect for which he had reserved himself, having been under a persuasion, for some years before, that he should see Mr. Horne become a Bishop. His discourse* on that occasion shewed him to be a true son and an able minister of the Church of England: and another discourse, originally delivered on a 30th of January, and reprinted since with large and curious annotations, has distinguished him for as firm and loyal a subject to his king and the laws of his country. Dr. Berkeley was

* This Sermon is now published, and may, not improperly, be bound up with this volume, if the reader pleases. The title of it is, An Inquiry into the Origin of Episcopacy, in a Discourse preached at the Consecration of George Horne, D. D. &c. &c.

very greatly eſteemed by his patron the late Archbiſhop Secker, with whom he had much influence; and he never ceaſed to take advantage of it, till he had obtained preferment from him for one of his old friends, who had no other proſpect. The father of Dr. Berkeley has been made known to the world by a few happy words of Mr. Pope: but the following anecdote, which is preſerved among the private notes of Biſhop Horne, will give us a more exact idea of his character. Biſhop Atterbury, having heard much of Mr. Berkeley, wiſhed to ſee him. Accordingly, he was one day introduced to him by the Earl of Berkeley. After ſome time, Mr. Berkeley left the room: on which Lord Berkeley ſaid to the Biſhop, "Does my couſin anſwer your Lordſhip's expecta-"tions?" The Biſhop, lifting up his hands in aſtoniſhment, replied, "So much underſtanding, ſo much "knowlege, ſo much innocence, and ſuch humility, "I did not think had been the portion of any but an-"gels, till I ſaw this gentleman." The paſſage is taken from Hughes's Letters. II. 2.*

Mr. Samuel Glaſſe, a ſtudent of Chriſt-church, who had the repute he merited of being one of the beſt ſcholars from Weſtminſter ſchool, was another of Mr. Horne's intimate friends, and continued to love and admire him through the whole courſe of his life.

* Dr. Berkeley, the excellent ſon of an excellent father, changed this world (in which he had ſeen much trouble) for a better, on the day of Epiphany 1795, before the firſt edition of this work went to the preſs.

The world need not be told what Dr. Glaſſe has been doing ſince he left the Univerſity, as a divine, as a magiſtrate, and as a teacher and tutor of the firſt eminence; of whoſe uſeful labours, the goſpel, the law, the church, the bar, the ſchools of learning, the rich and the poor, have long felt and confeſſed the benefit: and may they long continue ſo to do! although it may be ſaid, without any ſuſpicion of flattery, in the words of the Poet—*non deficit alter aureus*—a ſon, whoſe learning, abilities and good principles have already entitled him to the thanks of his country, and will ſecure his fame with poſterity.

This gentleman, the ſon of Dr. G. diſtinguiſhed himſelf very early in life by his uncommon proficiency in Hebrew literature, which procured him the favour of Dr. Kennicott, and a ſtudentſhip of Chriſt-church. He has ſince acquired a great addition of fame as a claſſical ſcholar, by his elegant tranſlation into Greek Iambics of Maſon's Caractacus, and Milton's Samſon Agoniſtes, adapted in form, and ſtyle, and manner, to the ancient Greek drama*. And he has recently ſhewn himſelf an elegant Engliſh writer, as well as a pious

* Though I ſpeak with reſpect of this, as a work of great ſcholarſhip, and even wonderful in a young man, I have my doubts, whether any Engliſhman can exhibit unexceptionable Greek verſification, in which a Critic cannot, with a microſcope in his hand, and a little jealouſy in his eye, diſcover flaws and pinholes; and that a Greek verſion of a fine Engliſh Poem, whoever produces it, will at laſt be but a bad likeneſs of a good thing: which may be ſaid without impeaching the

pious and well informed divine, by his publication of the Contemplations of Bishop Hall, in a form very much improved. He had prepared a Dedication of that excellent work to Bishop Horne; but the Bishop dying, while the work was depending, an advertisement is prefixed, which does great honour to his memory.

From Westminster-school there came, at an earlier period, a Mr. John Hamilton of University College, whose father was a Member of the Irish Parliament, and his mother a lady of high rank. This amiable young man, for the politeness of his behaviour, his high accomplishments, his vivacity of temper and readiness of wit, was a companion equally respectable and desirable; so nearly allied in disposition and abilities to the two characters of Mr. Watson and Mr. Horne, that a strict friendship grew up between them. The example of some seducing companions from Westminster-school had rendered him for a while dissipated and thoughtless: but when the time approached, in which he was required to prepare himself for holy orders, he determined to become a clergyman in good earnest; gave himself up to study and retire-

the parts or the diligence of any translator. When a man writes in a dead language, he does it at a great hazard: and I have heard this matter carried to such a nicety by a person of distinguished learning, as to suppose it dangerous, even in Latin composition, to put a noun and a verb together, unless you can find that noun and that verb actually standing together in some native Latin writer of allowed authority.

ment;

ment; and was known to rise frequently at four o'clock in a summer's morning, to read the works of St. Austin. With this disposition, it is no wonder he was ready to embrace every opportunity of deriving more light to his Christian studies. He therefore soon became a Hebrew student in common with his friends, and made a rapid progress in divinity. For a time he took upon himself the curacy of Bedington in Surrey: but he was soon advanced to the archdeaconry of Raphoe in Ireland, having first obtained a presentation to the valuable living of Taboyne; where, to the loss of the world, and the unspeakable grief of the author of these papers, to whom he was a most affectionate and valuable friend, he soon afterwards died. In the beginning of his indisposition, he had been almost miraculously restored at Bristol in the spring of the year 1754, just at the time when the Living was given to him by Lord Abercorn his relation, and the dignity superadded by the Bishop of the diocese. Ireland was a stage, on which his learning and principles, his active zeal, his polite manners and great abilities, were much wanted. They have at this time but a mean opinion of that kind of learning which this young archdeacon so much valued and affected. Had he lived, he might have done much good in bringing over many considerable persons to an attentive study of the Scripture, which had produced so happy an effect upon himself. But, alas! instead of this, it is now reported, that the country has been considerably hurt in its principles by some modern

 writings,

writings, which have lately come into vogue; of which it is not my buſineſs in this place to ſpeak more particularly.

It has given me great pleaſure, thus to take a review, haſty as it has been, of ſome of thoſe excellent perſons with whom Mr. Horne was connected in the days of his youth. A reader, who is a ſtranger to all the parties, may ſuſpect that I have turned my pen to the making of extraordinary characters; but I truſt he will take my word for it, that I have only made them ſuch as I found them; and ſuch as the late good Biſhop their friend would have repreſented them, had he been alive and called upon to do them juſtice. I am convinced, his own pen would have given more to ſome, not leſs to any: and that he would have mentioned others of whom I have not ſpoken; for certainly I might have added many to the collection; ſuch as, the Rev. John Auchmuty, whoſe father was Dean of Armagh, and who uſed to amuſe us with an account of his adventures at Tetuan in Africa, during his chaplainſhip under Admiral Forbes: Mr. James Stillingfleet, a grandſon to the celebrated and learned Biſhop of that name; firſt one of the Hebrew Exhibitioners at Wadham College; afterwards Fellow of Merton, and now Prebendary of Worceſter: Mr. George Downing, another Hebrew Exhibitioner at Wadham College, and now a Prebendary of Ely, whom Mr. Horne admired and reſpected for thoſe virtues and qualifications, which have endeared him to all his acquaintance. To theſe

I might

I might add Mr. Edward Stillingfleet, a Gentleman Commoner of Wadham; the Reverend John Whitaker, now ſo well known by his learned and valuable writings; with others of like character and literature, to none of whom do I mean any diſreſpect if I have omitted them. There was one very learned gentleman in particular, Mr. Forſter of Corpus Chriſti College, who publiſhed a beautiful quarto edition of the Hebrew Bible. He had the reputation of being a profound ſcholar, and was a great favourite with Bp. Butler, author of the celebrated *Analogy* &c. This learned man introduced himſelf to Mr. Horne's acquaintance, only for the opportunity of conferring with him on ſome principles which he had newly adopted in Philoſophy and Divinity. How far Mr. Horne and Mr. Forſter proceeded in the argument, I cannot exactly ſay; but this I well remember, that, when the *conſubſtantiality* of the *elements* came into queſtion, Mr. Forſter did not ſeem to think *that* doctrine improbable, which later enquiries have rendered much leſs ſo: and allowed, that if the public were once ſatisfied in that particular, he believed very few objections would be made to the philoſophical ſcheme of Mr. Hutchinſon*.

I am now to conclude with a character, which I introduce with ſome reluctance; but it is too remarkable to be omitted in an account of Mr. Horne's

* See Mr. Horne's Apology (hereafter to be ſpoken of) p. 35, 36; where this conference with Mr. Forſter is alluded to.

literary connections; and some useful moral attends it in every circumstance: the character I mean is that of the late Dr. Dodd. Humanity should speak as tenderly of him as truth will permit, in consideration of his severe and lamentable fate.

A similitude in their studies and their principles produced an acquaintance between Mr. Horne and Mr. Dodd: for when Mr. Dodd began the world, he was a zealous favourer of Hebrew learning, and distinguished himself as a preacher; in which capacity he undoubtedly excelled to a certain degree, and in his time did much good. After Mr. Dodd had been noticed in the University of Cambridge for some of his exercises, he made himself known to the public by an English poetical translation of Callimachus, in which he discovered a poetical genius. Of the Preface to the translation of Callimachus, which gives the best general account, that was ever given in so short a compass, of the Heathen Mythology, the greater part was written for him by Mr. Horne. It is supposed, with good reason, that Mr. Dodd was obliged to others of his friends for several useful notes on the text of Callimachus. He makes a particular acknowlegement to the Rev. Mr. Parkhurst, "from "whose sound judgment, enlarged understanding, un- "wearied application, and generous openness of heart, "the world has great and valuable fruits to expect." Archbishop Secker conceived a favourable opinion of Mr. Dodd, from his performances in the pulpit; and it was probably owing to the influence of the

Archbishop,

Archbishop, that he was appointed to preach the sermons at Lady Moyer's Lectures. But this unhappy gentleman, having a strong desire, like many other young men of parts, to make a figure in the world, with a turn to an expensive way of living; and finding that his friends, who unhappily were suffering under the damnatory title of *Hutchinsonians*, would never be permitted (as the report then was) to rise to any eminence in the Church; Mr. Dodd thought it more prudent to leave them to their fate, with the hope of succeeding better in some other way: and, to purge himself in the eye of the world, he wrote expressly against them; laying many grievous things to their charge; some of which were true, when applied to particular persons; some greatly exaggerated; and some utterly false; as it may well be imagined, when it is considered that the author was writing to serve an interest*.

There could be no better judge than Mr. Dodd himself

* When it was under deliberation whether any answer should be given to this book of Mr. Dodd, Mr. Horne objected to it in the following terms, which discover his great prudence and judgment. "Whoever shall answer it, will be under the necessity of appearing "as a partizan, which in these times should be avoided as much as "possible. I had much rather the name of Hutchinson were dropped, and the useful things in him recommended to the world, "with their evidence, in another manner than they have been. "Mankind are tired and sick (I am sure I am for one) with the "fruitless squabbles and altercations about etymologies and particularities. In the mean time, the great plan of Philosophy and "Theology, that must instruct and edify, lies dormant."

himſelf of the motives on which he had aſſumed a new character. He certainly did himſelf ſome good, in the opinion of thoſe, who thought he was grown wiſer: but being ſenſible how far he had carried ſome things, and how much he had loſt himſelf, in the eſteem of his old friends, he was anxious to know what ſome of them ſaid about him. He therefore applied himſelf one day to a lady of great underſtanding and piety, who knew him well, and who alſo knew moſt of them; deſiring her to tell him, what Mr. ſuch an one ſaid of him? He ſays of you, anſwered ſhe—*Demas hath forſaken us, having loved this preſent world:* with which he appeared to be much affected. Not that the thing had actually been ſaid, ſo far as I know*, by the perſon in queſtion; but ſhe, knowing the propriety with which it might have been ſaid, gave him the credit of it. There was a general appearance of vanity about Mr. Dodd, which was particularly diſguſting to Mr Horne, who had none of it himſelf; and the levity, with which he had totally caſt off his former ſtudies, being added to it, both together determined him to drop the acquaintance with little heſitation. He not only avoided his company, but conceiving a diſlike as well to his moral as to his literary character, is ſuppoſed to have given ſuch an account of him in one of the public papers, as made him very ridiculous, under the name of *Tom Dingle*. Not long afterwards Mr. Foote brought him upon the

* But I am now informed, it actually was ſaid.

ſtage

ſtage for a tranſaction which reflected great diſhonour upon a clergyman, and for which the King ordered him to be ſtruck off the liſt of his chaplains.

The revolt of Mr. Dodd, if he meant to raiſe himſelf in the world by it, did by no means anſwer his purpoſe. It brought him into favour with Lord Cheſterfield; but that did much more hurt to his mind, than good to his fortune. The farther he advanced in life, the more he became embarraſſed: and his moral conduct was commonly known to be ſo far depraved, that a late celebrated gentleman of Clapham, who was privy to it, is ſaid to have predicted ſome years before, that he would come to an untimely end. How unſearchable are the wiſdom and juſtice of divine Providence! The worldly policy of Dr. Dodd loſt him the friendſhip of ſome wiſe and good men, particularly of Mr. Horne, but procured for him the favour of Lord Cheſterfield; and that favour tempted him to another ſtep of policy, which brought him to his death. The memory of Dr. Johnſon is much to be honoured for the tender part he took in behalf of Dr. Dodd during the time of his affliction. And let it be remembered, in juſtice to his former friends, that few perſons were more deeply affected by his lamentable end than ſome of thoſe who had been under the neceſſity of dropping his acquaintance. I have it on the beſt authority, that one of them kept a ſolemn faſt till night on the day of his execution, and afterwards moralized very ſeriouſly upon his fate in one of the newſpapers of the time.

From

From this account of Mr. Horne's friends and acquaintance I return now to the hiftory of his ftudies. When a young man of a vigorous mind determines, in thefe latter days of the Church, to make himfelf learned, he is in great danger, from the books he may read, and the company into which he may fall; notwithftanding the integrity of his mind, and the purity of his intentions. If he join himfelf to a party, he will be under the influence of an affection, which is very properly called partiality; and which inclines him to favour the meafures of his party indifcriminately; and therefore does great hurt to the judgment. He is apt to praife and cenfure, to love and hate, not with his own fpirit, but with the fpirit of his party. With their fingularities, whatever they may be, he will find little fault; and, if they have errors, they are fuch as he will not foon difcover. To this danger Mr. Horne was expofed, as a reader of Hutchinfon. I fhall therefore defcribe it more particularly, and fhew how and by what means he efcaped it in all its parts, and preferved the independency of his underftanding: in doing which, if I can do it faithfully, I fhall certainly make myfelf of fome ufe to the public.

Mr. Hutchinfon fell into a new and uncommon train of thinking in Philofophy, Theology, and Heathen Antiquity; and appears to have learned much of it from the Hebrew, which he ftudied in a way of his own: but as he laid too great a ftrefs in many inftances on the evidence of Hebrew Etymology,

his

his admirers would naturally do the ſame: and ſome of them carried the matter ſo far, that nothing elſe would go down with them; till by degrees they adopted a mode of ſpeaking, which had a nearer reſemblance to cant and jargon, than to ſound and ſober learning. To this weakneſs thoſe perſons were moſt liable, who had received the feweſt advantages from a learned education. This was the caſe with ſome ſenſible tradeſmen and mechanics, who, by ſtudying Hebrew, with the aſſiſtance of Engliſh only, grew conceited of their learning, and carried too much ſail with too little ballaſt. Of this Mr. Horne was very ſoon aware; and he was in ſo little danger of following the example, that I uſed to hear him diſplay the foibles of ſuch perſons with that mirth and good humour which he had ready at hand upon all occaſions. With the like diſcretion and candour, he allowed to the Reverend Dr. Sharp of Durham all that could reaſonably be allowed, when he attacked the followers of Hutchinſon upon the Etymological quarter, where they ſeemed moſt vulnerable, or, where they might at leaſt be annoyed with moſt appearance of advantage: and he never, through the whole courſe of his life, was a friend to the etymological part of the controverſy; as it appears from his writings; in which Hebrew etymology, however he might apply to it for himſelf, is rarely if ever inſiſted upon. In ſome of his private letters, one of which has been already referred to in a note, he declared his mind very freely on the inexpediency of ſquabbling

about

about words, when there were so many things to be brought forward, which were of greater importance, and would admit of less dispute.

A farther danger arose from that custom, in which some of the followers of Mr. Hutchinson had too freely indulged themselves, of treating their opponents with oo great asperity and contempt. Hutchinson himself was very reprehensible in this respect, as well in his conversation as in his writings; and thereby lost much of that influence with men of learning, which he might have preserved, had he considered it as a duty to be more temperate and flexible in his manner of addressing the public. But he was a man of a warm and hasty spirit, like Martin Luther; who to certain modern speculations in Philosophy and Theology could preserve no more respect than Luther did to the errors of Popery. How far the circumstances they both were under, the zeal by which they were actuated, and the provocations they met with from the world, will justify them in the use of intemperate language, can be known only to God, to whom they must give an account. But whatever excuses may be made for the principals, we do not see how they can be extended to those who succeeded. Some of these however did claim for themselves the like privilege, and gave great offence to persons of cooler judgment. The world will not suffer things to be forced upon them. When men are angry, it is always supposed they have but little to say, and are provoked by a sense of the insufficiency of themselves and their cause.

It

It was a wiſe ſaying of Lord Coke, the famous lawyer, "Whatever grief a man hath, ill words work no good; "and learned counſel never uſe them." To this wiſe and excellent maxim the followers of Mr. Hutchinſon did not in general attend as they ought to have done. It filled them with indignation, to ſee how little they prevailed againſt the perverſe treatment of ſome ill-diſpoſed adverſaries: and, if they had found ſuch principles as they thought of uſe to themſelves, it was a mortification to ſee them overlooked and diſdained by others. But there was ſo much ſweetneſs in the natural temper of Mr. Horne, that no bitter weed could take root there; and the intemperance of others only ſerved to put him the more upon his guard; of which we have a happy example in his State of the Caſe between Sir Iſaac Newton and Mr. Hutchinſon. This was one of his earlieſt compoſitions; in which the argument is conducted throughout with perfect modeſty, civility, and a proper reſpect to all parties. I have heard him admire greatly that calmneſs for which the Chineſe are ſo remarkable, although it borders in ſome degree upon cunning or ſtupidity. "The "only way for a man to gain the favour of the Chineſe "is to ſet forth his reaſons in the cooleſt manner; that "people being of ſuch a diſpoſition, as to deſpiſe the "moſt rational arguments, if delivered with anger." The ſame, ſaid he, is true of mankind in general.

The learning, which diſpoſes us to affect a ſuperiority over other men is too generally attended by a forgetfulneſs of God: and it has therefore been well obſerved,

ſerved, that knowlege, though a good thing in itſelf, as light is when compared with darkneſs, is apt to puff us up: while charity, which is an humble and ſubmiſſive virtue, edifieth; that is, builds us up in the way of grace, and makes us better Chriſtians. So far as knowlege, though of the pureſt ſort, infuſes pride, juſt ſo far it extinguiſhes devotion. It was therefore objected to the new Hebrew ſtudents, that they were a carnal ſort of people, ſo full of ſcriptural learning, as to be much wanting in a due regard to ſcriptural piety. The intelligent reader will eaſily gueſs from what quarter ſuch an accuſation would ariſe. It came from thoſe who are apt to offend in another way; who ſuppoſe that an appearance of godly zeal, and a paſſion to ſave ſouls, will ſupply the defects of Chriſtian knowlege: but without it, there will not be Chriſtian prudence; and ſuch perſons, neglecting to inform themſelves, ſuffer under the want of judgment, and are carried into deluſion, of which they do not ſee the conſequences. Ignorant piety, like ignorant ingenuity, muſt go to ſchool, before it will be able to work ſurely and with good effect. It muſt itſelf be taught before it can be fit to teach others. The great Lord Bacon obſerved of the firſt Puritans, that they reaſoned powerfully on the neceſſity of a ſerious piety; and brought men well to the queſtion, *what muſt I do to be ſaved?* But when they had done this, they were at a loſs how to give them an anſwer. There is danger to man on every ſide: learning is tempted to overlook piety; and

and piety thinks there is no use of learning. Happy is he who preserves himself from both these errors: who, while he seeks wisdom, applies it first to the reformation of his own life, and then to the lives of other men! This appears to have been the persuasion of Mr. Horne; in whose earliest writings we find such a tincture of devotion, that some of his readers, who valued themselves upon their discernment, thought his warmth discovered a degree of enthusiasm; that he was devout overmuch; and consequently we have the testimony of such persons, that he was not wanting in Christian piety. Thus much at least may be affirmed, that he was in no danger of an outward formal religion, destitute of the vital spirit of Christianity.

There was yet another danger to be apprehended, and that of no small concern to a member of the Church of England. It happened, that among the admirers of Mr. Hutchinson there were many dissenters; who, with all the information they had acquired, did not appear (as might reasonably have been expected) to be much softened in their prejudices against the constitution of this Church.—With some of these Mr. Horne frequently fell into company; of which it was not an improbable consequence (and he afterwards was aware of it) that he might come by degrees to be less affected, than he ought to be, to the Church of which he was a member: especially as there was some jealousy already in the minds of Mr. Hutchinson's readers against their superiors both in Church and State, on account of the unfair and angry treatment (I may ſay, perſecution) ſome of them had ſuffered, and the diſlike and averſion which their principles had met with from perſons of eſtabliſhed reputation. The modeſt and civil Letter to a Biſhop, from the Lord Preſident of the Court of Seſſion in Scotland, the Honourable Duncan Forbes, had met with little or no attention; which, with many other ſlights and provocations, contributed to keep them in no very good humour: ſo that it was to be feared they would be too ready to hear, what others might be too ready to ſuggeſt. With ſome of our diſſenters, it is too much the cuſtom to turn the clergy of the Church and their profeſſion into ridicule; a ſort of behaviour which ſhould always be avoided by religious men, when religion is the ſubject. A piece was handed about, which calls itſelf a Dialogue upon Biſhops; a ſly and malignant invective, in a ſtrain of irony, and by no means deſtitute of wit, againſt the Prelates of this Church. The thing is written in the ſame ſpirit with the Martin Mar-Prelate of the old Puritans, though in a ſuperior ſtrain of irony; and had for its author a man whoſe name was Biron, a Diſſenting Teacher of eminence; whoſe works are collected together, and publiſhed, under the terrific title of *The Pillars of Prieſtcraft Shaken.* The Church of England, whoſe religion is here intended by the word *prieſtcraft*, never had a more willing adverſary than this man; unleſs it were *Gordon*, the author of the *Independent Whig*; whoſe writings, plentifully diſperſed there, contributed

not

not a little to the revolt of America, by rendering the Americans more diſaffected to the religion of the mother country.

So long as a connexion remained with the non-conforming readers of Mr. Hutchinſon, it was expected by them, that all Church-differences would be laid aſide, as matters of no ſignification; and that both parties would join hands againſt the common enemies of Chriſtianity. Things being thus diſpoſed, an occurrence intervened, to which Mr. Horne, as it appears from ſome of his letters, imputed the breach which afterwards took place, and his own deliverance, in conſequence of it, from all danger of fanatical infection.

Dr. Clayton, then Biſhop of Clogher in Ireland, in the year 1750, publiſhed his Eſſay on Spirit, with deſign to recommend the Arian doctrine, and to prepare the way for ſuitable alterations in the Liturgy. The favourers of hereſy are ſeldom found to be the enemics of ſchiſm: this author therefore, to ſtrengthen his party, diſtinguiſhed himſelf as a warm friend to the cauſe of the Sectarics; intimidating the Church with the proſpect of deſtruction, unleſs the ſafety of it were provided for by a timely compliance with the demands of its adverſaries. This Eſſay, being reported to come from a perſon of ſuch eminence in the Church, alarmed her friends and animated her enemies. It carried with it a ſhew of learning, and ſome ſubtilty of argument: an anſwer to it was therefore expected and wiſhed for.

It happened at this time, that I was settled at Finedon in Northamptonshire, as Curate to the Reverend Sir John Dolben; which I have reason to remember as a most happy circumstance in the early part of my life. In this situation I was frequently visited by my friend and fellow-student Mr. Horne. He came to me, possessed with a desire of seeing an Answer to this Essay on Spirit; and persuaded me to undertake it. All circumstances being favourable, no objection was made; and accordingly down we sat together for a whole month to the business. The house of my patron Sir John Dolben had an excellent library; a considerable part of which had descended from Archbishop Dolben; and it was furnished with books in every branch of reading, as well ancient as modern, but particularly in divinity and ecclesiastical history. In a country parish, without such an advantage, our attempt had been wild and hopeless: but with it, we had no fear of being at a loss concerning any point of learning that might arise. What Bishop Clayton (supposing him to be the author of an Essay on Spirit) had offered in favour of the non-conformists, obliged us to look into the controversy between them and the Church, which as yet we had never considered; and to consult such historians as had given a faithful account of it. This inquiry brought many things to our view, of which we had never heard; and contributed very much to confirm us in the profession to which we had been educated: but, at the same time, it raised in our minds some new suspicions against our non-conforming friends; and the occasion called upon us to say some things which it could not be very agreeable to them to hear, so long as they persisted in their separation. In every controversy, there will be some rough places, over which the tender-footed will not be able to pass without being hurt; and when this happens, they will probably lay upon others that fault which is to be found only in themselves. It happened as might be expected. When the Answer was published, great offence was taken; and they who had argued for us, as Christians, in a common cause, began now to shew themselves as enemies to the Church of England. They addressed themselves to us in such a strain, to the one by letter, to the other in conversation, as had no tendency to soften or conciliate; for it breathed nothing but contempt and defiance. It had therefore the good effect of obliging us to go on still farther in our inquiries, that we might be able to stand our ground. To this occurrence it was first owing, that Mr. Horne became so well learned in the controversy between the Church and the Sectaries, and was confirmed for life in his attachment to the Church of England*. It was another

* The following extract from a long letter will shew how his mind was employed at the time when it was written: "I have "been reading some of the works of Dr. George Hickes against the "Romanists. He is a sound and acute reasoner, and differs from "Leslie in this, that whereas Leslie's method was, to single out one "point which he calls the *jugulum causæ*, and stick to that; Hickes "follows them through all their objections; unravels their sophistry, "and

another happy circumſtance, that in the iſſue, by perſons of more impartiality, the Anſwer to the Eſſay on Spirit, on which we had beſtowed ſo much labour, was very ſavourably received; eſpecially in Ireland, where it was moſt wanted. The work was rendered more uſeful by the opportunity it gave us of explaining ſome abſtruſe articles in the learning of antiquity; particularly, the Hermetic, Pythagorean and Platonic Trinities; which the writer of the Eſſay had preſſed into his ſervice, to diſtract the minds of his readers, without pretending to know the ſenſe of them. We had the advantage of the author in this ſubject, from having been permitted to look into ſome manuſcript papers of a learned gentleman, who had ſpent ſeveral

" and confirms all he ſays with exact and elaborate proofs. He ſhews " the greateſt knowlege of primitive antiquity, of fathers, councils, " and the conſtitution and diſcipline of the Church in the firſt and " pureſt ages of it. This kind of learning is of much greater value " and conſequence than many now apprehend. What, next after the " Bible, can demand a Chriſtian's attention before the hiſtory of the " Church, purchaſed by the blood of Chriſt, founded by inſpired " apoſtles, and actuated by a ſpirit of love and unity, which made a " heaven upon earth even in the midſt of perſecution, and enabled " them to lay down their lives for the truth's ſake? Much I am ſure " is done by that cementing bond of the ſpirit, which unites Chriſtians " to their head and to one another, and makes them conſider them- " ſelves as members of the ſame body, that is as a church, as a fold of " ſheep, not as ſtraggling individuals.—What I ſee of this in a certain " claſs of writers determines me to look into that affair." Such a man as this, ſo far advanced in the days of his youth, would pay but little regard to ſhallow reaſonings and haſty language from the enemies of uniformity.

years

years of his life in ſtudying the myſteries of the ancient Greek Philoſophy; which, at the bottom, always proved to be Materialiſm. In this the ſpeculations of Heathen Philoſophers naturally ended; and ſo do the ſpeculations of thoſe moderns who follow them in their ways of reaſoning.

From our frequent intercourſe with the library above mentioned, we had the good fortune to meet with the works of the Rev. Charles Leſlie in two vols. fol. which may be conſidered as a library in themſelves to any young ſtudent of the Church of England; and no ſuch perſon, who takes a fancy to what he there finds, can ever fall into Socinianiſm, Fanaticiſm, Popery, or any other of thoſe more modern corruptions which infeſt this Church and Nation. Every treatiſe comprehended in that collection is incomparable in its way: and I ſhall never forget how Mr. Horne expreſſed his aſtoniſhment, when he had peruſed what Mr. Leſlie calls *the Hiſtory of Sin and Hereſy*; which, from the hints that are found in the Scriptures, gives an account how they, Sin and Hereſy, were generated among the Angels before the beginning of the world: "It is," ſaid he, "as if the "man had looked into heaven, to ſee what paſſed "there, on occaſion of Lucifer's rebellion."

In reading Mr. Leſlie's Socinian controverſy, he was highly amuſed with a curioſity, which the author by good fortune, though with great difficulty, had procured and preſented to the public in an Engliſh tranſlation from the Arabic. It is a letter addreſſed to the Morocco Ambaſſador, by two of the Socinian fraternity in England, who called themſelves *Two ſingle Philoſophers*, and propoſed a religious comprehenſion with the Turks: the ſaid Socinians having diſcovered, that the Turks and themſelves were ſo nearly of one opinion, that very little was wanting on either ſide to unite them in the ſame communion. The preſent very learned Biſhop of Rocheſter, Dr. Horſley, lighted upon the ſame thing many years afterwards, and was ſo much ſtruck with its ſingularity, that he has referred to it in his works, to ſhew how naturally the religion of the Socinians ends in the enthuſiaſm of Mahomet.

The ſight of Mr. Leſlie's two Theological folios prepared Mr. Horne for the reading ſuch of his Political works as ſhould afterwards fall in his way: and it was not long before he met with a periodical paper, under the title of *The Rehearſals*, which the author had publiſhed in the time of Queen Ann, when the Infidels and Diſſenters were moſt buſy; and had conceived ſtrong hopes (as they ſaid themſelves) of deſtroying the eſtabliſhed Church. This paper boldly encountered all their arguments; diſſected Sidney and Locke; confuted the republican principles, and expoſed all the deſigns of the party. That party, however, had, at that time, intereſt enough to get the paper, which bore ſo hard upon them, ſuppreſſed by authority; but not till the writer had done the beſt of his work; which made him boaſt, notwithſtanding what had happened, that he had ſown thoſe ſeeds of orthodoxy and loyalty in this kingdom, which

all

all the devils in hell would never be able to root out of it. This ſingular work, then lately re-printed in ſix volumes (1750) fell into the hands of Mr. Horne at Oxford, and was examined with equal curioſity and attention. According to his own account, he had profited greatly by the reading of it; and the work, which gave to one man of genius and diſcernment ſo much ſatisfaction, muſt have had its effect on many others; inſomuch that it is highly probable, the loyalty found amongſt us at this day, and by which the nation has of late been ſo happily preſerved, may have grown up from ſome of the ſeeds then ſown by Mr. Leſlie: and I have ſome authority for what I ſay*. This I know, that the reading of that work begat in the mind of Mr. Horne an early and ſtrict attention to thoſe political differences, and the grounds of them, which have at ſundry times agitated this country, and diſturbed public affairs.

In the year when the *Jew-Bill* was depending, and after it had paſſed the Houſe, he frequently employed himſelf in ſending to an evening paper of the time certain communications, which were much noticed; while the author was totally unknown, except to ſome of his neareſt acquaintance. By the favour of a great Lady, it was my fortune, (though then very young) to be at a table, where ſome perſons of the firſt quality were aſſembled; and I heard one of them † very

* No farther proof of this will be wanting to thoſe intelligent perſons, who have read the learned Mr. Whitaker's Real Origin of Government, one of the greateſt and beſt pieces the times have produced.

† Lord Temple.

earneſt

earneſt on the matter and ſtyle of ſome of theſe papers, of which I knew the ſecret hiſtory; and was not a little diverted when I heard what paſſed about them. To the author of thoſe papers the *Jew-Bill* gave much offence, and the *Marriage-Bill* not much leſs. He was highly gratified by the part taken in that perilous buſineſs by the Reverend William Romaine, who oppoſed the *Conſiderations* diſperſed about the kingdom in defence of the Jew-Bill, with a degree of ſpirit and ſucceſs, which reminded us of Swift's oppoſition to Wood's Half-pence in his Drapier's Letters.

Mr. Horne having entered upon his firſt Hebrew ſtudies, not without an ardent piety, he was ready to lay hold of every thing that might advance him in the knowlege and practice of the Chriſtian life. He accordingly made himſelf well acquainted with the ſerious, practical writings of the Reverend William Law, which, I believe, were firſt recommended to him by Mr. Hamilton, afterwards Archdeacon of Raphoe in Ireland, or by the Reverend Doctor Patten of Corpus Chriſti College. He conformed himſelf in many reſpects to the ſtrictneſs of Mr. Law's rules of devotion; but without any danger of falling, as ſo many did, after Mr. Law's example, into the ſtupendous reveries of Jacob Behmen, the German Theoſophiſt. From this he was effectually ſecured by his attachment to the doctrines and forms of the primitive Church, in which he was well grounded by the writings of Leſlie, and alſo of the Primitive Fathers, ſome of which were become familiar to him, and very highly eſteemed. But being ſenſible how

eaſy

easy it was for many of those who took their piety from Mr. Law, to take his errors along with it, he drew up a very useful paper, for the security of such persons as might not have judgment enough to distinguish properly, under the title of *Cautions to the Readers of Mr. Law** : and excellent they are for the purpose intended: they shew the goodness of his heart, and the soundness of his judgment.

Some worthy ladies, who were in the habit of reading Mr. Law, had from thence filled their heads with several of the wild notions of Jacob Behmen; and were zealous in making proselytes. A lady of fashion in Ireland, of the first rate for beauty, elegance and accomplishment, was going apace into this way, at the instance of a proselyting acquaintance. Her situation was known and lamented; and it was earnestly wished that somebody would undertake to open her eyes before she was too far gone. Mr. Horne, though much interested in the success of such an attempt, did not take the office upon himself, but committed it to a friend; and the paper produced the desired effect.

When the writings of Leslie, or Law, or Hutchinson, were before Mr. Horne, he used them with judgment and moderation, to qualify and temper each other: he took what was excellent from all, without admitting what was exceptionable from any. To his academical Greek and Latin he had added a familiar acquaintance with the Hebrew; and having found

* This paper is given in the *Appendix*.

his

his way to the Chriſtian Fathers, I conſider him now as a perſon furniſhed with every light, and ſecured from every danger, which could poſſibly occur to him as a member of the Church of England; and conſequently well prepared for any ſervice which the times might require of him. In Engliſh divinity he had alſo greatly improved himſelf by the writings of Dr. Jackſon, and Dr. Jeremy Taylor: from the latter of which, I ſuppoſe him to have derived much of that mildneſs and devotion, for which he was afterwards ſo conſpicuous*. The former, Dr. Jackſon, is a magazine of theological learning, every where penned with great elegance and dignity, ſo that his ſtyle is a pattern of perfection. His writings, once thought ineſtimable by every body but the Calviniſts, had been greatly neglected, and would probably have continued ſo, but for the praiſes beſtowed upon them by the celebrated Mr. Merrick of Trinity College in Oxford, who brought them once more into repute with many learned readers. The early extracts of Mr. Horne, which are now remaining, ſhew how much information he derived from this excellent writer; who deſerves to be numbered with the En-

* From many paſſages which might be produced from his private letters and his printed works, no Engliſh writer ſeems to have taken his fancy, and fallen in ſo exactly with his own diſpoſition, as Dr. Taylor; firſt in his Life of Chriſt, then in his Ductor Dubitantium or Rule of Conſcience, and afterwards in his Rule and Exerciſe of Holy Dying, which he calls a Golden Tract, and the author of it the inimitable Biſhop Jeremy Taylor. See his Commentary on Pſalm cxix. v. 71.

gliſh

glish Fathers of the Church. That there cannot be in the Church of England a useful scholar, unless he is precise in following the same track of learning, I will not presume to say: but this I shall always think, that if we are ever to see another Mr. Horne; a commentator, so learned; a preacher, so evangelical; a writer, so accomplished; a Christian, so exemplary; he must come out of the same school.

With his mind thus furnished, the time drew near when he was to take holy orders. This was a serious affair to him: and he entered upon it, as every candidate ought to do, with a resolution to apply the studies he had followed to the practice of his ministry; and, above all the rest, his study of the Holy Scripture. Soon after he had been ordained, on Trinity Sunday, 1753, by the Bishop of Oxford, he related the circumstance by letter to an intimate friend, not without adding the following petition, which is well worth preserving: "May he, who ordered Peter three times "to feed his lambs, give me grace, knowlege and "skill, to watch and attend to the flock, which he "purchased upon the cross, and to give rest to those "who are under the burden of sin or sorrow! It hath "pleased God to call me to the ministry in very trou-"blesome times indeed; when a lion and a bear have "broken into the fold, and are making havock among "the sheep. With a firm, though humble confi-"dence, do I purpose to go forth; not in my own "strength, but in the strength of the Lord God; and "may he prosper the work of my hands!" He came

to

to me then reſident upon the curacy of Finedon in Northamptonſhire, to preach his firſt ſermon: to which, as it might be expected, I liſtened with no ſmall attention; under an aſſurance, that his doctrine would be good, and that he was capable of adorning it to a high degree with beautiful language and a graceful delivery. The diſcourſe he then preached, though excellent in its kind, is not printed among his other works. Scrupulous critics, he thought, might be of opinion, that he had given too great ſcope to his imagination; and that the text, in the ſenſe he took it, was not a foundation ſolid enough to build ſo much upon. This was his ſentiment when his judgment was more mature; and he ſeems to me to have judged rightly. Yet the diſcourſe was admirable in reſpect of its compoſition and its moral tendency. Give me an audience of well diſpoſed Chriſtians, among whom there are no dry moraliſts, no faſtidious critics; and I would ſtake my life upon the hazard of pleaſing them all by the preaching of that ſermon. With farther preparation, and a little more experience, he preached in a more public pulpit, before one of the largeſt and moſt polite congregations at London. The preacher, whoſe place he ſupplied, but who attended in the church on purpoſe to hear him, was ſo much affected by what he had heard, and the manner in which it was delivered, that when he viſited me ſhortly after in the country, he was ſo full of this ſermon, that he gave me the matter and the method of it by heart; pronouncing at the end of it, what a writer of his life

ought

ought never to forget, that——"George Horne was, "without exception, the beſt preacher in England." Which teſtimony was the more valuable, becauſe it came from a perſon, who had, with many people, the reputation of being ſuch himſelf. This ſermon is preſerved; and if the reader ſhould be a judge, and will take the pains to examine it, he will think it merits what is here ſaid of it. The ſubject is the ſecond advent of Chriſt to judgment. The text is from Rev. i, 7. *Behold he cometh with clouds, and every eye ſhall ſee him, and they alſo which pierced him; and all kindreds of the earth ſhall wail becauſe of him. Even ſo. Amen.**

Beſides his talent for preaching, which from the beginning promiſed (and has now produced) great things; Mr. Horne had obtained ſo high a character at Oxford, for his humanity, condeſcenſion and piety, that his reputation came to the ears of a criminal in the Caſtle, under ſentence of death for one of the many high-way robberies he had committed. The name of this man was Dumas; he was an Iriſhman by birth; and his appearance and addreſs had ſo much of the gentleman, that he was a perſon of the firſt rank in his profeſſion. This man having heard of Mr. Horne, as a perſon remarkable for his ſenſe and goodneſs, requeſted the favour of his attendance; to which, on a principle of conſcience, he conſented; though the office was ſuch as would probably put the tenderneſs of his mind to a very ſevere trial. And ſo it

* See Serm. vol. I. Diſc. 6.

it proved in the event; his health being confiderably affected for fome time afterwards. I do not find among his papers any minutes of this affair preferved in writing*: and though he gave me a large account of it, to which I could not but liften with great attention, I cannot recollect fo much of it as I wifh to do, at this diftance of time. This I know, that he ufed to think anxioufly with himfelf day and night, in what manner he fhould addrefs this unhappy man, and what kind of fpiritual counfel would be moft likely to fucceed with him; for he found him, though ready and fenfible enough in all common things, deplorably deftitute of all religious knowlege. To the beft of my remembrance he always chofe to be quite alone with him when he attended; and by repeated applications, and conftant prayer, recommended by his mild and engaging manner, thought he had made fome confiderable impreffion upon his mind. In the laft conference before his execution, he thanked Mr. Horne very heartily for his goodnefs to him, and ufed thefe very remarkable words: "Sir, you may, perhaps, "wonder at what I am about to tell you; but, I do "affure you, I feel at this moment no more fenfe of "fear, than I fhould do if I were going a common "journey." To this Mr. Horne anfwered, that he was indeed very much furprifed; but he hoped it was upon a right principle. And fo let us hope: though the criminal was fcarcely explicit enough to give due

* But the prayers he compofed for the occafion are in one of his MSS.

ſatisfaction, whether this indifference proceeded from Chriſtian hope or conſtitutional hardneſs. The converſation between the Ordinary and the priſoner the evening before he ſuffered (as Mr. Horne related it, who was preſent at the interview) conſiſted chiefly in an exact deſcription of all the particulars of the ceremonial, which the priſoner was to go through in the way to his death; and of courſe had very little either of comfort or inſtruction in it. The feelings of that gentleman, who had attended the executions for ſeveral years, were very different from thoſe of his aſſiſtant; and he ſpoke of the approaching execution with as little emotion, as if Mr. Dumas had taken a place for the next morning in an Oxford coach. He even amuſed himſelf with telling them the ſtory of another unhappy criminal, who had nothing of the fortitude of Mr. Dumas; a perſon of the law, put to death for forgery, whoſe heart had failed him at the time of his execution: "There was poor *Paul*," (ſaid he) "we could not make him riſe in the morning— "he would not get up—I thought we ſhould never "have got him hanged that day," &c. Such is the effect of cuſtom and habit upon ſome minds!

Thus was Mr. Horne initiated early into the moſt difficult duty of the paſtoral charge, the viſitation of the ſick and dying: a work of extreme charity; but for which all men are not equally fit; ſome, becauſe they have too little tenderneſs; others, becauſe they have too much. It is a bleſſing that there are many helps and directions for thoſe who wiſh to improve themselves. The office in the Liturgy is excellent in its kind, but it doth not come up to all cases. Among the posthumous papers of Bishop Horne, I find an inestimable manuscript, which it is probable he might begin to compile for his own use about this time, and partly for the occasion of which I have been speaking. He was by no means unacquainted with the matter and the language of prayer; having shewn to me, as we were upon a walk one summer's evening in the country, when he was a very young man, that precious composition of Bishop Andrews, the first copy of which occurred to him in the library of Magdalen College; on which he set so great a value during the rest of his life, that, while he was Dean of Canterbury, he published, after the example of the excellent Dean Stanhope, his predecessor, a handsome English edition of it. The original is in Greek and Latin; and it happened some time after Mr. Horne had first brought the work into request, that a great number of copies of the Greek and Latin edition were discovered in a warehouse at Oxford, where they had lain undisturbed in sheets for many years. In the copy published after Dean Stanhope's form, the Manual for the Sick, though the best thing extant upon its subject, is wholly omitted: but in the posthumous manuscript I speak of, the whole is put together, with improvements by the compiler; and I wish all the parochial clergy in the nation were possessed of it.

We are now coming to a more busy period of Mr. Horne's life, the year 1756, when he was called upon

to

to be an apologiſt for himſelf and ſome of his friends, againſt the attack of a literary adverſary.

In the controverſy about Hebrew names, and their doubtful interpretations, in which the learned Dr. Sharp of Durham was prevailed upon (as it is reported, much againſt his will) to engage, Mr. Horne never interfered; as being of opinion, that, if all that part of Mr. Hutchinſon's ſyſtem were left to its fate, the moſt uſeful and valuable parts of it would ſtill remain, with their evidences from the Scripture, the natural world, and the teſtimony of ſacred and profane antiquity. He was likewiſe of opinion, that where *words* are the ſubject, words may be multiplied without end: and the witneſſes of the diſpute, at leaſt the majority of them, having no competent knowlege of ſo uncommon a ſubject, would be ſure to go as faſhion and the current of the times ſhould direct. That a zealous reader of the Hebrew, captivated by the curioſity of its etymologies, ſhould purſue them beyond the bounds of prudence, is not to be wondered at. Many Hebrew etymologies are ſo well founded, and throw ſo much light on the learning of antiquity, and the origin of languages, that no man can be a complete Philologiſt without a proper knowlege of them. The learned well know how uſeful Mr. Bryant has endeavoured to make himſelf of late years by following them: and yet, it muſt be confeſſed that, with all his learning, he has many fancies and peculiarities of his own, which he would find it difficult to maintain. If Mr. Hutchinſon and his followers have been ſometimes viſionary in their criticiſms, and carried things too far, it does not appear that the worſt of their interpretations are ſo bad as thoſe of ſome learned critics in the laſt century, who, from the allowed primævity of their favourite language, applied it without diſcretion to every thing. All the names in Homer's Iliad and Odyſſey were hebraized, and all his fables were derived from ſome hiſtory or other in the Bible: and this to ſuch a degree, as was utterly improbable, and even childiſh and ridiculous*. Such are the weakneſſes to which great ſcholars are ſubject, in common with other men; ſometimes for want of light, and ſometimes for want of diſcretion: and the greateſt ſcholars of this age are not without them. Dr. Horne, I have reaſon to think, did ſo much juſtice to the criticiſms of Dr. Sharp, as to read them carefully: which is more than I dare ſay of myſelf; and I may plead in my behalf the example of my learned and reſpectable friend Granville Sharp, Eſq. the ſon of the Archdeacon; who very ingenuouſly owned to me, that he had never read his father's books in the Hutchinſonian controverſy: perhaps, becauſe he is as little inclined to logomachy as I am. However, I have ſeen enough to diſcover from the general tenor of them, that it ſeems to have been the deſign of that learned author, to raiſe difficulties, and throw

* If the curious reader can meet with a book under the title of Ὁμηρος Ἑβραιζων, he will ſee this plan, of deriving all things from the Hebrew, carried to extremity. He may alſo find other examples, but not ſo extravagant, in Gale's Court of the Gentiles.

things

things into the ſhade: in which he has apparently ſucceeded. When I look into a writer of the Hutchinſonian perſuaſion, though I may ſuſpect his criticiſms, and diſlike his manner, I am animated by his zeal, and generally learn ſomething uſeful: but when I look into the criticiſms of Dr. Sharp, I learn nothing: I feel cold and diſſatisfied with all languages and all ſcience; as if the Scripture itſelf were out of tune, and divinity a mere diſpute. It is therefore my perſuaſion, that his writings have done little ſervice to Theology or Philology, but that they have operated rather as a diſcouragement; for who will labour, if there be no proſpect of coming to any determination one way or the other? That I am not taking a part againſt Dr. Sharp, but that Dr. Sharp did in this reſpect take a part againſt himſelf, is evident from his own words; which do plainly declare, that his object in writing againſt the followers of Hutchinſon was, to "prove the uncertainty of ſomething affirmed "to be certain." I know of ſome, who took the contrary part; endeavouring to prove "the certainty "of ſomething affirmed to be uncertain;" and I think they were more hopefully employed: for where uncertainty is the prize, what encouragement is there to ſtrive for it? Mr. Horne, who knew the value of his time, had no inclination to waſte any of it in this endleſs chace of verbal criticiſm: and I have reaſon to think, that, if there was any ſtudy in particular to which he took a complete averſion, it was

 the

the Hutchinsonian controversy about a few * Hebrew words.

Another dispute soon arose, after that of Dr. Sharp, which was of much greater concern; and so Mr. Horne thought, from the part he took in it. How he acquitted himself, the reader must judge when he has heard the particulars.

With many young scholars in the University of Oxford, the principles of Mr. Hutchinson began to be in such esteem, that some member of the University, who was in the opposite interest, or had no fancy to that way, made a very severe attack upon them in an anonymous pamphlet, intitled, *A Word to the Hutchinsonians;* and Mr. Horne, being personally struck at, as the principal object of the author's animadversions,

* I have here allowed more than I can strictly justify; and, by so doing, I have given advantage to some, and offence to others: I beg therefore to be rightly understood. In respect to Dr. Sharp, Mr. Horne was certainly of opinion, that the Doctor had left the more useful and valuable parts of Mr. Hutchinson's system untouched: so I myself have thought, and been assured from that day to this; and I believe the reader will himself be of the same opinion, if he duly considers the contents of my *Preface*. Whatever dislike Mr. Horne might express toward the verbal disputes of that time, no man could set a greater value than he did on Hebrew Learning discreetly followed and applied. That I may not be thought to leave so weighty a matter under an unjust statement, I have subjoined to this second Edition a letter which I wrote to a person of honour, recommending the study of the Hebrew language by showing its usefulness and excellence. I embrace the present occasion of making it public, and wish it may derive some vitality from the reputation of Bishop Horne.

ſions, was obliged to take up the pen in defence of himſelf and his friends. The public in general, and Mr. Horne in particular, by ſome very broad hints, gave the thing to Mr. Kennicott of Exeter College, a man of parts, and a clear agreeable writer, who had very juſtly acquired ſome fame for his ſkill in the Hebrew language. His two Diſſertations, one on the Tree of Life, and the other on the Sacrifices of Cain and Abel, were in many hands, and ſo well approved, that ſome farther and better fruit of his ſtudies might reaſonably be expected. As to the author of this anonymous pamphlet, I can affirm nothing poſitively from my own knowlege: I can only relate what was told me by Dr. Golding of New College, who was afterwards Warden of Wincheſter. From this gentleman I heard what had happened to himſelf in regard to the publication above mentioned, and what his own ſentiments were. Soon after it appeared, Mr. Kennicott accoſted him in a bookſeller's ſhop, "Dr. Golding, I give you joy, on being "the author of a very ingenious pamphlet, called A "Word to the Hutchinſonians."—"Indeed," ſaid Dr. Golding, "I was not the author of it; but I believe "you know who was." When an anſwer had appeared, with the name of Mr. Horne to it, Dr. Golding, meeting Mr. Kennicott in the ſtreet, ſaid, "Well, "Mr. Kennicott, and who is the author of the Word "to the Hutchinſonians *now*?" Which queſtion was only anſwered by a laugh. The Dr. Golding, of whom I am ſpeaking, had been a preacher much approved in the pulpit of the Univerſity, and had contended with ſome zeal for the principles of Hutchinſon: but had now the reputation of having forſaken them all; which report might poſſibly give occaſion to Mr. Kennicott's compliment; it being not improbable, that a perſon who could forſake them would make it his next ſtep (as Dr. Dodd afterwards did) to write againſt them. He had been an intimate friend to the above mentioned Mr. Watſon of Univerſity College, who had recommended him to travel as a tutor with the Earl of Dartmouth and Mr. North, afterwards Lord North and Lord Guilford, with whom he ſpent ſome time abroad. He was undoubtedly a man of learning and ability: but being under the repute of having renounced ſome principles he had once received, I was very deſirous to know how that matter might be: and Dr. Golding, at my requeſt, was ſo obliging as to do me the honour of a viſit, while I lived at a private houſe in Oxford. I told him plainly, that there were ſome opinions of Hutchinſon in Natural Philoſophy, which, when properly diſtinguiſhed, did appear to me to be true, and, as ſuch, worth recommending to the world: and that, as I had ſome intention of taking the office upon myſelf, I ſhould eſteem it as a great favour, if he, being a perſon of more years and experience, would communicate to me fairly thoſe objections, which had taken effect upon his own mind; that if I ſhould be ſtaggered with them, my deſign might be laid aſide. The Doctor was full of pleaſantry and good humour; gave

gave me the whole ſtory about the pamphlet, as above related, and ſpoke with great reſpect of Mr. Horne: but as to the particular object of my enquiry, his philoſophical *reaſons*, I could not ſucceed in drawing any one of them out of him, and am to this hour in the dark upon the ſubject. I ſhall not therefore indulge myſelf in ſpeculations and conjectures, for which I have no authority; but only remark in general, what all men of diſcernment know to be true; that, as a man's opinions have an influence upon his expectations in this world, ſo his expectations in this world may have an influence upon his opinions. Hoping that I ſhall be pardoned for a ſmall digreſſion, not quite foreign to the ſubject in hand, I return now to Mr. Horne and his Apology*, of which I ſhall give a ſhort view; but it is a work which cannot without injury be abridged; as comprehending a great variety of ſubjects in a ſmall compaſs.

The temper of it appears in the firſt page. The excellent Hooker had replied to a petulant adverſary in the following very ſignificant words: "Your next "argument conſiſts of railing and reaſons. To your "railing I ſay nothing: to your reaſons I ſay what "follows." "This ſentence," ſays the apologiſt, "I am "obliged to adopt, as the rule of my own conduct; "the author I am now concerned with having mixed "with his arguments a great deal of bitterneſs and "abuſe,

* The title is—"An Apology for certain Gentlemen in the Univerſity of Oxford, aſperſed in a late anonymous Pamphlet," &c. A new Edition, with a *new Preface*, is juſt publiſhed.

" abuse, which must do as little credit to himself as " service to his cause. He is in full expectation of " being heartily abused in return: but I have no oc- " casion for that sort of artillery; and have learned " besides, that *the wrath of man worketh not the right- " eousness of God.* Therefore, in the words of the " excellent Hooker, *to his railing I say nothing: to his " reasons I say what follows.*"

To the charge of being an Hutchinsonian, a name so invidiously applied, as a sectarian appellation, to himself and other readers of Hutchinson's writings, he answers, that, as Christians, they acknowlege no Master but one, that is Christ: that they were members only of The Church: and that, as all their reading had not formed them into a Sect, they ought not to have a mark set upon them. "Is it not hard measure," says he, "that when a clergyman only preaches the " doctrines and enforces the duties of Christianity from " the Scriptures, his character shall be blasted, and " himself rendered odious by the force of a name, " which, in such cases, always signifies what the im- " posers please to mean, and the people to hate? " There are many names of this kind now in vogue. " If a man preaches Christ, that he is the end of the " law, and the fulness of the gospel—'You need " not mind him; he is a Hutchinsonian.' If he men- " tions the assistance and direction of the Holy Spirit, " with the necessity of prayer, mortification, and the " taking up of the cross—'O, he is a Methodist!' " If he talks of the divine right of Episcopacy, with

" a word

"a word concerning the danger of Schifin—' Juft "going over to Popery!' And if he preaches obedi"ence to King George—' You may depend upon it, "he is a Pretender's man.' Many things may be "ridiculed under their falfe titles, which it would "not be fo decent to laugh at under their true ones."

As to their being a fect or combination of Separatifts from the Church-of-England Chriftians, "We "do," fays he, "moft fincerely difavow the name and "the thing. In the communion of the Church of "England we intend to die. To every zealous friend "and promoter of the intereft of Chriftianity, the "Scriptures, and the Church, we are ready cheer"fully to give the right hand of fellowfhip, whether "he be a reader of Mr. Hutchinfon *or not*," &c. "They tell men" (faid their accufer) "that they, and "they only, are the fervants of the moft high God, "who fhew forth the way of falvation:"—"they labour "to difcredit all other preachers." "By no means:" (fays the anfwerer) "they labour to difcredit all falfe "doctrines, preached by many who SHOULD preach "the gofpel. It is the complaint of hundreds of fe"rious and pious Chriftians, who never read or heard "of Mr. Hutchinfon, that there is at prefent a la"mentable falling off from the OLD way of preach"ing and expounding the word of God. And, if "there be fuch a defection from the primitive man"ner of preaching, the proper place wherein to fpeak "of it is an Univerfity, where preachers are educa"ted. If offence fhould be taken at this, I can on-

 "ly

" ly say, that, if any one will tell me how truth may " be spoken, in such cases as these, without offend- " ing *some*, I will spare no labour to learn the art of " it."

If any person wishes to know all the particular charges brought forward by this author, and how they are answered, he will find the pamphlet at large a very curious piece, and to that I would refer him: but some of these answers carry so much instruction, that I cannot refrain from extracting a few of them. To the charge of their insulting and trampling upon reason, under pretence of glorifying revelation, Mr. Horne answers: "The abuse, not the use, of rea- " son, is what we argue against. Reason, we say, " was made to learn, not to teach. What the eye is " to the body, reason or understanding is to the soul; " as saith the apostle, Eph. i. 18, having the eyes of " your understanding enlightened. The eye is framed " in such a manner as to be capable of seeing; rea- " son in such a manner as to be capable of knowing. " But the eye, though ever so good, cannot see with- " out light: reason, though ever so perfect, cannot " know without instruction. Therefore the phrase, " light of reason, is improper; because it is as ab- " surd to make reason its own informer, as to make " the eye the source of its own light: whereas rea- " son can be no more than the organ which receives " instruction, as the eye admits the light of heaven. " A man may as well take a view of things upon " earth in a dark night by the light of his own eye, as

" discover

" discover the things of heaven, during the night of " nature, by the light of his own reason," &c.

To another similar objection, often made against them, that they decry natural religion, it is answered, " To be sure, we do; because, at the best, it is a " religion without the knowlege of the true God, or " the hope of salvation; which is Deism: and it is a " matter of fact, that, from Adam to this day, there " never was, or could be, a man left to himself, to " make a religion of nature. It is, we know, a re-" ceived notion, that man, by a due and proper use " of his reasoning faculties, may do great things: " and so, by a due and proper use of the organs of " vision, he may know much of the objects around " him. But still, the pinching question returns: Is " it not light that enables him to make a due and " proper use of the one, and instruction of the other? " Shew us the eye that sees without light, and the " understanding that reasons upon religion without " instruction, and we will allow they both do it by " the light of nature. Till then, let us hear no more " of natural religion. And let me, on the subjects " of reason and nature, recommend two books: the " first, *Mr. Leslie's Short and Easy Method with the " Deists*; where the debate between them and the " Christians upon the evidence of revelation is brought " to a single point, and their cause overthrown for " ever. This most excellent piece, with the other " Tracts of the same author usually bound with it, " have, I thank God, entirely removed every doubt "from my mind: and, in my poor opinion, they "render the metaphyſical performances upon the "ſubject entirely uſeleſs. The ſecond book I would "recommend is *Dr. Ellis's Knowlege of Divine "Things from Revelation, not from Reaſon or Nature.* "In this book natural religion is fairly demoliſhed."

Mr. Horne and his friends were farther charged with "a great contempt for learning." "But that," ſays he, "depends upon the nature and kind of the "learning. Becauſe ſometimes a man is called a "learned man, who, after a courſe of ſeveral years' "hard ſtudy, can tell you, within a trifle, how ma-"ny degrees of the non-entity of nothing muſt be "annihilated, before it comes to be ſomething. See "King's Origin of Evil, ch. iii. p. 129, with the note. "That ſuch kind of learning as that book is filled "with, and the preſent age is much given to admire, "has done no ſervice to the cauſe of truth, but on "the contrary that it has done infinite diſſervice, and "almoſt reduced us from the unity of Chriſtian faith "to the wrangling of philoſophic ſcepticiſm, is the "opinion of many beſides ourſelves, and too ſurely "founded on fatal experience."—"As to thoſe who "are engaged in the ſtudy of uſeful Arts and Sci-"ences, Languages, Hiſtory, Antiquities, Phyſics, "&c. &c. with a view to make them handmaids to "divine knowlege; we honour their employment, "we deſire to emulate their induſtry, and moſt ſin-"cerely wiſh them good luck in the name of the "Lord." The Metaphyſical Syſtem alluded to above

was

was a book in great requeſt at Cambridge, between the years 1740 and 1750; and was extolled by ſome young men who ſtudied it, as a grand repoſitory of human wiſdom. The notes were written by Dr. Edmund Law, afterwards Biſhop of Carliſle. Having heard ſo high a character of it, I once ſat down to read it, with a prejudice in its favour. I afterwards ſhewed it Mr. Horne: and, when he had conſidered it, we could not but lament in ſecret, what he at length complained of in public, that a work ſo unfounded and ſo unprofitable ſhould have engaged the attention, and excited the admiration, of ſcholars intended for the preaching of the Goſpel. The account here given of it has ſomething of the caricature; but the leading principle of the book is in ſubſtance as the apologiſt has deſcribed it.

Whoever the author of the pamphlet was, he ſeems to have entered upon his work with a perſuaſion, that the gentlemen of Oxford, to whom he gives the name of Hutchinſonians, were in ſuch diſeſteem with the world, ſo little known by ſome, and ſo much diſliked by others, that any bold attack upon their characters would be ſufficient to run them down: and imagining that his book muſt have that effect, he foretells them how they muſt ſubmit, in conſequence of it, to "deſcend and ſink into the deepeſt humiliation," &c. This is not criticiſm, but unmerciful outrage; and the author has ſo much of it, that the apologiſt, having collected it together, concludes with a very pathetic remonſtrance: "Theſe, ſir, are *hard ſpeeches* againſt "men,

"men, of whom, their enemies themſelves, being "judges, muſt own, that they are ſound in the faith, "ſteady to the church, and regular in their duties— "Upon an impartial ſurvey of all that has been ſaid "or written againſt us—I muſt declare, that *neither* "*againſt the law, neither againſt the temple, neither* "*againſt Cæſar*, is it proved that we have *offended* "*any thing at all*," &c. &c.

The reader may perhaps obſerve upon what I have preſented to him, and he would ſee it more plainly, if he were to read the whole book, as I would adviſe him to do, that the diſpute relates chiefly to the foundations of religion. Of Mr. Hutchinſon we hear but little; his name was the match that gave fire to the train: but the queſtion ſeems really to have been this; whether Chriſtianity, in the truth and ſpirit of it, ought to be preſerved; or whether a ſpiritleſs thing, called by the name of Chriſtianity, would anſwer the purpoſe better: in other words, whether the religion of Man's Philoſophy, or the religion of God's Revelation, ſhould prevail. If this was the queſtion, a more important one was never agitated ſince the beginning of the Reformation; and every true Chriſtian hath an intereſt in the iſſue of it. The temper with which Mr. Horne conducted himſelf, though under very great provocation, is very much to be admired. There never was a piece of invective more and completely taken down than in the Apology; the matter of it is both inſtructive and curious: ſeveral points of divinity, more than my ſhort abſtract would admit, are truly and clearly ſtated: and as to the characters of the writer himſelf and his friends, we ſee the crimes of which they were accuſed, and the defence they were able to make; of which defence thoſe perſons could form no judgment, who had taken their opinion of the parties from the *Reviews* and other diſaffected publications of the time; unleſs they were wiſe enough to collect by inference, that where bad things were ſo much applauded, that which was diſpraiſed and outraged muſt have ſome good in it. As to myſelf, I freely confeſs, I am to this hour delighted and edified by that Apology; and, after ſo many years, I ſee no reaſon to depart from any one of its doctrines; but ſhould be thankful to God, if all the young clergy of this church were almoſt and altogether ſuch as Mr. Horne was when he wrote it; and I heartily rejoice that it is now republiſhed, that they may have an opportunity of reading it. And I would adviſe, if it were poſſible, they ſhould ſee what the learned Dr. Patten wrote in the ſame year; who was author of another Apology; which, with its defence againſt the Reverend Mr. Ralph Heathcote, diſplays the meekneſs of great learning againſt the vain bluſterings of great aſſurance*: and, to ſhew how the Reviews of this country impoſe upon the ignorant and the credulous, Mr. Heathcote was highly commended, and the character of Dr. Patten was

* What David Hume calls the Illiberal Petulance, Arrogance, and Scurrility of the Warburtonian School. See his Life, p. 21.

taken from the repreſentation of his adverſary, without reading his book*.

But I muſt now proceed to another cauſe, which made more noiſe in the world, and is in itſelf of ſuch importance that it ought never to be forgotten.

After his Apology, Mr. Horne took a part in the controverſy with Mr. Kennicott on the Text of the Hebrew Bible†; in which he and his friends ſo deeply intereſted themſelves, on a principle of conſcience as well as of literary evidence, that it is impoſſible for me to proceed in the taſk I have undertaken, without giving a plain and impartial account of what paſſed upon that occaſion; and it will afford me an opportunity of bringing to light an extraordinary character of whom the world never heard.

Mr. Kennicott having diſtinguiſhed himſelf as a perſon learned in the Hebrew; a propoſal was ſet on foot by himſelf and his friends for collating the Text of the Hebrew Bible with ſuch manuſcripts as could *now* be procured; in order to reform the Text, and prepare it for a new tranſlation to be made from it into the Engliſh language. Mr. Kennicott explained at large the nature of this deſign, and attempted to prove

* Veſtra ſolum legitis, veſtra amatis: cæteros, cauſâ incognitâ, condemnatis. See the Crit. Rev. for April 1756. In the year 1759 Dr. Patten preached another ſermon before the Univerſity, which he printed. In this the ſubject of his two former pieces is continued, and the argument carried on farther, and well ſupported.

† In a Pamphlet publiſhed in 1760, entitled, A View of Mr. Kennicott's Method of correcting the Hebrew Text, &c.

prove the necessity of such a measure, in some learned dissertations on the state of the printed Hebrew Bibles. The design came at length to maturity; Mr. Kennicott himself was appointed the sole conductor of it; and such powerful interest was made in its behalf, that persons of the first honour and eminence supported it by an annual subscription to a very great amount. Manuscripts were collected from all parts of the world; and a company of collators were employed under the eye of Mr. Kennicott at Oxford; who gave an annual account, attested by Dr. Hunt the Hebrew professor, of the state of the collation. The subscription was continued, and the work went on for several years. A new Hebrew Bible was at length printed in folio; a copy of the first volume of which came to the library of the Sorbonne while I was at Paris in the year 1776, and was shewn to me by Mr. Asseline the Hebrew professor of that time*.

Far be it from me to speak with disrespect of an undertaking, which had the encouragement of so many great, so many good, and so many learned persons; who must be supposed to have acted with the best intention, in consequence of such reports as were laid before them; for many of them certainly had no judgment of their own upon the subject. But Mr. Horne, and some other readers of Hebrew, never

* After the Revolution of 1789 this gentleman was made Bishop of Bologne by the King; but by reason of the increasing troubles, he went to Brussels, and afterwards into Germany. He is universally spoken of as a person of great worth and learning.

approved of the design from the beginning; and Dr. Rutherforth of Cambridge, a man of no small erudition, wrote professedly, and with some asperity, against it; or, at least, against the way in which he thought it would be executed. Some of the considerations they went upon were these following:

1. That the design was dangerous, and had a bad aspect. A new translation of the Bible into English had been strenuously recommended some years before by suspected persons with an ill intention*. That such persons, being not well affected to the Church of England or its doctrines, would probably interfere with all their heart and interest, to turn the design to their own purposes. For it was evident by the intention of Dr. Kennicott at first, that there should be both a New Hebrew Text, and a New English Version: and I am rather of opinion, that Mr. Horne and his friends, by their remonstrances, however apparently unnoticed, might have some little share of merit in preventing it.

2. It hurt and alarmed them, to see a learned gentleman plead and argue, as if he had a victory to obtain

* It appears from a Life of Dr. Sykes, p. 354, that the Socinians had great hopes from a new English Version of the Bible, by which *all our present learned illustrations of the S. S. were to be superseded*—all things were to become new—*the disciples were to become one fold*, and the *absolute unity of the peerless majesty of God was to be maintained by the whole community of Christians.*—Socinianism alone was to introduce Paradise and the Millennium. The Socinians of Poland had a translation made; but it did not answer their purpose. See Mosheim's Hist. of Socinianism.

tain by proving the corruption of the Hebrew Text, and it were the game he was hunting after; for this did not look as if the glory of God was the object in view, but rather his own emolument, as a collator—οπȣ το συμφερον, εκει το ευσεβες.

3. They were of opinion, that the attempt was ſuperfluous; becauſe the exactneſs of the Maſoretical Jews had guarded and ſecured the Text of their Bible in ſuch a manner, that no other book in the world had ever been ſo guarded and ſecured: that therefore there could not be room for any great alarm upon the ſubject.

4. That Cardinal Ximenes and his aſſiſtants, about two hundred years before, had carefully collated the Hebrew Text with manuſcripts, older and better than were now to be met with in the world; and had exhibited a printed Hebrew Text, as perfect as could be expected or need be deſired: becauſe, by Mr. Kennicott's own confeſſion, no ſuch errors occurred in the Text as affected any point of doctrine; the various readings being chiefly to be found in dates and numbers, which are of leſs importance and more uncertain notation. That therefore, what Cardinal Ximenes had done in a better manner and with greater advantages, would now be done with more difficulty, and probably to leſs effect.

5. They apprehended, that the diſpute about the Hebrew Text, the Samaritan Pentateuch, &c. had been ſufficiently agitated and judiciouſly ſtated by Carpzov of Leipſic in his writings againſt Whiſton;

ſo far at leaſt as to ſhew, that no great things were to be expected from any adventurer, who ſhould afterwards take the ſame ground. Carpzov's book was thought ſo uſeful and ſatisfactory, that Moſes Marcus, a converted Jew, had tranſlated it into Engliſh.

6. A conſideration which had great weight with Mr. Horne was that of the probable conſequence of an undertaking ſo conducted as this was likely to be. Unbelievers, Sceptics, and Heretics, of this country, who had affected ſuperior learning, had always been buſy in finding imaginary corruptions in the Text of Scripture: and would in future be more bold and buſy than ever; as the work of confounding the Text by unſound criticiſm would be carried on with the ſanction of public authority, and the Bible left open to the experiments of evil-minded critics and cavillers. For beſides the collating of manuſcripts, the collator, in his Diſſertations, had opened three other fountains of criticiſm, by which the waters of the Sanctuary were to be healed: the Ancient Verſions, the Samaritan Pentateuch, and Sound Criticiſm. Having conſidered theſe in their order, Mr. Horne ſets before his readers above twenty inſtances from Mr. Kennicott's own books, as a ſpecimen of his manner of proceeding; to ſhew "what "an inundation of licentious criticiſm was breaking "in upon the Sacred Text." Theſe inſtances are ſuch as fully juſtify his reflections; which the reader may find at p. 12, &c. of his View of Mr. Kennicott's Method, &c.

Such were the conſiderations on which Mr. Horne and

and his friends opposed Mr. K.'s undertaking; and, it is hoped, nothing has appeared to their disadvantage. In the progress of the controversy, some other considerations arose, which served to confirm them in the part they had taken. They observed that Mr. Kennicott changed his ground; first urging the necessity of a *new Text* for the purpose of a new English Version; and afterwards giving it up, without assigning his reasons. Another fact arose, which was palpably contrary to his own principles. When the design was to come forward, he had objected to the labours of Cardinal Ximenes, as being ineffective, because he admitted manuscripts furnished by Jews: but, when the work was to be carried on, he himself made Jews his agents to collect manuscripts for him in foreign parts, and admitted them, so far as we know, without reserve: and with this remarkable difference, that the Jews of the Cardinal were turned Christians; whereas the Jews of Mr. Kennicott were still in their unbelief—except one; and he was of a character so extraordinary, that the reader cannot be displeased if I give some account of him; without which, so great a curiosity would, in all probability, be lost to the world. While the work of collation was going forward, it so happened, that Mr. Kennicott and his work, and Mr. Horne, and some of the friends to both, fell into difficulty and danger, from a man whose name was Dumay; a person, who having been encouraged upon benevolent motives in the beginning, proved in the issue to be not much better than the Dumas, who had been attended in the Caſtle at Oxford; and of whom it is ſtill uncertain, whether he did not come to the ſame untimely end. It was my fortune to be the firſt perſon in the Univerſity of Oxford that took notice of him, and the laſt that received any intelligence about him after he left this country; and it is doubtful to me whether any body is better acquainted with his character and hiſtory than myſelf. He was a French Jew, born upon the borders of Lorrain, and had received ſuch an education as enabled him to underſtand Hebrew, and to write it with conſummate excellence. He could turn his hand to drawing, and any other work of art: he had the ingratiating addreſs of a Frenchman, with an appearance of ſincerity; but with the unprincipled mind of a Jew; ſo that there was no depending upon him. Before he was twenty years of age, he appeared at Oxford as a petty Jew-merchant, whoſe whole ſtock conſiſted of a few ſeals, pencils, and other trinkets. His civility drew my attention, and I took him to my chambers, to inquire what he had learned. I ſoon found his qualifications conſiderable, and, for his excellence in writing Hebrew, ſet him to work, with deſign to preſerve his performances as curioſities; and I have ſeveral of them by me at this time. His ingenuity ſoon procured him more friends, of whom Mr. Horne was one of the moſt conſiderable; by means of which he gained a moderate livelihood; and ſome pains were taken with him occaſionally, with the hope of bringing over a perſon of ſo much Jewiſh knowlege to ſome ſenſe

of

of Christianity. After he had led this sort of life for some time, he returned to visit his relations in France; having first prevailed on me to write him a testimonial of his late behaviour, to procure him a favourable reception; from which it seems probable, that he had left his friends in consequence of some misdemeanor. While he was abroad, he turned Christian, and received baptism from a priest of the Church of Rome, under the name of Ignatius. Then he went into the army of the King of France; promoted desertion among his comrades, quarrelled with his officer, and ran him through the body, but without killing him. Just at this juncture, the army in which he served came to an engagement with Prince Ferdinand, and he was taken prisoner. But the Prince having heard something of his history, and understanding it would be certain destruction to him if he were sent back to his own party, gave him a passport to England, with a recommendation to Mr. De Reiche, the Hanoverian Secretary at St. James's; a very worthy friendly gentleman, who had been a considerable benefactor to Dumay, till he found him at length a dead weight upon his hands, and grew tired of him. In the year 1761, after the famous transit of Venus, he presented himself to Mr. Horne at Magdalen College with terribly sore eyes; and being asked what was the matter, he answered, that he had suffered in his eyesight by looking at the sun: for having omitted to furnish himself as other people did for the occasion, he had made all his observations through a crack in

his

his fingers, and had nearly put his eyes out. I do not recollect at what time he entered into his employment under Mr. Kennicott, who certainly found him very well qualified for his purpose in point of ability and industry, but high spirited, turbulent, and discontented; so that, after he had been a year or two at the work of collating Hebrew manuscripts, he quarrelled with his employer, threw himself out of his work, and came with his complaints to me in the country, desiring to shew me some extracts he had made from the collations, that I might be a witness with him to the futility of the undertaking. The specimen he produced was not to the advantage of it; but it was not easy to judge, how far the fidelity of a person in an ill humour was to be depended upon. None but the collator himself could determine with precision. I advised him by all means to return to Mr. Kennicott, make his peace with him, and go on quietly with his business. Which he did; but after a perfidious manner; playing a false game between two parties; and carrying stories from the one to the other as it suited his purpose, till all his friends found reason to be afraid of him, and Mr. Kennicott (now Dr. Kennicott) was under the necessity of dismissing him. So he left the occupation of a collator, formed a plan for forging Hebrew manuscripts, with all the appearances of antiquity, and putting them off for genuine, to shew how the world might be imposed upon. Somebody in compassion to his distress recommended him as an assistant to a charitable gen-

tleman

tleman at a ſchool in Bedfordſhire, for which employment he was well qualified; but there alſo, after he had given much trouble, he miſcarried. At length he got into ſome place of truſt, which gave him an opportunity of making off with a ſum of money: for, with all his ingenuity and induſtry, and without any one expenſive vice, yet, as if ſome dæmon had purſued him, he ſo ordered his affairs, that, having now a wife and child to maintain, he was very ſeldom far from beggary: whence one would hope he did ſome things rather from diſtreſs than malignity; though it muſt be owned, that upon the plea of his own wants, he could juſtify himſelf to his own conſcience in any act of perfidy againſt the beſt of his benefactors; his conduct being exactly the ſame to his friends and his enemies, if his affairs required it. With what he had thus got he went over to Paris; where, by means of his own Hebrew papers, and ſome others which he had carried away with him, he had the addreſs to introduce himſelf to a ſociety of Hebrew ſcholars among the Capuchin Friars of St. Honoré; and amongſt them all they fabricated a work, in the French language, which came over into England under the title of *Lettres de M. l'Abbé de **** Ex-profeſſeur en Hébreu en l'Univerſité de ***, au Sr. Kennicott Anglois.* It has Rome in the title, as if it had been there printed, but it was ſold at Paris; and its date is 1771. This pamphlet is ſevere, both in its reflections and its examples, on the work of collation, ſo celebrated in England, that people would hear nothing againſt it; and I was told, that the bookſeller who traded in foreign books refuſed to take this into his ſhop: and yet ſome of its aſſertions are but to the ſame effect with thoſe of Mr. Horne in his View; the ſubſtance of which the reader may ſee from the quotation in the margin*. This piece was afterwards tranſlated into Engliſh by a worthy gentleman, who was ſtruck by its facts and arguments; and a ſmall anonymous pamphlet was publiſhed ſoon after its appearance, apologizing for the ſilence of Dr. Kennicott, and alleging that he had *no time to anſwer it*.

While I was at Paris, I inquired of Mr. Aſſeline, the Hebrew profeſſor at the Sorbonne, whether he had ever ſeen ſuch a perſon as I deſcribed Dumay to be? He anſwered that he had ſeen him, but that he was gone off from Paris, and he ſuppoſed nobody knew what was become of him. When I inquired farther, who had been his friends, he confeſſed that the Capuchins of St. Honoré were ſuſpected to have been the compilers and editors of his book. Now the reader has heard my ſtory, let him conſider, whether he can recollect a more extraordinary character, than that of this Jew, Chriſtian, Papiſt, Proteſtant, Soldier, Scrivener, French, Engliſhman! If it ſo happened that he ſurvived his *fourberies*, he may have proved

* Il ne reſtera pas un ſeul mot dans la Bible Hebraïque dont on puiſſe garantir la ſincérité. Sentez donc les ſuites de votre entrepriſe: il n'en réſultera qu'un ouvrage mal conçu, peu conforme aux regles de la ſaine critique, totalement inutile, et plus propre à éblouir par un vain etalage de prétendues corrections, qu'à inſtruire par des raiſonnemens ſolides. P. 12.

to

to be a serviceable hand, and have acted some useful part upon the stage of the French Revolution*.

Neither Mr. Horne nor his friends could ever be persuaded, that, under the present state of the printed Hebrew Text, the labours of an Hebrew collator were at this time wanted by the Christian world; or that the experiment, from the face with which it made its appearance, would not be attended with some danger: and it might be owing (as I have said) to their pressing remonstrances, that the plan of a new Text, and a new English Translation, was laid aside. How far they were right in apprehending evil from it to the Christian cause, doth not appear from any consequences which have yet followed, and we hope, it never will. The edition makes a very fine book, which will do honour to the memory of the editor, and, with its various readings, may be a very innocent one, if used with discretion. My learned and worthy friend the late Rev. Mr. Parkhurst (the last edition of

* This man is frequently spoken of in Dr. Horne's Letters; from one of which, of March 1770, I take what follows: "The "Sieur Dumay is a curious rogue indeed! The subject is so pregnant, that I could with pleasure put out my candles, to pass the "evening in meditation upon him and his proceedings, since we had "first the honour of knowing him, when he talked so much of "Titus and the copper fly. If the best men are most imposed upon (as "some say they are) we may, I think, without vanity, esteem ourselves to be a tolerably good sort of people." N. B. The Jews have a foolish legend, that when Titus had destroyed Jerusalem, God Almighty, to be revenged on the enemy of his people, sent a copper fly for his punishment, which crept up his nose, and fed upon his brain, till it had killed him.

whose Hebrew Lexicon was patronized by Dr. Horne after he was made a bishop) speaks of it with due respect: his words are these—"The principal *various* "*readings* in Dr. Kennicott's Hebrew Bible have been "carefully noted, and are submitted to the reader's "consideration and judgment. And it is hoped that "the use which is here made of that elaborate work "cannot fail of being acceptable to every serious and "intelligent inquirer into the sense of the Hebrew "Scriptures." See the advertisement to the third edition.

Of the friendly way in which Dr. Kennicott and Dr. Horne lived together, forgetting all their former disputes, yet without changing their opinions on either side, so far as I have been able to discover, I have already spoken: but the cause of learning and religion is still, and ever will be, so deeply concerned in the argument between them, that it well deserves to be remembered and understood; and for this reason only I have spent so many words upon it. I may therefore hope to be pardoned, if I still go on to do as much justice as I can to Dr. Horne's side of the question, by adding one weighty reason, which he had (though he did not say much about it) for his suspicions in regard to the good effect of the collating system*. He thought it would be of disservice to turn the minds of the learned more toward the

* In Bishop Hurd's late Life of Dr. Warburton, Dr. Lowth is reflected upon for his expectations from the labours of Dr. Kennicott.

letter

letter of the Bible, when they were already too much turned away from the ſpirit of it. The beſt fruits of divine wiſdom may be gathered from the word of God, in any language, and in any edition. To what the Scripture itſelf calls the ſpirit of the Scripture, the learned of late days were become much more inattentive than in paſt ages. The Puritans of the laſt century ſet a proper value upon it, and ſome of them did well in diſplaying it: but when their formal manners, with their long prayers, and their long graces, were rejected, their interpretations of the Scripture, and with them all ſounder interpretations of the kind, fell into diſrepute; for men are ſuch haſty reformers, that if they caſt out evil, they caſt out ſome good along with it. When tares are plucked up, the wheat is always in danger.

To this cauſe another may be added. The perſons, who ſince that time have riſen into chief repute for parts and learning, had nothing of this in their compoſitions; ſuch as Clarke, Hoadley, Hare, Middleton, Warburton, Sherlock, South, William Law, Edmund Law, and many others, who have flouriſhed ſince the Reſtoration: they either did not know it, or did not reliſh it, and fell totally into other ways of ſtudying and reaſoning: after which it was naturally to be expected in their diſciples, that the ſpirit of the Scripture ſhould be leſs regarded. This actually did happen, and to ſuch a degree, that many did not even know what was meant by it. Somebody was wanting to revive the knowlege that was loſt: but, alas!

alas! when this was attempted, the door was ſhut. This ſort of learning, the beſt and the greateſt of which the mind of man is capable in this life, had been ſo long aſleep, that it ſeemed likely never more to awake. Accordingly, when Mr. Horne ſat down to write his Commentary on the Pſalms, which proceeds throughout upon the true principle, he was under great anxiety of mind about the reception of it by the world; and expreſſed his fears in the Preface to the work, telling his readers "he is not inſenſible "that many learned and good men, whom he does "not therefore value and reſpect the leſs, have con-"ceived ſtrong prejudices againſt the ſcheme of in-"terpretation here purſued; and he knows how little "the generality of modern Chriſtians are accuſtomed "to ſpeculations of this kind.—In the firſt age of the "Church, when the apoſtolical method of citing and "expounding was freſh upon the minds of their "followers, the author cannot but be confident, that "his Commentary, if it had then made its appear-"ance, would have been univerſally received and "approved as to the general deſign of it, by the "whole Chriſtian world," &c. &c. How unfortunate it is that ſuch ſtrong prejudices ſhould be conceived againſt that mode of interpretation, in which Chriſtians differ from Jews! But ſo it is; and ſo long as it is the cuſtom for learned men to employ their time and talents, as the Maſorites did, and more reputation is to be obtained by picking and ſifting of letters, than by the apoſtolical method of opening the ſenſe and

and ſpirit of them, the evil will be rather increaſing than diminiſhing. When faſhion invites, vanity will always follow; critic will ſucceed to critic, and he that is the boldeſt will think himſelf the greateſt, till all due veneration for the Bible is loſt, and the Text is cut and ſlaſhed, as if it were no longer a living body, but the ſubject of a Lecture in Surgeons' Hall. While the rage of editing prevails, and the ſtate of the copy is the grand object, we have then too much reaſon to apprehend, that the ſpirit of life, which is ſtill to be found, even in the worſt copies and pooreſt editions, will be leſs regarded and underſtood. We ſhould have but a mean opinion of the gardener, who ſhould always be clearing and raking his borders, but never raiſing any thing from them to ſupport the life of man. Thus, if collating ends in collation, the tendency of it may be bad, though it be ever ſo well executed: and I believe this was, at the bottom, the chief objection againſt it in the mind of Mr. Horne. He was ſhy of ſpeaking too plain, through a fear of giving offence; but the time has now many greater dangers than that of offending ſome few modern critics and editors.

I relate it as a ſingular occurrence, that when the mind of Mr. Horne was firſt filled with the deſign of commenting upon the Pſalms, he ſhould meet with a traveller in a ſtage-coach, who was in principle the very reverſe of himſelf. The man gave his judgment with all freedom on all ſubjects of divinity, and among the reſt on the uſe of the Pſalms in the ſervice of the Church. The Pfalms of David, he faid, were nothing to us, and he thought other compofitions might be fubftituted, which were much more to the purpofe than David's Pfalms. He happened to be fpeaking to a perfon, who could fee deeper than moft men into the ignorance and folly of his difcourfe, but was wife enough to hear him with patience, and leave him to proceed in his own way. Yet this poor man was but the pattern of too many more, who want to be taught again, that David was a Prophet, and fpeaks of the Meffiah where he feems to be fpeaking of himfelf; as the apoftle St. Peter taught the Jews, in the fecond chapter of the Acts, and thereby converted three thoufand of them at once to the belief of Chrift's refurrection.

There is another modern way of criticifing upon the Scripture, to which Mr. Horne had no great affection, as thinking it could never be of much fervice: I mean that cuftom, which has prevailed fince the days of Grotius, of juftifying and illuftrating the things revealed to us in the Scripture from *heathen* authorities. I had feen too much of this among fome of my acquaintance, perfons of no mean learning, but who, inftead of employing themfelves in the more fuccefsful labour of comparing fpiritual things with fpiritual, in order to underftand them, were diligent in collecting parallel paffages from Heathen authors, to compare them with the Scripture; as if the fun wanted the affiftance of a candle; or the word of God was not worthy to be received, but fo far only as we are able to reconcile it with the wiſdom of Greek and Roman authors. He was rather of opinion, with a certain writer, that the Bible will explain all the books in the world, but wants not them to explain it. St. Paul did not think it improper, on certain occaſions, to refer to Heathen authorities*, and make his uſe of them for the confirmation of his own doctrine; but this was done when he was arguing with Heathens, not with Chriſtians. There is not the ſame propriety, when his ſublime chapter on the reſurrection is compared (as I have ſeen it) with Plato's doctrine of generation and corruption. Take the Heathen doctrine of the origination of mankind, and compare it with the ſacred hiſtory of Adam in Paradiſe, and it will ſoon appear how little the one wants the help of the other.

> Quum prorepſerunt primis animalia terris
> Brutum et turpe pecus, glandem atque cubilia propter
> Unguibus et pugnis, dein fuſtibus, atque ita porro
> Pugnabant armis, quæ poſt fabricaverat uſus:
> Donec verba, quibus voces ſenſuſque notarent,
> Nominaque invenere—— HOR.

It was a doctrine of the Heathen poets, that men, when firſt made, were *without ſpeech*, creeping on all four like beaſts, living upon acorns, and lodging like ſwine in a foreſt: whereas, when we conſult the Bible, we find the firſt man converſing with his Maker, placed under a ſtate of inſtruction and probation, and in a condition but little lower than an

* See Acts xvii. v. 23. 28.

angel. What muſt the conſequence be, when an attempt is made to reconcile theſe two accounts, and melt them down together? Yet was this actually done by the learned Dr. Shuckford, as it may be ſeen in the laſt-written Preface to his Connexion; where the hiſtory of Adam, and of Eve, and of Paradiſe, and the Intercourſe of Man with his Creator, is commented upon and illuſtrated from Ovid and Tully, and Mr. Pope's poetical ſyſtem of Deiſm, called *an Eſſay on Man*; till the whole is involved in obſcurity, and becomes even childiſh and inſignificant; as if it had been the deſign of the critic to expoſe the ſacred hiſtory to the contempt of blaſphemers and infidels. This abuſe of learning Mr. Horne could not ſee without a mixture of grief and indignation: he is therefore ſuppoſed to be the perſon who, in a little anonymous pamphlet, made his remarks on this unworthy manner of handling the Scripture. While he was young, his zeal was ardent, and his ſtrictures were unreſerved. Yet I can never perſuade myſelf, that it was the intention of Dr. Shuckford to put a ſlight upon the Bible; though he certainly has made the Moſaic account as ridiculous in ſimplicity, as Dr. Middleton did in malice. I rather think he was betrayed into the miſtake by a prevailing cuſtom of the age. When the learned are leſs ſtudious of the Scripture, and become vain of other learning, it may eaſily be foreſeen how the Scripture muſt ſuffer under their expoſitions; and, if they do not foreſee it, we would refer them for evidence

evidence to the Supplemental Discourse on the Creation and Fall of Man, by Dr. Shuckford. The reformer, who dares to censure a corrupt practice, can never be well received by the parties who are in fault. This was the lot of Mr. Horne and his friends. The candle, which they had lighted at the Scripture, and held up to shew some dangers and absurdities in modern learning, was blown out, and they themselves were accused as persons of great zeal and little understanding. How often do we see, that when men *should* be reformed, and are *not*, they are only provoked past remedy! This being, upon the whole, but an unpleasant subject, I shall proceed to one that will entertain us better.

A letter of July the 25th, 1755, informed me that Mr. Horne, according to an established custom at Magdalen College in Oxford, had begun to preach before the University, on the day of St. John the Baptist. For the preaching of this annual sermon a permanent pulpit of stone is inserted into a corner of the first Quadrangle; and, so long as the stone pulpit was in use (of which I have been a witness) the Quadrangle was furnished round the sides with a large fence of green boughs, that the preaching might more nearly resemble that of John the Baptist in the wilderness; and a pleasant sight it was: but for many years the custom hath been discontinued, and the assembly have thought it safer to take shelter under the roof of the chapel. Our fore-fathers, it seems, were not so much afraid of being injured by the falling of a little rain, or the blowing of the wind, or the ſhining of the ſun upon their heads. The preacher of 1755 pleaſed the audience very much by his manner and ſtyle, and all agreed that he had a *very fine imagination:* but he was not very well pleaſed with the compliment. As a *Chriſtian teacher*, he was much more deſirous that his hearers ſhould receive and underſtand, and enter into the ſpirit of the doctrines he had delivered; but in this he found them ſlower than he wiſhed, and laments it heavily in a private letter. Two ſermons on the ſubject of St. John the Baptiſt were printed, and many others ſucceeded which were not printed: for the author, at laſt, on a review of what he had done, thought it more adviſable to throw the matter out of that form, and caſt an abridgment of the whole into the form of *Conſiderations:* on which performance I have already ſpoken my mind, and, I believe, the mind of every competent judge, in the beginning of this work. (See Pref. Epiſt. p. iv.) I can only ſay here, that if there be any Chriſtian reader, who wiſhes to know what a ſaint is, and aſpires to be one himſelf, let him keep before his eyes that beautiful and finiſhed picture of St. John the Baptiſt, to the executing of which but one perſon of the age was equal. But behold how this was deſcribed by the *Critical Reviewers* of the time! "In the Conſiderations," they ſay, "there "are ſome judicious and ſolid remarks relative to "practice, but *nothing to engage the attention of a curious, inquiſitive, or critical reader.*" They might

have

have ſaid the ſame of the Sermon on the Mount. It looks as if they would have been better pleaſed with a diſſertation upon the manner in which the wild honey was made and collected for John to eat*, properly interſperſed with quotations from Athenæus and other authors, to ſhew the learning of the writer,

* Many examples might be given, to illuſtrate the diſtinction between *Chriſtian* Divinity, by which men are edified, and *curious* Divinity, by which they are only amuſed and entertained. We read in the goſpel, Luke xix. 4. That Zaccheus climbed up into a ſycamore tree, to ſee Jeſus paſs by, and was led by that circumſtance to repentance and ſalvation. When this caſe is conſidered by the *Chriſtian Divine*, he dwells upon the circumſtance of Zaccheus's deſiring to ſee the Saviour of the world, and the ineſtimable bleſſing of being called by him, as Zaccheus was, to a ſtate of ſalvation. But when the *curious Divine* hears that Zaccheus climbs up into a tree, he climbs up after him; not to ſee what he ſaw, but to examine the nature of the tree, and aſcertain to what ſpecies of plants, botanically conſidered, it properly belongs.

In this example we have two very different modes of treating the Scripture. No man that loves learning will condemn the critical diſquiſitor: let him purſue his inquiries; there is no harm in them: but when he preſumes, as from an upper region, to diſdain the Chriſtian Divine, as unworthy of all commendation, he pays too great a compliment to his own importance, and raiſes a very juſt ſuſpicion againſt his own religious principles. The caſe of Zaccheus is conſidered in the *Chriſtian* way by Biſhop Hall (ſee Mr. Glaſſe's edition, vol. iii. p. 219) and matter enough for the *critical way* may be found in the Voyages of Frederick Haſſelquiſt, p. 129, et alib. The ſame *inquiſitive* perſon was, as he tells us, very ſolicitous to diſcover what *kind of tree in particular* David had his eye upon in the *firſt Pſalm*: which never can be diſcovered, if his expreſſions, as they ſeem, have an alluſion to the *Tree of Life*. See our author's Commentary on the Firſt Pſalm; who inclines to this opinion.

and that, perhaps, but impertinently introduced. When there is a party always ready, and always upon the watch, to hinder the ſucceſs of every good attempt, and miſlead the ignorant on ſubjects of the firſt importance, ſuch a writer as the author of thoſe Conſiderations had little chance of eſcaping. Their artifices had been ſo well obſerved and underſtood by him, that he was able to predict their proceedings. When I had printed a diſcourſe on the Moſaic Diſtinction of Animals in the Book of Leviticus, which had coſt me much reſearch and meditation, under the title of Zoologia Ethica, in which I had traced the *moral intention* of that curious inſtitution, he foretold me how it would be repreſented to the public; that the critics would ſelect ſome part of the work, which was either ambiguous in itſelf, or might be made ſo by their manner of exhibiting it, and give that as a ſpecimen of the plan, to diſcourage the examination of it. "The paſſage (ſaid he), at page 19, &c., about "the camel and the ſwine will probably be ſelected "by the Reviewers, given to the reader without a "ſyllable of the evidence, and then the whole book "diſmiſſed with a ſneer." In a few months after, his prediction was ſo exactly verified, that one would have ſuſpected him to have been in the ſecret. "If "you look into the Critical Review, you will be "tempted to think I wrote the article on the Zoolo-"gia, to verify my own prediction. Without giving "the leaſt account of your plan, and the arguments "by which it is ſo irrefragably ſupported and demon-

"ſtrated,

" ſtrated, the ——— give the very paſſage about " the ſwine and the camel, and conclude the whole " ſcheme to be viſionary, and *problematical*, as they " phraſe it*." Thus is a malignant party gratified, and the public is beguiled by falſe accounts: the deception may continue for a time; but truth and juſtice generally take place at laſt.

There is a portion of the New Teſtament, very intereſting and full of matter, on which the author of the Conſiderations, ſoon after he was in holy orders, beſtowed much thought and labour; I mean the eleventh chapter of St. Paul's Epiſtle to the Hebrews. On this he compoſed at leaſt twenty ſermons; which are all excellent; but being more agreeable to the ſpirit of the firſt ages than of the preſent, he was not forward, though frequently ſolicited, to give them to the world. He objected, that they wanted to be reviewed with a more critical eye, and even to be recompoſed; and that this would be a work of time. Toward the latter end of his life, however, he ſet about it, but got no farther than through the third diſcourſe. The firſt is on the Character of Abel, the ſecond on Enoch, the third on Noah. Of theſe I have the copy, and hope it will be publiſhed. Whoever looks at them, will wiſh he had lived to ſatisfy his mind about all the reſt. They would

* The date of the letter from which this extract is taken is Feb. 12, 1772. The work, thus unfairly treated, I ſent to the learned Biſhop Newton, a writer of profound ſkill in the language of the Scripture; who allowed that I had proved the *moral intention* of that law which is the ſubject of it.

certainly

certainly have been improved by fuch a revifion; yet, perhaps, not fo much as he fuppofed. Firft thoughts, upon a favourite fubject, are warm and lively; and the language they bring with them is ftrong and natural; but prudence is apt to be cold and timorous; and, while it adds a polifh, takes away fomething from the fpirit of a compofition.

But the greateft work of his life, of which he now began to form the defign, was a *Commentary on the whole Book of Pfalms.* In the year 1758, he told me how he had been meditating on the Book of Pfalms, and had finifhed thofe for the firft day of the month, upon the following plan*: 1. An analyfis of the Pfalm, by way of argument. 2. A paraphrafe on each verfe. 3. The fubftance digefted into a prayer. "The work (faid he) delights me greatly, "and feems, fo far as I can judge of my own turn and "talents, to fuit me the beft of any I can think of. "May he, who hath the *keys of David*, profper it in "my hand; granting me the knowlege and utterance "neceffary to make it ferviceable to the Church!" Let any perfon of judgment perufe the work, and he will fee how well the author has fucceeded, and kept up the fpirit of it to the end. His application of the book of Pfalms is agreeable to the teftimony fo repeatedly given to it, and the ufe made of it, in the New Teftament. This queftion is ftated and fettled beyond a doubt, in a learned preface to the work.

* This plan he afterwards thought proper to alter, and, as it is judged, for the better.

The

The ſtyle is that of an accompliſhed writer; and its ornaments diſtinguiſh the vigour of his imagination. That all readers ſhould admire it as I do, is not to be expected; yet it has certainly met with great admiration; and I have ſeen letters to him, from perſons of the firſt judgment, on the publication of the book. It will never be neglected, if the church and its religion ſhould continue; for which he prayed fervently every day of his life. When it firſt came from the preſs, Mr. Daniel Prince, his bookſeller at Oxford, was walking to or from Magdalen College with a copy of it under his arm. "What have you "there, Mr. Prince?" ſaid a gentleman who met him. "This, ſir, is a copy of Dr. Horne's Pſalms, "juſt now finiſhed. The Preſident, ſir, began to "write *very young*: but this is the work in which he "will always live." In this Mr. Prince judged very rightly: he will certainly live in this work; but there are many others of his works, in which he will not die, till all learning and piety ſhall die with him.

His Commentary on the Pſalms was under his hand about twenty years. The labour, to which he ſubmitted in the courſe of the work, was prodigious: his reading for many years was allotted chiefly to this ſubject; and his ſtudy and meditation together produced as fine a work, and as finely written, as moſt in the Engliſh language. There are good and learned men, who cannot but ſpeak well of the work, and yet are forward to let us know, that they do not follow Dr. Horne as an interpreter. I believe them; but

but this is one of the things we have to lament: and, while they may think this an honour to their judgment, I am afraid it is a ſymptom that we are retrograde in theological learning. The author was ſenſible, that, after the pleaſure he had received in ſtudying for the work, and the labour of compoſing and correcting, he was to offer what the age was ill prepared to receive. This put him upon his guard; and the work is in ſome reſpects the better for it, in others not ſo good; it is more cautiouſly and correctly written, but perhaps not ſo richly furniſhed with matter as it might have been. Had he been compoſing a novel, he would have been under none of theſe fears: his imagination might then have taken its courſe, without a bridle, and the world would have followed as faſt as he could wiſh.

The firſt edition in quarto was publiſhed in the year 1776, when the author was vice-chancellor; and it happened, ſoon after its publication, that I was at Paris. There was then a Chriſtian Univerſity in the place! and I had an opportunity of recommending it to ſome learned gentlemen who were members of it, and underſtood the Engliſh language well. I took the liberty to tell them, our church had lately been enriched by a Commentary on the Pſalms; the beſt, in our opinion, that had ever appeared; and ſuch as St. Auſtin would have peruſed with delight, if he had lived to ſee it. At my return the author was ſo obliging as to furniſh me with a copy to ſend over to them as a preſent; and I was highly

gratified

gratified by the approbation with which it was received. With thofe who could read Englifh, it was fo much in requeft, that I was told the book was never out of hand; and I apprehend more copies were fent for. Every intelligent Chriftian, who once knows the value of it, will keep it, to the end of his life, as the companion of his retirement: and I can fcarcely wifh a greater bleffing to the age, than that it may daily be better known and more approved.

About the time when it was publifhed, that fyftematical infidel, David Hume, died. It had been the aim of his life, to invent a fort of Philofophy, that fhould effect the overthrow of Chriftianity. For this he lived; and his ambition was to die, or be thought to die, hard and impenitent, yea, and even cheerful and happy; to fhew the world the power of his own principles: which however were weakly founded, and fo inconfiftent with common fenfe, that Dr. Beattie attacked and demolifhed them in the life-time of the author. Special pains were taken by Hume himfelf, and by his friends after him, to perfuade the world, that his life, at the laft ftage of it, was perfectly tranquil and compofed: and the part is fo laboured and over-acted, that there is juft caufe of fufpicion, even before the detection appears. Dr. Horne, whofe mind was ever in action for fome good end, could not fit ftill, and fee the public fo impofed upon. He addreffed an anonymous *Letter to Dr. Adam Smith* from the Clarendon Prefs; of which the argument is fo clear, and the humour fo

easy

eaſy and natural, that no honeſt man can keep his countenance while he reads it, and none but an infidel can be angry. While Dr. Adam Smith affects to be very ſerious and ſolemn in the cauſe of his friend Hume, the author of the Letter plays them both off with wonderful effect. He alludes to certain anecdotes concerning Mr. Hume, which are very inconſiſtent with the account given in his Life: for at the very period, when he is reported not to have *ſuffered a moment's abatement of his ſpirits*, none of his friends dared to mention the name of a certain *author* in his preſence, leſt it ſhould *throw him into a tranſport of paſſion and ſwearing:* a certain indication that his mind had been greatly hurt; and nobody will think it was without reaſon, if he will read the Eſſay on Truth by Dr. Beattie; which is not only a confutation of Hume's Philoſophy; it is much more; it is an extirpation of his principles, and delivers them to be ſcattered like ſtubble by the winds.

The Letter to Dr. Adam Smith, like the Eſſay of Dr. Beattie, has a great deal of truth, recommended by a great deal of wit: and if the reader has not ſeen it, he has ſome pleaſure in ſtore. We allow to the memory of Dr. Adam Smith, that he was a perſon of quick underſtanding and diligent reſearch, in things relating merely to this world; of which, his Inquiry into the Cauſes of the Wealth of Nations will be a laſting monument; and it is a work of great uſe to thoſe who would obtain a comprehenſive view of buſineſs and commerce: but when he ſet up Mr.

Hume as a pattern of perfection, and judged of all religion by the principles of that philosopher, he was very much out of his line.

The Letter was followed in course of time by *Letters on Infidelity*; which are very instructive and entertaining, and highly proper for the preventing or lessening that respect which young people may conceive unawares for unbelieving philosophers. It has been objected by some readers of a more severe temper, that these Letters are occasionally too light*: and I must confess, I should have been as well pleased, if the story of Dr. Radcliffe and his man had been omitted: but there is this to be said, that these are not sermons, but familiar letters; that Dr. Horne considered the profession of infidelity, as a thing more ridiculous and insignificant in itself, than some of his learned readers might do; that, as it appeared in some persons, it was really too absurd to be treated with seriousness; and, as Voltaire had treated religion with ridicule instead of argument, and had done infinite mischief by it, justice required that he and his friends should be treated a little in their own way†. Besides, as infidels have nothing to support them

* In his preface to these Letters, the author has endeavoured to obviate this objection; and we think he has done it very sufficiently.

† One of the severest reflections, that ever came from the pen of Dr. Horne, was aimed, as I suppose, at this Mr. David Hume: yet it is all very fair. This philosopher had observed, that all the *devout* persons he had ever met with were *melancholy*: which is thus answered: "This might very probably be; for, in the first place, "it

them but their vanity, let them once appear as ridiculous as they are impious, and they cannot live. They can never approve themſelves, but ſo far only as they are upheld and approved by other people. To treat them with ſeriouſneſs (as W—— has treated G——) is to make them important; which is all they want. The opinions of Mr. Hume, as they are diſplayed in theſe Letters, are many of them ridiculous from their palpable abſurdity: but, it muſt be owned, they are ſometimes horrible and ſhocking; ſuch as, that man is not an accountable but a neceſſary agent; conſequently, that there is no ſuch thing as ſin, or that God is the author of it: that the life of a man and the life of an oyſter are of *equal* value*: that

" it is moſt likely, that he ſaw very few, his friends and acquaintance " being of another ſort; and, ſecondly, the ſight of *him* would make " a devout perſon melancholy at any time." Serm. vol. iii. p. 96. Theſe Letters are a demonſtration that all devout perſons are not melancholy.

* It is a fundamental doctrine in the Creed of *Materialiſm*, that nature conſiſts of *matter* and a *living ſubſtance* of which all living creatures *equally* partake; and which, when it dies in a carcaſe, is continued in the reptiles that feed upon it. The origin of individual life, in every form, is from the general animation of the world; on which the philoſophers of antiquity ſpeculated; and ſome inconſiderate Chriſtians have taken it up on their authority. You have it in Virgil:

Principio cœlum, ac terras, campoſque liquentes,
Lucentemque globum Lunæ, Titaniaque aſtra
SPIRITUS intus alit: totamque infuſa per artus
MENS agitat molem, et magno ſe corpore miſcet.
INDE hominum pecudumque genus, VITÆQUE volantum.

And

that it may be as criminal to act for the preservation of life, as for its destruction: that as life is so insignificant and vague, there can be no harm in disposing of it as we please: that there can be no more crime in turning a few ounces of blood out of their course (that is, in cutting one's throat) than in turning the waters of a river out of their channel. What is murder? It is nothing more than turning a little blood out of its way. And so the Irishman said, by the same figure of rhetoric, that perjury was nothing more than kissing a book, or, as he worded it, smacking the calveskin. This is the sage Mr. Hume! whom Dr. Adam Smith delivers to the world, after his death, as a perfect character; while a man of plain sense, who takes things as they are, would think it impossible that any person, who is not out of his mind, should argue at this rate: Mr. Hume seems to me to have borrowed from the school of the old Pyrrhonists much of that system which he is supposed to have invented. They made all things indifferent, and doubted of every thing, that there might be nothing true or real left to disturb them. The chief good they aimed at in every thing, was what they called ἀταραξια, a state of undisturbance or tranquillity, in which the mind cares for nothing: and it was the

And in Mr. Pope's Essay on Man,

All are but parts of one stupendous whole,
Whose body Nature is and God the soul, &c.

Ep. i. 267, &c.

What follows is in exact conformity with the principle of Virgil, and of our philosophical Deists.

ambition of Mr. Hume to be thought to have lived and died in this state; but by all accounts his ἀταραξία was not quite perfect*. His object was undoubtedly the same with that of the Pyrrhonists, and he pursues it by a like way of reasoning. The speculations of these men were so copious, that there is matter enough left for another Mr. Hume to set himself up with, and pass for an original. Of all the sects of antiquity this was the most unreasonable; though pretending to more wisdom than all the rest. That, which was but folly under Heathenism, turns into desperation and madness under the light and truth of Christianity. Where all was blind tradition, or wild conjecture, there might be some excuse for fixing to nothing; but to affect *undisturbance*, after what is now revealed, concerning death and judgment, and heaven and hell, is to try how far a man can argue himself out of his senses. What angels may think of such a person, I do not inquire: but how must evil spirits look upon that man, who sleeps or laughs over the things at which they tremble; and then calls himself a *Philosopher!*

Of the Letters on Infidelity, the first half is employed

* Pliny the Natural Historian has rightly observed, that Philosophers, through the affectation of apathy, divested themselves of all human affections; that this was the case with Diogenes the Cynic, Pyrrho, Heraclitus, and Timon of Athens; the last of whom actually sunk into a professed hatred of all mankind. "Exit hic animi tenor aliquando in rigorem quemdam, torvitatemque naturæ duram et inflexibilem; adfectusque humanos adimit, quales *apathes* Græci vocant, multos ejus generis experti." Nat. Hist. lib. vii. c. 19.

ployed on Mr. David Hume; the latter half on a more modern adventurer; who, to be revenged on the Bishops of this Church, put together a miscellany of objections against the Scripture and the Christian religion. The Right Reverend Bench had procured an Act of Parliament against the Sunday-Clubs, which met together on the evening of the Sabbath-day, to indulge themselves, and corrupt an audience, with blasphemous disquisitions and disputations. For thus cruelly disturbing the amusements of infidelity, the Bishops are represented as the vilest of persecutors: whips, tortures, racks, and all the implements of the Holy Office, are introduced to confirm the accusation; from all which a stranger to the case might suppose it a common thing with the Prelates of this country, to break the bones of Infidels, or roast them alive: and all this is for nothing else, but that they had seasonably and wisely provided, that the Christian religion, in a Christian country, should not be trampled under foot, upon the Sabbath-day.

The objections this man hath brought together are very well taken off: but if Christians are bound to answer, so long as infidels will object, who never wish to be satisfied, and are probably incapable of being so, their lot would be rather hard, and much of their time unprofitably spent. The Gentlemen of the Long Robe attend the court, not to answer the scruples which felons may entertain about the principles of justice, but to administer the law; otherwise their work would never be done: and it is the busineſs of the clergy to preach the Goſpel to the people: it was the part of God, who gave the word, to prove it to the world by prophecies and miracles. The prophecies are as ſtrong as ever; ſome of them more ſo than formerly: and miracles are not to be repeated for proof, after the world hath once been perſuaded. All is then left to teſtimony and education. Before Moſes gave the law, he ſhewed ſigns and wonders: but, when the law was once received, parents were to tell their children, and confirm the truth by the memorials that were left of it. It therefore lies upon our adverſaries to ſhew, how it came to paſs, on any of *their* principles, that men like themſelves, as much diſpoſed to make objections, ſhould receive the Scripture as the word of God in the ſeveral nations of the world, and receive it at the peril of their lives: a fact which they cannot deny. Let them alſo try to account for it, on their own principles, how the Jews have been ſtrolling about the world for ſeventeen hundred years, as witneſſes to the Scripture, and to the ſentence therein paſſed upon themſelves. Till they can do theſe things, it is nothing but an evaſion to cavil about words and paſſages; a certain mark of prejudice and perverſeneſs. They know they cannot deny the whole; but, as they muſt appear to be doing ſomething, they flatter their own pride by keeping up a ſkirmiſh, and perplex weak people, by raiſing difficulties about the parts. This was the expedient on which Mr. Voltaire beſtowed ſo much labour. It does not appear

to

to me that he really thought the facts of Christianity to be false; but that his vanity and perverseness tempted him to ridicule the Bible, without denying in his mind that God was the author of it: in fact, that he was a *Theomachist*, who hated the truth, knowing it to be such, and braved the authority of Heaven itself: or, in the words of Herbert, that he was a man,

> Who makes flat war with God, and doth defy
> With his poor clod of earth the spacious sky.

If a religion, to which the nature of man is so hostile, did actually make its way without force, and against the utmost cruelty and discouragement from the world; *that* fact was a miracle, including within itself a thousand other miracles.

See, on the other hand, how Paganism, Mahometism, and modern Atheism, were and are supported and propagated: the Pagan Idols by ten bloody persecutions, with every act of outrageous mockery and insult, for want of reasons and miracles: the religion of Mahomet (a sort of Christian Heresy) by rewards of sensuality and the power of the sword; that is, by force and temptation: the Atheism of France by farcical representation and ridicule of truth, assisted in the rear by imprisonments, murders, and confiscations. These be thy gods, O Infidelity, by the power of which thy kingdom is established in the world! These efforts of violence shew the weakness of false reason, and the strength of that which is true; and demonstrate, that men were prevailed upon by true evidence, and rational persuasion, to receive the Christian faith. Here lie the merits of the cause in a small compass: and let all the infidels upon earth lay their heads together, and give a direct answer. Swift assures us, from his own observations, and I believe very truly, that a man was "always vicious before he became an unbeliever;" and that "reasoning will never make a man correct an opinion, which by reasoning he never acquired." Some service, however, is done to the cause of piety, and defensive weapons are put into the hands of those whose minds are as yet uncorrupted, when the malice or ignorance of an infidel is exposed by an examination of his objections: the corruption of *his* mind is thereby displayed in such a manner, that even a child may see it: and therefore we are much obliged to Dr. Horne, for answering the doubts of infidels, and for seasoning his answer with such wit and spirit, that the work, in some parts of it, has the force of a comedy: it should therefore be put into the hands of young people, that they may see how foolish some men are, when they pretend to be over-wise. The Letter to Dr. Priestley from an Under-graduate, that to Dr. Adam Smith on the Character of David Hume, and the Letters on Infidelity, are three choice pieces upon the same argument, which should always go together. But suppose infidelity is answered, the business is not all done: we have still the *believing unbeliever* to contend with, of whom there is but little hope. The Christian evidence can certainly have

have no effect on thofe that deny it: but that it fhould have fo little effect on fome that believe it, and even argue and difpute well for it, this is the greateft wonder of all: but fo the matter ftands. There is a fort of people amongft us, who believe Chriftianity as a *fact*, while they deny it as a *truth*: and fuch perfons may do more harm, and be themfelves as far from the kingdom of heaven, as the open unbeliever: the Gofpel affures us, that he and the hypocrite will have their portion together. Prieftley afferts the *facts* of Chriftianity againft the Philofophers of France, while he believes no more of its *truth* than the Sadducees of Jerufalem did, who yet never denied that God had fpoken unto Mofes. That men profeffing Chriftianity fhould be under temptations to vice, we can eafily underftand: but that their minds fhould believe and deny, at the fame time, concerning the fame thing, *there* is the difficulty. May it be faid, that the mind has antecedently admitted a principle, which militates againft the *truth* while it does not militate againft the *fact*? God knows how the matter is: but I fee too much of it in the world.

Though the imagination of Dr. Horne was fometimes at play when the *Speculum* of Infidelity was in his hand, his heart was always ferious: thence it came to pafs, that the compofition of fermons was a work never out of his mind; and it was the defire and the pleafure of his life to make himfelf ufeful in the pulpit wherever he went. The plan which he commonly proposed to himself in preaching upon a passage of the Scripture was that of giving, 1. The literal sense of it: then, 2. The interpretation or spirit of it: and 3. The practical or moral use of it, in an application to the audience: and he was of opinion, that one discourse, composed upon this plan, was worth twenty immethodical essays; as being more instructive in the matter, more intelligible in the delivery, and more easily retained in the memory. Yet, after long practice, he came to a determination, that no method was more excellent, than that of taking some narrative of the Scripture, and raising moral observations on the several circumstances of it in their order. His Sermon on Lot in Sodom, vol. II. disc. i. and on Daniel in Babylon, vol. II. disc. viii. are of this kind. The Noble Convert, or History of Philip and the Ethiopian Eunuch, vol. II. disc. iii. is another. The Paralytic, and the Woman taken in Adultery, belong to the same class. One of the most skilful and excellent preachers this Church could ever boast, was the late Dr. Heylyn, a Prebendary of Westminster. His discourse on the Canaanite was considered by Dr. Horne as a most perfect and elegant model of a sermon, on a miracle, or any other portion of the Scripture; he pronounced it to be succinct, clear, and forcible, with nothing in it superfluous or tiresome: and, it came into his mind, on reading it, that another after the same model might be composed on the Samaritan Woman and the discourse our Saviour held with her. This he

lived

lived to execute. It is ſtill among his unpubliſhed diſcourſes, and is itſelf worthy to be printed, as a ſpecimen of *this manner*.

There are certainly different modes of preaching, all of which are good in their way: ſome are moſt proper for one ſubject, ſome for another. One of theſe is that of Jeſus Chriſt himſelf; who, from preſent occaſions, and circumſtances of time and place, made uſe of the opportunity to raiſe ſuch doctrines as were wanting for the inſtruction of his hearers: the mind being under the beſt preparation for the conceiving of truth, when that truth is raiſed from the objects of its preſent attention. We ſee our Saviour at a well of water (a precious object in hot countries) diſcourſing on the waters of life, to a perſon who came, in the heat of the day, to draw the water of the well. After this example did Dr. Horne, when he was by the ſea-ſide at Brighthelmſtone, take *the Sea* for the ſubject of a ſermon; one of the moſt ingenious he ever compoſed; and, without queſtion, peculiarly ſtriking to the audience, who had the object before their eyes*. This naturally reminds me of a reflection he made, when, with other young people of the Univerſity, he attended a courſe of Chemical Lectures at Oxford. It was the cuſtom of Dr. Alcock to carry his pupils over ſuch ground, as rendered the ſcience of great ſervice to every perſon of a learned profeſſion. The laſt lecture

* See vol. III. diſc. iv.

was

was upon *poiſons:* and the ſubject required, that ſnakes ſhould be produced upon the table, and made to bite poor harmleſs animals to death; whoſe cries, and howlings, and convulſions, after the wounds given, were extremely affecting, and made ſome of the ſpectators ready to faint. On which he obſerved afterwards—"*that* would have been the moment, to "have delivered a theological lecture on the *Old Ser-* "*pent* of the Scripture—that hath the *power of death* "—and firſt brought it, with all its fatal ſymptoms "and miſeries, into the world!" And he judged right; it would have been better underſtood, and more felt, at that time, than at any other; for it is not to be calculated, how much the mind is aſſiſted in its contemplations by the ſenſes of the body, giving life to its ideas, and working irreſiſtibly upon the paſſions.

His opinion concerning the duties of a preacher is to be found in the Preface to the firſt volume of his Sermons, expreſſed in the words of Fenelon. He conſidered alſo, but never printed, the faults and abuſes which every preacher ſhould ſtudy to avoid: and, as it may be of much ſervice to ſome readers, I ſhall take the liberty of mentioning them in this place:

> Let thoſe teach others, who themſelves excel,
> And cenſure freely who have written well.

"A preacher ſhould avoid rambling upon general

"or

"or trivial ſubjects; ſuch as are not to the purpoſe; "not adapted to the wants and occaſions of the au-"dience, which are always to be conſidered.

"He ſhould beware of polemical and wrangling "compoſitions.

"He ſhould not mix things ſacred and profane to-"gether, from an oſtentation of learning. Such "learning is quite out of place. Alſo a diſcourſe, "conſiſting of critical remarks, is fitter for an editor "than a preacher. See Heylyn, I. 155. with the Pre-"face to Maſſillon's Petit Carême; and the note in "Oſwald's Common Senſe, vol. I. for ſome very uſe-"ful obſervations on this part of the ſubject.

"To be always dwelling on the expedience, neceſ-"ſity, and evidence of revelation, is to ſuppoſe that the "audience conſiſts of Deiſts: for ſuch diſcourſes have "no effect on any but Deiſts, and rarely upon them.

"There may be a fault alſo, in dwelling too much "on the elementary and catechetical doctrines, and "not (as the apoſtle expreſſes it) *going on unto perfection.*

"It is always bad to treat religious ſubjects in a "dull, dry way; neglecting the imagery, energy, and "perſuaſive elocution of the Scriptures.

"Nor is it better to diſcourſe on morality in a rigid, "legal, and comfortleſs manner, without firſt warm-"ing and animating the mind to the practice of it by "motives of faith and love. St. Paul, in 1. Cor. xv. "diſcourſes, for fifty-ſeven verſes together, on the "animating doctrine of the Reſurrection of Chriſt, "and in one ſingle verſe, the laſt in the chapter, "conveys the moral of the whole.

"Much

"Much time and labour are frequently loſt in proving what all the hearers allow: as for example, the obligation they are under to do their duty, inſtead of ſhewing and expoſing the various modes of ſelf-deceit, by which they contrive to elude the obligation, and live in contradiction to their principles. Pleas and pretences of this ſort ſhould be collected, ſtated, and anſwered in a cloſe lively manner, till the hyprocrite is completely unmaſked, driven out of his ſtrong holds, and obliged to ſurrender at diſcretion. Maſſillon is admirable at this, and it makes the general plan of his ſermons.

"The word of God is abuſed by preachers, when it is accommodated and made ſubſervient to the corruptions of the time. It is then an inſtrument for the gratifying of their vanity, or procuring wealth and promotion. Such a traffic with the word is like that of Judas, when he ſold Chriſt for money.

"All affected elegance, and trifling conceits, are to be avoided, as having a bad effect upon the audience, who are tempted to forget the errand they came upon, and to ſuppoſe that the preacher, appearing to have no ſenſe of the greatneſs of his ſubject, is not in earneſt.

"Too great familiarity of expreſſion, with coarſe images, taken from low ſubjects, are fulſome. Dr. South has ſome excellent obſervations in vol. IV. p. 40, on the words, *Every ſcribe inſtructed into the kingdom of God*, &c.

"In what is called an application, at the end of a ſermon, the preacher makes a tranſition by the

"ſhorteſt

"shortest way, from the subject to the audience, and "shews them their duty from what has been said. A "writer, strong in his expressions, affirms, that a ser-"mon *without an application* does no more good than "the *singing of a skylark*: it may teach, but it does "not impel; and though the preacher may be under "concern for his audience, he does not shew it, till he "turns the subject to their immediate advantage."

These observations, upon the composition of sermons, are so much the more valuable, because we have them from a most excellent preacher, who had formed himself upon the rules he has given for others. He is a good farmer, who raises a good crop; but he is a better, who teaches others also to do the same; and the public are more obliged to him. If these precepts were properly attended to, the people would soon know how to distinguish between a sound teacher and an unlearned enthusiast; the Methodists would decrease, and the Church would be edified. If something had been added against errors in the pronunciation of sermons, I should have been glad to communicate it: but, as I find nothing to this purpose, I shall venture but a single remark upon the subject. Every preacher wishes to be *understood* as well as heard; but many are deficient in this respect, for want of a distinct articulation; which might easily be acquired, if they would attend to a simple rule, without the observation of which no man's delivery can be perfect. It is well known, that a piece of writing may be understood, if all the vowels are omitted;

omitted; but, if the vowels are ſet down, and the conſonants omitted, nothing can be made of it. Make the experiment upon any ſentence: for example; *judge not, that ye be not judged.* Take out the vowels, and it will ſtand thus—*jdg nt tht y b nt jdgd*: This may readily be made out: but take away the conſonants, and nothing can poſſibly be made of it—*ue o a e e o ue.* It is the ſame in ſpeaking as in writing: the vowels make a noiſe, and thence they have their name, but they diſcriminate nothing. Many ſpeakers think they are heard, if they bellow them out: and ſo they are; but they are not underſtood; becauſe the diſcrimination of words depends upon a diſtinct articulation of their conſonants: for want of conſidering which, many ſpeakers ſpend their breath to little effect. The late Biſhop of Peterborough, Dr. Hinchcliffe, was one of the moſt pleaſing preachers of his time. His melodious voice was the gift of nature, and he ſpake with the accent of a man of ſenſe, (ſuch as he really was in a ſuperior degree;) but it was remarkable, and, to thoſe who did not know the cauſe, myſterious, that there was not a corner of the church, in which he could not be heard diſtinctly. I noted this myſelf with great ſatisfaction; and, by watching him attentively, I perceived it was an invariable rule with him, to do juſtice to every conſonant, knowing that the vowels will be ſure to ſpeak for themſelves. And thus he became the ſureſt and cleareſt of ſpeakers; his elocution was perfect, and never diſappointed his audience. In this reſpect, most preachers have it in their power to follow him: his sense, and his matter, and the sweetness of his tone, were such as few will attain to. He was a prelate, to whom I owed much respect; and I am happy in giving this testimony to his excellence.

The last literary work which Dr. Horne proposed to execute, while Dean of Canterbury, was a formal Defence of the Divinity of Christ against the Objections of Dr. Priestley; in which it was his intention to shew, how that writer had mistaken and perverted the Scripture and the Liturgy.

I have often wondered secretly, why this good man should have felt as if he was called upon to encounter a writer of Dr. Priestley's disposition, who had already passed under the strong hand of Dr. Horsley, and would have been humbled for the time to come, had he been blessed with any feeling. That Dr. Priestley is a man of parts, a versatile genius, and of great sagacity in philosophical experiments, is well known and universally allowed: but let any person follow him closely, and he will see, that if ever there was a wise man, of whom it might be said, that *the more he learnt, the less he understood*, it will be found true of Dr. Priestley. His vanity made him believe, that he was wise enough to enlighten, and powerful enough to disturb, the world: he was therefore for ever busy at one of these or the other; a Volcano, constantly throwing out matter for the increase of heresy, schism, or sedition, and never to be quenched by disputing. It is the way of the world, to make

their

their eſtimate of a man from his parts and abilities; but it is more wiſe and juſt to meaſure him by the uſe he makes of them, to the benefit or the hurt of mankind: for the beams of the ſun are uſed to warm and animate; while the brightneſs of lightning is to ſhatter and conſume. So long as Dr. Prieſtley felt nothing (or ſeemed to feel nothing), it had a bad effect upon him, and made him more troubleſome, that ſuch perſons as Dr. Horſley and Dr. Horne ſhould enter the liſts againſt him: it made him appear more formidable in the eye of the public, and ſo it tended to gratify the prevailing paſſion of his mind. So far indeed as he deceived and diſturbed others, a compaſſionate regard to *them* might be the motive with thoſe who diſputed with him.

In the year 1786 Dr. Horne preached a ſermon at the Primary Viſitation of the Archbiſhop at Canterbury, on the duty of *contending earneſtly for the Faith*; and, when this was printed, together with another diſcourſe on the Trinity, he ſubjoined an advertiſement, declaring his intention to anſwer the objections againſt the Divinity of Chriſt, which had been urged of late. "Indulgence," ſaid he, "is re-"queſted as to the article of *time*: I cannot write ſo "*faſt* as Dr. Prieſtley does; and I wiſh to execute "the work with care and attention; after which it "ſhall be left to the judgment of the learned, the "pious, and the candid, of all denominations." At the cloſe of this year, he alludes to the advertiſement, in a letter from Canterbury: "You ſee the taſk I

have

"have undertaken." And here nobody will wonder, that as he had given me his assistance in the first work I published, and its chief merit had been owing to that circumstance, he should demand of me in return any service he thought it in my power to execute: he therefore goes on, "It is undertaken in "confidence of your friendly aid; and I should be "happy, as we began together with Clayton, if we "might end together with Priestley." For the sake of Dr. Horne, I was ready to work under him, in any capacity he should prescribe: but it always appeared to me, that Priestley was a person of too coarse a mind to be the proper object of a serious argument. That he had borrowed most of his objections, I had very little doubt; and that his remarks on Jews, Gnostics, Ebionites, Plato, Philo, and Justin Martyr, were not original; there being a magazine in store, to which the orthodox of this country do but rarely apply themselves. If this could have been pointed out, it would have done more toward the curing of his readers, and given more mortification to himself, than the most laboured confutation of the matter in the four volumes of his Objections.

Dr. Horne, I am very sure, had a mean opinion of Priestley's originality as a scholar: he speaks of him under the character of a man, *who is defying all the world, and cannot construe a common piece of Greek or Latin**. I find another note concerning him,

* Letter, Aug. 22, 1786.

with the date of 1788 affixed to it, taken from Dr. Johnſon, who ſpoke his opinion of Prieſtley to Mr. Badcock in theſe words; "You have proved him "as deficient in probity as he is in learning." Mr. Badcock had called him an *Index-ſcholar:* but Johnſon was not willing to allow him even that merit; ſaying, that he borrowed from thoſe who had been borrowers themſelves, and did not know that the miſtakes he adopted had been anſwered by others*. There was an expectation about this time, that a controverſy would break out between Prieſtley and Gibbon; of which an arch Quaker ſpoke thus: "Let "thoſe who deny, and thoſe who corrupt, the true re-"ligion of Jeſus Chriſt, fight it out together; and "let his faithful followers enjoy their mutual over-"throw†."

In the eyes of all reaſonable men, the Church of England could want but little defence, in a literary way, againſt an adverſary ſo enflamed with political hatred againſt it, and openly avowing a deſign to undermine and blow up its foundations, as with an exploſion of *gunpowder*‡. When it comes to this, the diſpute is no longer literary: the perſon, who carries it on in this way, ſhould be conſidered (if a

* See the Gentleman's Magazine for July 1785, p. 596.

† Ibid. p. 600.

‡ It was an obſervation of Dr. Horne, upon the curious ſermon on Free Inquiry, that the author ſpoke of this Powder-plot againſt the Church of England with as much certainty as if he had *held the lantern*.

gentleman)

gentleman) as a person of an unsound mind; if *not* a gentleman, then as an object of the penal laws of his country, if it should have any against such offenders. One, who is so wild and dangerous in his politics, must be a counterfeit in his Christianity; who, being *detected*, is thereby sufficiently *answered*.

On these considerations, without any view to the sparing of my own trouble, I was as well pleased to see, that the design of writing farther against Priestley was not prosecuted with vigour. How much had been collected for this purpose, I do not find; yet I know that the subject had been long and often in the mind of Dr. Horne; who told me when at Nayland in the year 1789, he had satisfied himself in respect to every objection from the Liturgy, exeept one; and that was from an expression in the Athanasian Creed, which sounded like Tritheism; the Creed affirming each person *by himself to be God and Lord.* I ventured to assure him, that the passage gave me no trouble, because I did not consider it as a metaphysical assertion, but as a plain reference to the words of the Scripture; which to each person of the Godhead, distinctly taken *by himself*, so far as that can be done, does certainly give the titles both of *God* and *Lord**. In this, therefore, instead of depending on the Creed, we only depend, as that does, upon the words of the Scripture. With this he was

* See John, xx. 28. Acts, v. 4. and xxviii. 25. and many other like passages.

ſatisfied, and allowed that ſuch an intention in the Creed removed the difficulty.

The laſt conſiderable affair in which he concerned himſelf while Dean of Canterbury, was an application from the Biſhops of the Epiſcopal Church of Scotland; three of whom, in the year 1789, came up to London, to petition Parliament for relief from the hard penalties under which they had long ſuffered. This they ventured to do, in conſideration of the loyalty and attachment they had lately profeſſed toward the King and the Conſtitution.

It was my lot likewiſe not to be an unconcerned ſpectator in this buſineſs. Through an intimacy which had long ſubſiſted between myſelf and a gentleman of great worth and learning in the county of Kent (the Reverend Nicholas Brett, of Spring-Grove) I became acquainted with the Biſhop of Edinburgh, Dr. Abernethy Drummond of Hawthornden, and had frequently correſponded with him. As ſoon as he came to London with his colleagues on the buſineſs aforeſaid, he wrote me word of his arrival, and explained the cauſe of the journey they had undertaken. Being myſelf of too inconſiderable a ſtation to be of any immediate ſervice to them in a matter of ſuch importance, I thought it the moſt prudent ſtep I could take, to forward the letter to a great perſon: who, with his uſual goodneſs and diſcretion, undertook to be an advocate for them; together with many other perſons of high reſpectability;

bility; and their petition was at length brought to ſuch an iſſue, as excited great thankfulneſs in the petitioners, though it did not exactly come up to the wiſhes they had formed at ſetting out.

There was no ſmall difficulty in making ſome perſons underſtand, who and what theſe poor petitioners were: and the caſe, notwithſtanding all that has paſſed, may ſtill be the ſame with many at this day. I therefore hope to be excuſed, if I enlarge a little in this place on their hiſtory and character, as they appeared, and were known to Dr. Horne; whoſe good opinion will be remembered as an honour, and may be of ſome uſe to them hereafter.

He had conſidered, that there is ſuch a thing as a pure and primitive Conſtitution of the Church of Chriſt, when viewed apart from thoſe outward appendages of worldly power, and worldly protection, which are ſometimes miſtaken, as if they were as eſſential to the being of the Church, as they are uſeful to its ſuſtentation. The hiſtory of the Chriſtian Church, in its early ages, is a proof of the contrary; when it underwent various hardſhips and ſufferings from the fluctuating policy of earthly kingdoms. And the ſame happened to the Epiſcopal Church of Scotland, at the Revolution in 1688; when Epiſcopacy was aboliſhed by the State, and the Preſbyterian form of Church-Government eſtabliſhed*. By this eſtabliſhment

* It is notorious, that the violence of the adverſe party againſt the

establishment the Bishops were deprived of their Jurisdiction, and of all right to the Temporalities of their Sees. But in this forlorn state they still continued to exist, and to exercise the spiritual functions of their episcopal character: by means of which, a regular succession of Bishops, and episcopally-ordained Clergymen, has been kept up in Scotland, under all the disadvantages arising from a suspicion of their being disaffected to the Crown, and attached to the interest of an exiled family. While attempts were making in behalf of that family, a variety of circumstances rendered it impossible for them to remove this suspicion, notwithstanding the many inconveniences and hardships to which it exposed them. All they could do was to conduct themselves in such a quiet manner, as might at length convince the Government, they had nothing to fear from a Scotch Episcopal Church, and consequently that there was no necessity for the execution of those severe laws, which on different occasions had been enacted against it.

At last the happy period came, which was to relieve them from this embarrassing situation. The wisdom and clemency of his present Majesty's Government encouraged them to hope, that an offer of

the Episcopal Church in Scotland began *before* the Government under King William was settled: when it could not be known by experience whether they would join with it or not. Before the Convention met, their Clergy were forcibly driven from their churches, and their possessions seized.

their

their allegiance would not be rejected: and, as ſoon as they could make that offer in a conſcientious manner, they had the ſatisfaction to find by the King's anſwer to their addreſs that it was graciouſly accepted: in conſequence of which, they could not but hope, that the Britiſh Legiſlature would take their caſe into conſideration, and ſee the expediency of relieving both Clergy and Laity of the Epiſcopal Communion in Scotland from the penalties to which they were expoſed in the exerciſe of their religion.

With this hope, three * of their Biſhops, as I have ſaid, came to London in the year 1789; and, notwithſtanding the ample recommendations they brought with them from their own country, they found it a work of time to make themſelves and their application properly underſtood. It would have been barbarous, after the die was caſt, to have thrown any diſcouragements in their way: but I was of opinion, from the beginning, that they were come *too ſoon*: more preparation was requiſite than they were aware of. The penal laws had reduced the Scotch Epiſcopal Church to a condition ſo depreſſed and obſcure, that it could ſcarcely be known to exiſt, but by ſuch perſons as were previouſly acquainted with its hiſtory. Among theſe, none entered more willingly and warmly than the then good Dean of Canterbury. As ſoon as he heard of the arrival of the Scotch

* Dr. John Skinner, Biſhop of Aberdeen; Dr. Abernethy Drummond, Biſhop of Edinburgh; and Dr. William Strachan, Biſhop of Brechin.

Biſhops at London, he was anxious to let them know how heartily he approved of the object of their journey, and kindly offered every aſſiſtance in his power to bring the matter to a happy concluſion. He paid them every mark of attention both at London and Oxford; and, when they ſet out on their return to Scotland, without having attained their object, he expreſſed, in very affectionate terms, his concern at their diſappointment, and told them at parting not to be diſcouraged; for, ſaid he, "your cauſe is good, "and your requeſt ſo reaſonable, that it cannot long "be denied."

In February 1791, after having taken his ſeat in the Houſe of Lords as Biſhop of Norwich, he wrote a friendly letter to Biſhop Skinner of Aberdeen, aſſuring him and the other members of the Committee for managing the buſineſs of the Epiſcopal Church of Scotland, that any help in his power ſhould be at their ſervice: and ſpeaking of their applying anew to both Houſes of Parliament, he ſaid, "It grieved "him to think they had ſo much heavy work to do "over again; but buſineſs of that ſort required pati-"ence and perſeverance."

It was ſaid about this time, that the Lord Chancellor, Thurlow, withheld his conſent to the Scotch Epiſcopal Bill, till he ſhould be ſatisfied by ſome of the Engliſh Prelates, that there really were Biſhops in Scotland. When Biſhop Horne was waited upon with this view by the Committee of the Scotch Church, and one of them obſerved, that his Lordſhip could

aſſure

assure the Chancellor they were *good Bishops*, he answered, with his usual affability and good humour, "Yes, Sir, much better bishops than I am."

A clergyman of Scotland, who had received English ordination, applied to him, wishing to be considered as under the jurisdiction of some English Bishop; that is, to be, in effect, independent of the Bishops of Scotland in their own country; but he gave no countenance to the proposal, and advised the person who made it quietly to acknowlege the Bishop of the diocese in which he lived, who, he knew, would be ready to receive him into communion, and require nothing of him, but what was necessary to maintain the order and unity of a Christian Church; assuring him, at the same time, that, if he were a private clergyman himself, he should be glad to be under the authority of such a Bishop. One anecdote more upon this subject, and I have done.

From the present circumstances of its primitive orthodoxy, piety, poverty, and depressed state, he had such an opinion of this Church, as to think, that, if the great Apostle of the Gentiles were upon earth, and it were put to his choice with what denomination of Christians he would communicate, the preference would probably be given to the Episcopalians of Scotland, as most like to the people he had been used to. This happened, as I perfectly recollect, while we were talking together on the subject of the Scotch Petition, on one of the hills

near

near the city of Canterbury, higher than the pinnacles of the Cathedral, where there was no witneſs to our diſcourſe but the ſky that was over our heads; and yet, when all things are duly conſidered, I think no good man would have been angry, if he had overheard us.

If the reader ſhould wiſh to know more of the people of this communion, let him conſult an Eccleſiaſtical Hiſtory of the Church of Scotland, by Mr. Skinner, father to the preſent worthy Biſhop of Aberdeen; a hiſtory comprehending a plain and unaffected detail of facts very intereſting and amuſing: and I hope he will alſo be convinced by the narrative I have here given, not only that the Biſhops of Scotland are true Chriſtian Biſhops, but that the Biſhops of England, from the part they kindly took in the affair, do little deſerve the clamour which ſome have raiſed againſt them, as if they were ſo dazzled by their temporalities, as to loſe ſight of their ſpiritual character, and bury the Chriſtian Biſhop in the Peer of Parliament.

The year 1789 was the fatal period, when French infidelity, with all the enthuſiaſtic fury of fanaticiſm, which it had affected to abhor, roſe up to deſtroy all regal authority, to extirpate all religion, to ſilence with the halter or the axe all that were not with them; and, in conſequence of their ſucceſs at home, undertook to ſhake, and diſſolve, if poſſible, all the kingdoms of the world. When this tremendous form of wickedneſs firſt appeared, it happened that I was at Canterbury,

Canterbury, on a viſit to the Dean; and being called upon to preach in the Cathedral, I took the ſubject of the time, and freely delivered my own ſenſe of it; which is now, I believe, the univerſal ſenſe of all that are true friends to this country. But ſome perſons, to whoſe affairs a ſimilar Revolution in England would have been of great ſervice, were very much offended; and one of them abuſed me groſsly for it in a Newſpaper. Not many weeks after, the Dean himſelf, on a Court holiday, took the ſame ſubject in the ſame pulpit; in conſequence of which, the ſame perſon that had reviled me was heard to declare, that his ſermon ought to be *burned by the hangman*. When he informed me by letter of this accident, he obſerved upon it in his eaſy way, that, as our doctrines, in bad times, would certainly bring us, both to the lamp-poſt, it might then be ſaid of us "in their death they were not divided." The character of the man, who had treated us with all this inſolence, was ſo vulnerable from its infamy, that ſome other perſon, who was intimately acquainted with his exploits, paid off our ſcores to the laſt farthing, by expoſing them to the public in a paper of the time. In ſo doing, he verified a wiſe obſervation, which I once received from a traveller in France, who had ſeen and knew more of the world than any I ever met with: "The man," ſaid he, "who injures me without provocation, will never be "able to contain himſelf without injuring others in like "manner; ſome of whom will be ſure to pay off my "ſcores,

"scores, and save me the trouble: and in the course "of my life, I never yet found, but that somebody or "other, in due time, revenged my quarrel, far be-"yond its value, upon that man whose ill manners "and insolence I had patiently neglected*."

The life of Dr. Horne, during his episcopate, affords but few incidents considerable enough to be here related: but there was one, which became the subject of much conversation between him and some of his friends. In the summer of the year 1790, he was upon a visit at the seat of a gentleman in Norfolk, for whom he had a great regard. I met his Lordship there, by his appointment; and it so happened, that, during our visit, Mr. John Wesley was upon his circuit about the counties of Norfolk and Suffolk, and came to a market-town very near us. Here he had many followers; and, being desirous of preaching to a large congregation, he sent some of his friends to the minister of the place, to ask for the use of the parish church for the forenoon of the next day. The clergyman was under some difficulty how to conduct himself; but, recollecting that the Bishop of the diocese was near at hand, he advised them to go and ask his permission. The messengers accordingly went; and the Bishop sent them back to the clergyman with this answer: "Mr. "Wesley is a regularly ordained Clergyman of the "Church of England; and, if the Minister makes no

* The two discourses here spoken of are to be found in Bishop Horne's Sermons, vol. IV. disc. xvi. Jones's Sermons, vol. II. disc. i.

"objection,

"objection, I ſhall make none." So it was determined that Mr. Weſley ſhould preach in the church the next day. As I never had an interview with that extraordinary man, and had often deſired to meet him, I would have taken this opportunity; eſpecially as there was a matter of no ſmall importance, concerning which I had a queſtion to aſk him. But being at this time an attendant upon the Biſhop of the dioceſe, we did not know how it might appear, and were unwilling to run the hazard of ſuch reports as might have been raiſed upon the occaſion. But our friend, at whoſe houſe we then were, being of the Laity, was under none of our difficulties; and a more intelligent perſon for the purpoſe was no where to be found. I therefore requeſted him to get to the ſpeech of Mr. Weſley in private, after the ſermon ſhould be over, and to aſk him in my name the following queſtion; "Whether it was true, as I had been aſſured, "that he had inveſted two gentlemen with the *Epiſ-* "*copal* character, and had ſent them, in that capa- "city, over to America?" With ſome difficulty our friend obtained a private audience; and, after ſome ſhort civilities had paſſed, he put his queſtion. At firſt, Mr. Weſley was not direct in his anſwer; but by degrees he owned the fact, and gave the following reaſon for it; that, as ſoon as we had made peace with America, and allowed them their independence, all religious connexion, between this country and the independent colonies, was at an end; in conſequence of which, the Sectaries fell to work to

increaſe

increaſe their ſeveral parties, and the *Anabaptiſts* in particular were carrying all before them. Something therefore was to be done, without loſs of time, for his *poor people* (as he called them) in America: and he had therefore taken the ſtep in queſtion, with the hope of preventing farther diſorders. The fact being not denied, the gentleman, who, for a layman, is as able a church-caſuiſt as moſt of his own or any other order, began to inquire a little farther into the caſe, with the deſire to know, how Mr. Weſley had ſatisfied his own mind in this matter, and what grounds he had gone upon. But as they were proceeding, ſome of his friends, either being impatient of any delay, or ſuſpecting that ſome miſchief might be going forward, came abruptly into the room, and reminded Mr. Weſley that he had no more time to ſpare. Thus the conference was ended, and our friend was obliged to take his leave. Some time afterwards (for we had left his houſe that morning) he gave us this account, as nearly as I can recollect; and having been preſent at Mr. Weſley's ſermon, was ſo well pleaſed, that he wiſhed half the clergy of the Church of England had preached the ſame doctrines, with the ſame zeal and devotion*.

In this preaching of Mr. Weſley, and the ſubject of the conference, when compared together, we have the character of Methodiſm complete: *it is Chriſtian godlineſs without Chriſtian order*. It is pity we could not obtain Mr. Weſley's own ſenſe of the commiſſion

* Let us hope that the *other* half *do* preach them.

with

with which *his* Bishops were sent out: but, as we were disappointed in that, we must inquire for ourselves, and answer as well as we can, without his help. The case obliges us to ask these two questions: 1. With what view this was done? and 2. By what authority? By Mr. Wesley's own account, this was his expedient for the preventing of confusion: whence we may gather, that he supposed confusion was not to be prevented among Christians, but by retaining the order of Bishops: and farther that unity had, in his opinion, been preserved among his own people by their relation to the Episcopacy of the Church of England, from which neither he nor they did ever profess themselves to be in a state of separation. Of this many proofs might be given. Their present application to the Bishop of the diocese was a confession of his authority, and signified a desire of acting under it: and Mr. Wesley had presented himself at the communion in the Cathedral Church at Bristol, and had received it from the hands of Bishop Bagot, as the Bishop himself informed me. Mr. Wesley might perhaps have considered farther, that, if Bishops were wanting in America for the preservation of unity among his people, and he himself did not send them, nobody else ever would: for, as the British Government did not send them, when it had power so to do, it was little to be expected they would attempt it when they had none. I cannot say what use he might make of the dispute between Dr. Mayhew, an American Dissenter, and Archbishop Secker, about the sending

ſending of Biſhops from hence to America; which I have always conſidered as the beginning and cauſe of the revolt that ſoon followed: this, I ſay, I do not know, and it would be vain to ſpeculate: therefore, let us now aſk the ſecond queſtion, by what *authority* he ſent Biſhops to America?

There are but two poſſible ways of putting men truly into the miniſtry: the one is by *ſucceſſion*; the other by immediate revelation or appointment from God himſelf. Paul received his commiſſion to preach, not *of man* nor *by man*, but of God; who *put him into the miniſtry*. Other miniſters of the Goſpel receive their commiſſion by impoſition of hands, from thoſe who had received it before. In this latter way of ſucceſſion, no man can poſſibly give that which he hath not received. Mr. Weſley, being himſelf but a preſbyter, could no more make a biſhop, than a member of the Houſe of Commons can make a member of the Houſe of Lords, who is made by creation from the King: the *leſs is bleſſed of the greater*, not the greater of the leſs. And, as this could not be done by Mr. Weſley in virtue of what he *was*, it muſt have been done in virtue of what he *thought* himſelf to be; a vicar-general of heaven, who was above all human rules, and could give a commiſſion, by a ſuperior right veſted in his own perſon. If he acted of himſelf, as John Weſley, a preſbyter of the Church of England, he acted againſt all ſenſe and order; and, by taking upon himſelf what no man can take, he would introduce in the iſſue more confuſion than he would prevent. The end will never be proſperous, when we do evil that good may come; and, if it doth not pleaſe God to uphold his own work in his own way, no man can do it for him. He may ſeem to do ſomething, but it will not laſt: he works upon a principle, the tendency of which is not to edification but to diſſolution. If Mr. Weſley did not act as of himſelf, but as by immediate revelation from God, and by the primary authority of Jeſus Chriſt in his Church, then he was an Enthuſiaſt, in the ſtricteſt and fulleſt ſenſe of the word; and any other perſon, or any hundred perſons, might act as he did, if they could think of themſelves as he thought of himſelf. But all ſuch confuſion was foreſeen and prevented, by the rules and orders of a Church, viſibly appointed and viſibly continued. When any people, whoever they are, think they can act with God againſt the rules of God, they are either become Rationaliſts, who do all by human authority, and deny all ſpiritual communication between God and man; or Enthuſiaſts, who think the Inſpiration or Spirit of the Goſpel has ſet them above the forms of the Church; which perſuaſion terminates in Spiritual Republicaniſm. In the Chriſtian ſociety, two things are to be kept up with all diligence; theſe are unity and piety. The man who ſhould ſuppoſe, that unity without piety will be ſufficient to carry him to heaven, would be under a great miſtake, and he would be juſtly condemned and deſpiſed for it. But is not he, who ſuppoſes that piety without unity will carry him to heaven, under as great (and, if he believes the Apoſtle, as dangerous) a miſtake* ? The ſubject merits great conſideration: but I ſay no more of it in this place. It reminds me of an anecdote I heard ſeveral years ago, and I believe Biſhop Horne was my author. When John and Charles Weſley began their new miniſtry, one of them went to conſult with Mr. William Law, as a perſon of profound judgment in ſpiritual matters; and, when the caſe had been opened, and the intention explained, Mr. Law made anſwer: "Mr. Weſley, if you wiſh to reform the "world and ſpread the Goſpel, you muſt undertake "the work in the ſame ſpirit as you would take a "Curacy in the Peak of Derbyſhire; but, if you pre-"tend to a new commiſſion, and go forth in the ſpi-"rit and power of an Apoſtle, your ſcheme will end "in Bedlam."

John Weſley was a wonderful man in his way: his labours were abundant and almoſt incredible†: in

* See and conſider the xiith and xiiith chapters of 1 Cor. the xiiith as a continuation of the xiith. Some excellent hints will be found on this ſubject in the Cautions to the Readers of Mr. Law, printed in the Appendix.

† Among his own people, he ſeemed to do more than he did. Of this I was informed by a bookſeller, who like others had been injured in his trade by the encroachments of Mr. Weſley in the way of *book-making:* and I was witneſs to ſome inſtances of this myſelf. He put his name to a Tranſlation of Thomas a Kempis, as if the Tranſlation had been his own: but a friend ſhewed me an old Tranſlation, with which it agreed, ſo far as we could ſee, in every word. He put his name to a Compendium of Philoſophy, though

in many reſpects he did good; he made thouſands of people ſober and godly: and, while he was doing good, he avoided evil; he avoided (at leaſt in words) the ſin of ſchiſm: he took the Chriſtian ſide, in ſtating the *origin of power*, againſt the Republicans of America; for which he was abuſed as an *old fox*, who only wanted to be made a biſhop. But with all this, he raiſed a ſociety on ſuch principles as cannot preſerve its unity; and thence, in effect, its exiſtence. I now underſtand, that partly from the loſs of their leader, and partly from the confuſion of the times, they have embraced ſome bad opinions; in conſequence of which, with little or no relation to the Church, they will not much longer be diſtinguiſhed from other diſſenters, and may in time be as bad as the worſt of them. When the lamp is broken, the ſnuff may lie burning for a time; but the ſupply of oil being gone, the light can be of no long continuance. If the Methodiſts would keep what they have got, and prevent their own ruin, they muſt do as Mr. Weſley did: they muſt preſerve ſome relation to the

though he tells us curiouſly in the Preface, it was taken from the work of a Profeſſor at Jena in Germany: yet he muſt be allowed great merit in amplifying the work. He ſold a work of mine, as if it had been an original work, partly copied, and partly put into Engliſh verſe, without aſking the conſent, or making a word of acknowlegement, in the Title or a Preface, to the author. He was free to produce any poſſible good from any labour of mine, without being envied: but ſuch proceedings have too much the appearance of party-craft to conſiſt well with honeſt unaffected piety.

Church, ſo long as any Church ſhall remain to which they may be related.

About a year after the accident of the Sermon and the Conference, a Life of Mr. Weſley was publiſhed by a Mr. Hampſon, in which the fact of ſending out biſhops is confeſſed. This book Biſhop Horne had procured; and, taking it out of his pocket as we were walking together in his garden at Norwich, he turned to the paſſage and ſhewed it me; and afterwards he put it into his Charge, which was the laſt work he printed before his death: and this brings me to the end of his *literary life*.

For the ſake of thoſe who admire Biſhop Horne's works, and were not acquainted with his perſon, it may be proper, before I conclude, to ſay ſomething of his *natural life*. When he firſt came to the Univerſity of Oxford, he was quite a boy; but being at a time of life when boys alter very faſt, he ſoon grew up into a perſon ſo agreeable, that, at the opening of the Radcliffe Library, when all were aſſembled and made their beſt appearance, I heard it ſaid of him, that there was not then a handſomer young man in the Theatre. But he was not of a ſtrong and muſcular conſtitution; and, from the diſadvantage of being very near-ſighted (quite helpleſs without the uſe of a glaſs) he did not render himſelf more robuſt by the practice of any athletic exerciſe. Amuſements of that ſort gave him more trouble than they were worth, and he never purſued them with any alacrity. It is related

related of Bishop Bull, that he was not addicted to any innocent pleasure, which is often necessary to unbend the mind, and preserve the body in health and vigour. The only diversion (if it may be called a diversion) to which this great man was addicted, was the enjoyment of agreeable conversation: and the same was the favourite amusement of Dr. Horne to the end of his life. I wish every young man, who is intended for a scholar, had some good or some necessary reason for not being led away by any sort of recreation. It was of service to his mind, that he was no fisherman, no shooter, no hunter, no horseman: the cultivation of his understanding was therefore carried on with less interruption, and his improvements were rapid. While on horseback he seemed to be in more danger than other young men: and he had a friend, who was so much concerned for his safety, that he sometimes rode after him, to watch over him, without letting him know of it. But so it happened, notwithstanding his vigilance, that he saw him suffer one bad fall, upon a dirty road, into a deep slough, and another upon very hard ground in the middle of the summer. His horse was then upon a gallop, and the fall pitched him upon his forehead; but, by the protection of a good Providence, the blow only gave him a head-ach, which soon went off without any other ill effect. When he came at last to be a Bishop, the friend, who had formerly been his attendant, reminded him of these accidents, and observed upon them, "My Lord, I "saw you fall twice, I have seen you rise three

 "times;"

"times:" meaning, that he had firſt riſen to be Preſident of Magdalen College, then to be Dean of Canterbury, and afterwards Biſhop of Norwich. The year after he came to Oxford, he fell ſick of the ſmall-pox, which proved very favourable, and he was removed to a houſe upon the hill at Headington for an airing; where his recovery had raiſed his ſpirits to ſuch a pitch, that his friends could not but obſerve the growing vigour of his mind, and augurate that his wits were intended for ſome very active part upon the ſtage of human life, as it afterwards proved.

In the year 1758 he was appointed junior Proctor of the Univerſity; on the 27th of April, 1759, he took the degree of B. D. and on the 28th of January, 1764, that of D. D. His health continued tolerably good, till the time of his proctorſhip: and here it ought in juſtice to be remembered, that he made one of the beſt Proctors ever known in the Univerſity of Oxford. He was ſtrict in the exerciſe of his office; but his ſtrictneſs was accompanied by ſo much mildneſs and goodneſs, that he was equally beloved and feared. His duty called upon him to viſit and inſpect the houſes of poor and diſorderly people; in one of which he took the meaſles, and ſuffered much by that diſtemper. The time at which this accident happened was in one reſpect rather unfortunate; for he was confined at the time when he ſhould have reſigned his office by a perſonal attendance in the Theatre. Dr. Thurlow, the late Biſhop of Durham, being at that time *Collector*, delivered the Latin ſpeech, at the cloſe of which he ſpoke to

this

this effect: "As to the late Proctor, I shall speak "of him but in few words, for the truth of which I "can appeal to all that are here present. If ever "virtue itself was visible and dwelt upon earth, it "was in the person who this day lays down his office." Which words were followed by an universal clapping. It was fortunate in one respect that he was not present; for thus it came to pass, that full justice was done to his character.

On the 27th of January 1768, on the death of Dr. Jenner, he was elected President of Magdalen College: in 1771 he was appointed Chaplain in ordinary to his Majesty; which appointment he held till he was preferred to the Deanry of Canterbury, on the 22d of September 1781: and on the 7th of June 1791 he was consecrated Bishop of Norwich in Lambeth Chapel, on the translation of Dr. Bagot to the see of St. Asaph. After he became President of Magdalen College, he adhered to the interest of Mr. Jenkinson (now Earl of Liverpool) a little to the disturbance of his academical peace. Mr. Jenkinson had been one of his contemporaries at University College: a gentleman, who, from his first appearance in the University, always promised to *do* something, and to *be* something, beyond other men, of his time. It was not possible that two such young men as he and Mr. Horne could be near neighbours without being fond of each other's company. The friendship once formed was ever after preserved: and when Mr. Jenkinson, though well known to be of what was then called the Court party, offered himſelf to repreſent the Univerſity in Parliament, his two friends, the Preſident of Magdalen, and the Maſter of Univerſity College, voted for him without ſucceſs. Their departure on this occaſion from what was then thought the *old* and proper intereſt of the Univerſity, brought upon them ſome animadverſions from a few of the warmeſt advocates on the other ſide; and little ſcurrilous witticiſms flew about againſt them both in the news-papers; which, ſo far as their own perſons were concerned, had little effect upon either, but that of exciting their laughter; and they have often been heard to make themſelves merry with ſeveral paſſages of that time.

Soon after he was advanced to the Preſidentſhip of Magdalen College, he married the only daughter of Philip Burton, Eſq. a lady for whom he always preſerved the moſt inviolate affection. By her he had three daughters; of whom the eldeſt is married to the Rev. Mr. Selby Hele, and the youngeſt to the Rev. Mr. Hole. The unmarried daughter reſides with Mrs. Horne, at Uxbridge. The former reſidence of this family near Windſor introduced him to the acquaintance of ſeveral great and reſpectable characters in that neighbourhood, particularly Sir George Howard, who received, and may probably have preſerved, many of his letters*.

* I recollect in this place an accident which happened to one of his letters. He correſponded formerly with Mr. Price of Epſom, whoſe lady was the ſiſter of Andrew Stone, Eſq. By a miſtake one of theſe letters fell into the hands of Mr. Stone; and it happened to contain ſome free remarks upon the lives and characters of

courtiers.

In the year 1776 he was appointed Vice-chancellor of the Univerſity, and continued in that office till October 1780. His vice-chancellorſhip introduced him to the acquaintaince of Lord North, then Chancellor of the Univerſity: a nobleman, who to a fine temper and pleaſant wit, had added ſuch good principles and uſeful learning, that he found in Dr. Horne a perſon exactly ſuited to his own mind: and I ſuppoſe it owing to the united intereſt of Lord North and the preſent Earl of Liverpool, that he was made Dean of Canterbury. When this happened, he would willingly have quitted his cares at Oxford, and taken up his reſidence in Kent, his native county; but that a friend, to whoſe judgment he owed reſpect, would not agree to the prudence of ſuch a ſtep. As for the Dean himſelf, worldly advantage was no object with him; he lived as he ought; and, if he was no loſer at the year's end, he was perfectly ſatisfied. This I know, becauſe I have it under his own hand, that he laid up nothing from his preferments in the Church. What he gave away was with ſuch ſecrecy, that it was ſuppoſed by ſome perſons to be little: but, after his death, when the penſioners, to whom he had been a conſtant benefactor, roſe up, to look about them for ſome other ſupport, then it began to be known who and how many they were. He complained to one of

courtiers. When this was lamented as an unfortunate circumſtance, "No, no," ſaid Mr. Price, "no misfortune at all—very proper "thoſe buſy gentlemen in high life ſhould ſee what learned men "think of them and their ſituation."

his

his moſt intimate friends, how much it was out of his way to diſcover ſuch objects as were worthy and proper, becauſe he deſcended ſo little into commerce with the world; yet, ſaid he, let any body ſhew me, in any caſe, what ought to be done, and they will always find me ready to do it. So far as he knew, he did good; and often attempted it, when he could not know; which is more or leſs the caſe with every charitable man. The diſcernment of objects is the privilege of God alone; who yet doeth good unto all, where we know it not.

As often as he was at Canterbury, his time paſſed very pleaſantly: he was in his native country: the families of the place and the neighbourhood ſhewed him the greateſt reſpect, and were delighted with his company and converſation: if he could have indulged himſelf, with prudence, as he wiſhed to do, he would have fixed himſelf there for the remainder of his life: but he ſtill ſubmitted to the unſettled life of a pilgrim, between the two ſituations of his College and his Deanry: with every thing that lay between Oxford and Canterbury he was acquainted, and with little beſides. In the year 1788 his conſtitutional infirmities began to increaſe upon him: "I have "been more than ever haraſſed (ſaid he) this year, "for four months paſt, with defluxions on my head "and breaſt; they have driven me to take the benefit "of the Headington air, this charming ſeaſon*, "which, by God's bleſſing, will enable me to get

* The letter is dated May 20, 1788.

" clear for the summer, I believe. But, as I grow " older, I shall dread the return of winter. Do you " know what could be done in the way of preserva- " tive? My good friends of the Church wish me to " continue here, and engage to do the business of the " Midsummer Chapter without me. I am urged to " get once more upon a *horse*—as much like an ass " as possible. Long disuse hath now been added " to an original awkwardness: however, by keep- " ing to a gentle pace, I shall avoid *going off*, as you " remember it was my hap once to do, like a frog " from a board." The visiting of some watering-place, Brighthelmstone, or Ramsgate, for the benefit of sea-bathing, had often been of great service to him. But notwithstanding all that could be done, he grew old faster than his years would account for, being now only in his fifty-seventh year: so that when a design was formed of making him a bishop, he felt himself by no means inclined to undertake the charge of so weighty an office; and it was not till after much reasoning with himself, that he was prevailed upon to accept it. I do not remember, that I ever took upon me, while this affair was depending, to throw in one word of advice, for it or against it; but rather that I left all things to work, as Providence should direct*. It was a sincere affliction to

* Very soon after the nomination of Dean Horne to the See of Norwich, a clergyman of that city, calling upon a clergyman of the city of London, said to him, " Report tells us, that the Dean of " Canterbury

to me, when I attended him at Norwich, to see how his limbs began to fail him. The Palace there is entered by a large flight of steps; on which he observed one day, "Alas! I am come to these steps, at a time "of life, when I can neither go up them nor down "them with safety." However, he resisted his infirmities with a degree of resolution. He accustomed himself to walk early in the garden by my persuasion; and assented to it, in his pleasant way, with these words: "Mr. William, (for so it had been his custom to call me for many years) "I have heard you "say, that the air of the morning is a *dram to the* "*mind:* I will rise to-morrow and *take a dram.*" That the faculties of his mind did not fail, in the way it was imagined, so long as he remained at Norwich, I could shew by the contents of the last letter he wrote to me, within a few weeks of his death; in which there is the same humour and spirit as had distinguished him in the prime of his life. That he was not subject to fits of weakness in his mind, I do not say: he could not persevere in a train of thought, as he used to do, but applied himself by short intervals,

"Canterbury is to be our Bishop." "Yes," said the London clergyman, "so I hear, and I am glad of it, for he will make a truly "Christian Bishop."—"Indeed! replied the other: well, I do "not know him myself, being a Cambridge man; but it is cur"rently reported at Norwich that he is a Methodist."—The same clergyman, when he became acquainted with his Bishop, was much delighted with him; and afterwards lamented his death as a great loss to the Christian Church in general, and to the Diocese of Norwich in particular.

as

as his ability would permit; and in that way he could execute more than we ſhould have expected from him, under his bodily infirmities. From two viſits to Bath he had received ſenſible benefit, and was meditating a third, when I left him in the autumn of 1791, which he had been requeſted not to defer too long. At my departure from Norwich, he carried me in his coach about ten miles; and we converſed by the way on the ſubject of his Charge, of which his mind was full, and which he was then beginning to print. When I had made him a promiſe to meet him during his next viſit at Bath, he ſet me down at Lodden, and I betook myſelf to my horſes. That moment will for ever dwell, like a black ſpot, upon the mind, in which we had the laſt ſight of a beloved friend. After this parting I never ſaw him more. His company I can now ſeek only in his writings; which are almoſt my daily delight. His journey to Bath, contrary to the perſuaſion of his friends, was deferred too long. Yet he had ſtill ſuch remaining vigour in his mind, that he did not intend to make his viſit to Bath an idle one; but ſelected from his manuſcript Sermons a ſufficient number to compoſe a volume, and took them with him, intending to employ a printer at Bath upon them. To this he was partly encouraged by an obſervation his good and affectionate lady had made upon him, from the experience of ſeveral years, that he never ſeemed to be ſo well as when he had printers about him; of which ſhe had even then ſeen a ſtriking example at Norwich. But, alas! while he was upon the road, he ſuffered a paralytic ſtroke, and, though very ill, finiſhed his journey. Mrs. Horne after this wrote me a letter full of hope, that, as the Biſhop could walk to the pump-room daily, he would ſtill recover: in conſequence of which, I went with ſome courage to London, intending to go on from thence to Bath; but was informed, as ſoon as I arrived in town, that he was not expected to continue many days: and the next day brought us the melancholy news of his death.

My worthy friend and pleaſant companion, the Reverend Charles Millard his chaplain, was with him at Bath, and was witneſs to many affecting paſſages which happened toward his latter end. Bad as he was, if Mrs. Horne entered the room, he ſpoke to her with his uſual cheerfulneſs; although a ſtupor commonly oppreſſed him, under which his mind wandered, and his ſpeech was confuſed: but from what could be underſtood, his thoughts were always at work upon ſome heavenly ſubject. When it was propoſed that the Holy Communion ſhould be adminiſtered to him by his chaplain, "By all "means," ſaid he, "you cannot do a better thing." In this ſervice he joined with great devotion, and when it was ended, "Now," ſaid he, "I am bleſſed "indeed*!"

On the Friday before his death, while his houſe-

* The letter of Mrs. Elizabeth Salmon, deſcribing this ſcene, is well worth reading, and is given in the Appendix.

keeper

keeper was in waiting by his bed-ſide, he aſked her, on what day of the week the *ſeventeenth* day of the month would fall? She anſwered, on Tueſday. "Make a note of that," ſaid he, "in a book:" which, to ſatisfy him, ſhe pretended to do. This proved to be the day on which he died—as quietly as he had lived. From this occurrence, a rumour got abroad, as if he had received ſome fore-warning of the time of his death. To this I can *ſay* nothing; but I can *think*, without any danger of being miſtaken, that if ever there was a man in theſe latter days, who was worthy to receive from above any unuſual teſtimony due to ſuperior piety, he was that man.

The affliction of his family was much relieved at this time by the friendly and charitable viſits of the celebrated Mrs. Hannah More, who was then at Bath, and well knew how much was due to the memory of the departed Biſhop.

One of his Lordſhip's chaplains attended him to his grave, and then returned in ſorrow to Norwich: his other chaplain paid the tribute due to his memory in a plain monumental inſcription. Both of them can unite in declaring, as they do with pleaſure, that the loſs to the Dioceſe of Norwich, and to themſelves in particular, hath been repaired far beyond their expectations, in the perſon of their preſent Dioceſan, the reſpectable and amiable ſucceſſor of Dr. Horne. May his days be as long and as happy, in his preſent ſituation, as thoſe of his predeceſſor were few and evil!

The

The inſcription is upon the tomb where he was buried, in the church-yard at Eltham in Kent, the reſidence of his father-in-law Mr. Burton; and the ſame is repeated upon a Tablet of Marble affixed to a pillar on the north ſide of the choir of the Cathedral Church at Norwich; of which the following is a copy:

Sacred to the Memory of
The Right Reverend GEORGE HORNE, D. D.
Many Years Preſident of Magdalen College in Oxford,
Dean of Canterbury,
And late Biſhop of this Dioceſe:
In whoſe Character
Depth of Learning, Brightneſs of Imagination,
Sanctity of Manners, and Sweetneſs of Temper
Were united beyond the uſual Lot of Mortality.
With his Diſcourſes from the Pulpit, his Hearers,
Whether of the Univerſity, the City, or the Country Pariſh,
Were edified and delighted.
His Commentary on the Pſalms will continue to be
A Companion to the Cloſet,
Till the Devotion of Earth ſhall end in the Hallelujahs of Heaven.
His Soul, having patiently ſuffered under ſuch Infirmities,
As ſeemed not due to his Years,
Took its flight from this Vale of Miſery,
To the unſpeakable Loſs of the Church of England,
And his ſurviving Friends and Admirers,
January 17, 1792, in the 62d Year of his Age.

Thus have I brought this good man to his end, through the labours and ſtudies of his life; in all which his example may be attended with ſome happy effect on thoſe who ſhall make themſelves acquainted with his hiſtory. In writing it I have not permitted myſelf

myſelf to conſider, what ſuppreſſions or alterations would have rendered it more agreeable to ſome people into whoſe hands it may fall. As truth will generally ſucceed beſt in the end, I have made the ſtory ſuch as I found it. I have concealed nothing out of fear; I have added nothing out of malice; and muſt now commit what I have written to that variety of judgment, which all my other writings have met with.

Some ſlight reports have been thrown out, which, without ſuch an explanation as I have in readineſs, might be underſtood to the diſadvantage of his memory. A ſhort life of him was written in the year 1793*, by the Reverend Mr. Todd, a clergyman of the Church of Canterbury, who has ſpoken very highly of him, but not above his character in any one reſpect. Yet ſome writer in a periodical publication could not content himſelf without making invidious compariſons, and inſinuating to the public that Mr. Todd had been guilty of exaggeration; but I may appeal to the feelings of the reader, whether it be not a worſe miſtake, in ſuch a caſe as the preſent, to depreciate with an ill deſign than to exaggerate with a good one; even ſuppoſing Mr. Todd to have done ſo; which to me doth not appear. I take Mr. Todd to be a man who loves the Biſhop's writings; and I take his cenſor to be a man who loves them not: and though I have enlarged on many things much farther from my own knowlege, than it was

* In a volume intitled Some Account of the Deans of Canterbury, &c. &c. by Henry John Todd, M. A.

possible or proper for Mr. Todd to do, I would nevertheless advise my readers to consult his account, which I believe to be very accurate in respect of its *dates*, and in the titles, and the particular circumstances which gave occasion to the several pieces, which were written by Dr. Horne, at the different stages of his life.

It has been hinted to me that Dr. Horne had embraced a sort of philosophy in the early part of his life, which he found reason to give up toward the latter end of it. Before it can be judged how far this may be true, a necessary distinction is to be made. I do not recollect, that his writings any where discover a professed attachment to the Hebrew criticisms of Mr. Hutchinson; and I could prove abundantly, from his private letters to myself, that he was no friend to the use of such evidence either in philosophy or divinity. But that he ever renounced or disbelieved *that* Philosophy, which asserts the true *agency* of nature, and the respective uses of the *elements*, or that he did not always admire, and so far as he thought it prudent insist upon it and recommend it, is not true. And I need not here appeal to any of his private letters, because some of his most serious and premeditated compositions assert this in terms sufficiently plain and strong. In his Commentary on the last Psalm he shews us what idea he had formed of the natural world. On the words, *Praise him in the firmament of his power*, he has the following comment: "which "power is more especially displayed in the formation

"of

"of the firmament, or expanſion of the material "heavens, and their inceſſant operations by means "of the light and the air, of which they are compoſed, "upon the earth and all things therein. Theſe are "the appointed inſtruments of life and motion in the "natural world, and they afford us ſome idea of that "power of God unto ſalvation, which is manifeſted "in the Church by the effects produced on the ſouls "of men, through the gracious influences of the "light divine, and the ſpirit of holineſs, conſtituting "the firmament of God's power in the new creation." In this paſſage it is the author's doctrine, that the firmament ſignifies the ſubſtance of the material heaven; and that this ſubſtance is compoſed of light and air. And farther, that theſe are the appointed inſtruments of life and motion in the natural world: that they give us an idea of the power of God, who acts in the œconomy of grace by the divine light and ſpirit, the Son and Holy Ghoſt, as he acts in nature by the operation of the air and light upon all things; and that thus the two kingdoms of grace and nature are ſimilar in their conſtitution, and confirm one another. In this doctrine, the doctrine of a philoſophy which the world does not generally receive, the author of the Commentary perſevered to the laſt day of his life. And why ſhould he not, when it is palpably true? Whoever aſſerts the agency of nature, and the offices of the elements as here deſcribed, need be afraid of no contradiction: he ſtands upon a rock, and has all nature to ſupport him; and the

 long

long experience of mankind, however it may loſe itſelf in the endleſs mazes of chemiſtry, and leave what is uſeful, to hunt after what is new, does yet all tend to confirm this univerſal principle, that matter acts upon matter, and that the world and all things therein are moved, ſuſtained, and animated, by the agency of the heavens upon the earth. The perſuaſion was once almoſt univerſal in this country, that matter is inveſted with attraction, repulſion, and gravitation, as *immaterial* principles: but this perſuaſion hath very much abated of late years; and it ſhould never be forgotten, that Newton himſelf left the queſtion open. It was indeed once thought that the motion of a ſecondary planet, or ſatellite, was a caſe which demonſtrated the neceſſity of attraction: but ſince that time, the phenomena of electricity have taught us, that æther can act from an opake body as from a luminous one; and therefore, that the ſame element may move both the primary and ſecondary: of which diſcovery philoſophers had no conception when gravity firſt came into faſhion. Our Royal Society have therefore expreſſed a diſpoſition to admit ſuch a cauſe of motion, if it can be reaſonably applied to the caſe. Sir John Pringle recommended it to be examined whether there be not a certain fluid acting as the cauſe of gravity, and of the various *attractions*, and of the animal and vital motions: and it has been argued by other members of the ſociety concerning the ſolar ſyſtem, as if it were *now* more apparent than heretofore, that an æther is diſperſed through

through all ſpace, which gives to bodies a tendency from its denſer to its rarer parts. In this the followers of Newton and Hutchinſon are now ſo nearly agreed, that it is to be lamented that ſcience ſhould ſuffer by any of their diſputes, or that the name of any perſon ſhould be held in contempt upon that account; particularly of ſo excellent a perſon as Dr. Horne. Why this good man ſhould be reported to have renounced what Newton himſelf, if he had ſeen what we have ſeen, would probably have adopted and carried on in his ſuperior way, I cannot underſtand. Therefore I diſtinguiſh once more, that the philoſophy, which Dr. Horne profeſſed, did not depend on doubtful interpretations of the ſcripture, but was confirmed by reaſon and experience, as it was argued in his State of the Caſe between Newton and Hutchinſon; from which he never departed, and from which no ſenſible man could depart. In philoſophy, thus defined and limited, he and I were always of a mind. Of myſelf I will ſay but little; and that little ſhould have been omitted, if I had not been forced upon an explanation, which I did not expect. For the proof of ſuch a ſyſtem of nature as Newton was not averſe to, I publiſhed a large quarto volume, above ſeven hundred copies of which are diſperſed about the world; and there muſt be learned and ingenious men to whom the thing is not unknown. Againſt ſome particulars there may be weighty objections; but againſt the general plan, I never yet ſaw one, that would trouble me for five minutes to anſwer it. Yet it does not follow, that people will ſee as we do. Where things have a new appearance, the world muſt have time; and the author who propoſes them muſt wait with patience, and bear with every kind of oppoſition and defamation; the latter of which is never to be underſtood as an unpromiſing ſymptom: for it ſhews that an adverſary is in diſtreſs, when he anſwers any thing, in ſuch words, as will equally anſwer every thing. From the books of foreigners I learn, that attraction and repulſion are not in ſuch eſtimation as they were fifty years ago. And at home, the ingenious Mr. George Adams, who has been a ſtudent and practitioner in Natural Philoſophy for more than twenty years, has found it neceſſary to adopt the new agency of nature, and has made his uſe of it through the whole courſe of a large work, which may be conſidered as an Encyclopædia in Natural Philoſophy, taking a larger circuit than has yet been attempted by any writer upon the ſcience. Other ingenious men may in time (as I am confident they will) follow his example; till it ſhall be no longer thought an *honour* to Dr. Horne that he *renounced* this Philoſophy, but that he did *not* renounce it.

If the reader will not be diſpleaſed with me I will tell him a ſecret, which he may uſe as a key to decypher ſome things not commonly underſtood. Between that philoſophy which maintains the agency of the heavens upon the earth, and the religion revealed to us in the Bible, there is a *relation*, which

renders

renders them *both* more credible. By a person with the Christian religion in his mind, this philosophy is more easily received; and if any one sees that this philosophy is true in nature, he will not long retain his objections against Christianity: but here is the difficulty; *he* will never begin, who resolves never to go on. But of any reasonable person, whose mind is still at liberty, let us ask, why it should be thought a thing incredible, that the creation of God should confirm the revelation of God? By which I would be understood to mean—that the world which we *see* should be a counterpart to the world of which we have *heard*, and in which we *believe*? Many in this age see the force of that great argument in favour of Christianity, which is drawn from the analogy between the kingdom of Nature and the kingdom of Grace, and admire it above all other things. Dr. Horne in particular had such an opinion of it, and conceived such hopes from it, that he used to say, and did say it late in life, that if Priestley should ever become a believer in the doctrine of the Trinity, it would be from the *Hutchinsonian philosophy*. To such a declaration as this, which the reader may depend upon, I can add nothing better, or more to the purpose, than a passage, from one of his manuscripts, concerning the religious use that may be made of Mr. Hutchinson's writings; and I am persuaded he persevered, to the day of his death, in the opinion there delivered. The passage is as follows:

"Cardinal Bellarmine wrote a small treatise, in-

 "titled,

"titled, *De ascensione mentis in Deum per scalas rerum* "*creatarum*, which he valued more than any of his "works, and read it over continually with great plea- "sure, as he says in the preface to it. A work of that "kind may be done in a far better and more complete "manner, by the key Mr. Hutchinson has given, "than has ever yet been done, and the natural and "spiritual world made to tally in all particulars. Such "a work would be of standing use and service to "the Church, and be a key to Nature and the S S, "teaching all men to draw the intended instruction "from both. For this purpose, the S S should be "read over, and the texts classed under their respec- "tive heads; and in reading other books, all just "applications of natural images should be extracted "from them, particularly where there are any good "divisions of an image into its parts and heads, as "much will depend on method and regularity. For "the blessing of God on such an undertaking, with- "out which all will be in vain, the Fountain of all "wisdom and Father of lights is humbly and fervently "to be implored, to enlighten the understanding, and "purify the heart, that it may be counted worthy, "through the merits of the dear Redeemer, to under- "stand the mysteries of the new creation shadowed "by the old, and explained in the S S. of eternal "truth, and be enabled to declare it to the people "unadulterated with any private imaginations, to the "glory of God, the edification of the church, and his "own salvation."

On the other hand, there are in this age philoſophical opinions, in which infidelity triumphs: and certain it is they have too plain an affinity to the atheiſtical doctrines of Epicurus aud Democritus, if they are not the ſame thing; and therefore ſuch an evil-minded wit as Voltaire caught at them with eagerneſs. He foreſaw how, with a little of his management, they might be turned againſt all religion, and lead to the abolition of all divine worſhip: he therefore ſtrained every nerve to magnify and recommend them: his induſtry in this reſpect was wonderful; and we find, by fatal experience, how far it has anſwered his purpoſe. The philoſophers of France have now ſeated themſelves upon the clouds, from whence they look down with contempt upon every degree of Chriſtian belief;—conſidering even Newton himſelf as an example of the weakneſs of human nature for believing the Scripture! Where will this end?

There is another report againſt the name of our good Biſhop, which wants explanation. The learned adverſary of the amiable Biſhop Hurd, and of the Reverend Mr. Curtis of Birmingham, and the friend of Dr. Prieſtley, a judge of all men and of all things, took occaſion, ſoon after the death of Biſhop Horne, to give us *his* character of him, in a note to a book he was then publiſhing; in which note many things are ſaid well, and like a ſcholar: but there is one thing which, though well ſaid, is not juſt to the Biſhop's memory; who is there reported to have *diffuſed a*

colouring

*colouring of elegance over the wild, but not unlovely, visions of enthusiasm**. Where could the gentleman find these *wild visions?* In the State of the Case between Newton and Hutchinson, the author argues from the words of each, and confirms what he says by fact and reason. The whole is written with the utmost coolness of temper, and without once appealing to any ambiguous evidence. In his sermons, his sense is strong, his language sweet and clear, his devotion warm, but never inflated nor affected: and, from the editions through which they pass, it is plain the world does see, and will probably see better every day, that they are not the discourses of a *varnisher of visions.*

* The *Socinian* notion of *enthusiasm* being a curiosity which deserves to be known, I shall give it to the reader in this place. I have a book before me, published by a Mr. E——n in the year 1772: a man, who seems no natural fool, but has made himself much worse than one through a conceit of superior Christian wisdom. He delivers it to us as a doctrine of the orthodox, that "if our "belief were not attended with some *difficulties to our reason*, there "would be no merit in our believing;" and then adds, "such men "I shall not scruple to call enthusiasts; and to argue the case with "them, would be like trying to convince the poor straw-crowned mo-"narch of Bethlehem—who is a king, because he *knows* he is a king." This gentleman tells us his mind fairly and plainly; for which we are obliged to him: but now let us try by his rule the faith of our Father Abraham. He believed in his old age, that his seed should be as the stars of heaven, from a wife that was barren; and this is the belief which was accounted to him for righteousness. Here the reason and experience of all mankind were contrary: against hope he believed in hope: here were not only *difficulties to reason*, but an actual impossibility to reason. The promise might have been given before,

In his Commentary on the Pfalms, he has followed the plan of the writers of the New Teftament, and of the Primitive Church, in applying them as prophecies and delineations of the perfon of Chrift and of the Chriftian œconomy. If he is judged to have betrayed any enthufiafm in *fo* doing, it is only becaufe he happened to write in the eighteenth century; when Chriftian learning, under the notion of improving it, is greatly corrupted; the Fathers of the Church but little known*, and lefs relifhed; and the zeal and piety of the Reformation very much abated. Erafmus was juft fuch another enthufiaft in his divinity as

before, while Abraham was young: but it pleafed God to defer it till he was old, when reafon could not receive it; and from this circumftance only his faith was meritorious. No, fays the Socinian; this man, by my rule, was an *enthufiaft*, no more to be argued with than the *monarch of bedlam*, &c.

What the mind of that man can be made of, who receives the Scripture as the word of God, and denies that *faith* has merit in admitting what is attended with *difficulties to reafon*, it is as hard for me to underftand, as it is for him to receive the Articles of the Church of England; and yet, if he has fpoken of himfelf truly, I cannot deny the fact: and as this man is but a pattern of other Socinians, I do fuppofe it to be the opinion of them all, that the proper act of *faith* in a Chriftian is an act of *enthufiafm*.

* I was therefore pleafed with a feafonable attempt to revive the reading of the Chriftian Fathers, by the Rev. Mr. Kett, in the Notes and Authorities fubjoined to the fecond edition of his very ufeful and learned Bampton Lectures, p. iii. where he recommends to the Ecclefiaftical Student a Selection from the writings of the Greek and Latin Fathers. I could add other names and other pieces; but thofe he has mentioned are very fufficient.

Dr.

Dr. Horne; and is frequently found to have diffused a like colouring of elegance over like interpretations of the Scripture: in which, however, he is not always either so elegant, or so successful, as the late Bishop his follower: yet for this, in the days of better divinity, when *faith* and *piety* were more in fashion, Erasmus was never reputed an enthusiast. A little warmth of *devotion* is very excusable in a Christian writer; and we apprehend that a very strong conviction of the wisdom and excellence of Christianity is necessary to the making of a good divine—Ου δει μετριως κεκινημενον απτεσθαι.

When a man of learning censures without justice, he opens a door for the free remarks of others upon himself. But I search not into the gentleman's writings, for any examples of severity, scurrility, adulation, perplexity of principle, smoke and smother, pedantry and bombast: let others look for such things, who take delight in finding them. For my own part, I would rather wish that my learned friend, when he is throwing his fine words about, would consider a little beforehand, how unworthy it may be found to attempt to lessen in any degree the good effect of such a character as that of Dr. Horne upon the Christian world, in its present declining condition and dangerous situation: and how much more it would be for his honour to use the eloquence he is master of, rather in promoting than in hindering its influenee. He knows too much of the world to be ignorant, that in this age, when so many counterfeits

are

are abroad, when ſome are ſo wild, and others ſo ſqueamiſh, no wound is ſo cruel upon a religious man, as the imputation of a wild enthuſiaſtic fancy: a fault wantonly imputed by the vicious and the ignorant, to unexceptionable perſons, only becauſe they have a little more religion than themſelves: and if ſuch perſons have made it their buſineſs, like Dr. Horne, to be deep in the Scripture, they will always be in danger from thoſe who are not ſo. Heathens accuſed the firſt Chriſtians of atheiſm and ſacrilege, becauſe they would not worſhip idols; and abuſed them as haters of mankind, only becauſe they avoided evil communications, and refuſed to be *conformed to this world.* Voltaire had no name for the Chriſtian faith, but that of ſuperſtition or fanaticiſm. There is a very uſeful and judicious diſſection of enthuſiaſm, by Dr. Horne himſelf, the beſt I ever met with, juſt publiſhed in a compilation by a ſociety for a *Reformation of principles,* which if gentlemen will condeſcend to examine, they may be better able to diſtinguiſh properly betwixt thoſe who *are* enthuſiaſts and thoſe who are *called* ſo.

All good men are walking by the ſame way to the ſame end. If there are any individuals, who by the ſhining of their light render the path more plain and pleaſant, let us agree to make the moſt we can of them, and be *followers of them, who through faith and patience inherit the promiſes.*

THE END.

APPENDIX.

APPENDIX.

The last Letter of the Reverend Robert Welbourne, Rector of Wendlebury in Oxfordshire.

[Referred to p. 45.]

Dear Jones,

YOU make it a doubt, whether I am a letter in your debt, or you in mine. This is a gentle rebuke for my silence; for so I must take it, conscious as I am of my own default; and, yet excusable, if frequent returns of pain and sickness may plead in my behalf. In these circumstances I have been as it were *oblitus meorum* for some months, and am therefore the more obliged to you for not applying to me the latter part of the sentence. In the month of July, had I not been prevented by a very bad fit of the stone, I was engaged to have been at ———, not without some hopes of seeing you: but it was not to be so: they now tell me I must, and I find it necessary to keep as quiet as I can. Arrived as I am at the age of man, I do not presume upon much time to come. My chief concern now is to make such an exit as my

 friends

friends would wiſh me; which, by the grace of God, and their prayers and my own, I hope to do. The manuſcript you ſpeak of, as you ſeem to ſet a value upon it more than it deſerves, I thought to have redeemed with a fair copy; but as I am now not likely to do ſo, you may keep or deſtroy it as you pleaſe. The heavy expenſe of your late removal muſt I think diſable you from proceeding to your degree, ſo ſoon as you intended. If his Grace of Canterbury conſiders his own bounty as the impediment, he cannot do leſs than grant you a faculty from Lambeth. If I ſhould ſee our Archdeacon Potter, as I hope to do in October, I ſhall give him a broad hint to that purpoſe. Wiſhing you health and proſperity, with my beſt reſpects to Mrs. J. I am, dear ſir,

Moſt affectionately yours,

Wendlebury, Sept. 7, 1764. ROBERT WELBOURNE.

This was followed, in the month of December afterwards, by a letter from Mr. Horne, which gives a very affecting account of this good man's death.

"OUR good old friend, *Robertus Wendleburienſis*, took his leave of this world about five weeks ago. His diſorder was in the bowels, through which he had no paſſage for ten days. But it was effected by putting him into a warm bath, and he was brought back from the gates of death; at which he expreſſed ſome regret, as having hoped that his pains and ſor-

rows

rows were at an end. But a relapſe ſoon carried his weather-beaten veſſel to its deſired haven of reſt and peace. He died in ſtrong faith, lively hope, and perfect charity, having received the Euchariſt from the hands of the Maſter of Univerſity College, who adminiſtered to him *in extremis*, and during his whole ſickneſs. He deſired that a little water might be mixed with the wine in the ſacramental cup: and this was the only particularity. Large bundles of papers, bound up by himſelf for that purpoſe, were burnt, according to his order. A few Sermons were left to his Nephew, who was executor. He bequeathed his gold and ſilver medals to Mr. Gilpin, and ſome copper ones to Chriſt-Church. It is obſervable, that he had kept a moſt exact account of his expenſes from the time when he was eighteen years of age. He once lent 1000l. to Dr. ——, which, as he took no ſecurity for it, he loſt by the Doctor's death, both principal and intereſt. He ordered ſcarves, rings, hat-bands and gloves, for the proper perſons who attended his funeral. Thus we muſt leave the body of our friend in the duſt, and his ſpirit in the boſom of faithful Abraham, waiting for the happy day of their re-union and glorification."

The manner in which Dr. Horne treats this melancholy ſubject is ſo tender and affecting, that I ſhall here add another letter, which he wrote to another intimate friend, upon a like occaſion.

To W. S.

12th Feb. 1780.

WE are all much affected by the melancholy tidings communicated in your letter. They are indeed such as I have expected to hear many times; but, when they come, it seems as if one had never expected them in earnest. And yet, when the first feelings are over, we cannot be concerned for the person departed, but for ourselves only. Her sufferings were long and heavy, and, therefore, we cannot in reality be sorry to find she is released from them. For many years she was in the furnace, and it was more than usually heated. Melted down at length, and purged from dross, she is formed anew, a vessel for the heavenly temple, and does not now wish to have suffered less in the day of trial and probation. Let us copy her patience and resignation, which were truly exemplary, and prepare to follow in God's good time. Having paid the tribute of grief that is due, let us return, with fresh vigour, to the duties of life, and prepare to answer those calls, which our faith and our country, our church and our king will shortly, I think, make upon us all.

Another letter to the same, on another subject.

To W. S.

2d July, 1788.

IN reading Gibbon, I was astonished to meet with so much gross and vulgar obscenity, from the pen of a *refined* and *elegant historian* and *philosopher*; and

and had thoughts of ſtringing the paſſages together, and preſenting them to the public. I did not much like the dirty work, and am therefore glad to be prevented by ſome one, who has done it with great gravity, in the Gentleman's Magazine for June, under the ſtyle of—"Selection from Mr. Gibbon's "*learned* and *entertaining* Notes," &c.—Who the *late prelate* was, that uſed to talk *bawdry* in Greek, I know not, but think it muſt have been ———; for they do not always go together.—In the xlviith chapter (the laſt of the fourth volume) Gibbon has diſplayed all his ſkill to expoſe church-polemics and churchmen, on the ſubject of the Incarnation, and the different opinions and councils holden concerning it. He has taken great pains to inveſtigate and ſtate all the niceties and minutiæ of the diſpute (as indeed he had done before in the caſe of the *Logos* and the Trinity) and ſets off as if moſt ſeriouſly intereſted in the cauſe; his ſtyle more flowing than uſual, and ſometimes riſing to a degree of ſublimity, as if inſpired by the ſubject. It would be worth your while, when you have two or three hours upon your hands, to read over the two chapters, as they ſtand by themſelves, detached from the civil hiſtory, and form a ſort of *whole* on thoſe great and much debated points of theology.—The ſtory of the degenerate Greeks, the fooliſh emperors and profligate empreſſes, is tedious and tormenting to read; but the chapters on Arabia, Mahomet, the Saracens, Caliphs, Cruſades, Tartars and Turks, are very curious and informing; though ſhocking to the imagination are the repeated carnage of the human race, and devaſtations of the globe, firſt by one ſet of ſavages and then by another. When to theſe you add the inteſtine quarrels and bitter animoſities between the Greeks and Latins, till, at the laſt ſiege of Conſtantinople by the Turks, one of the Greeks in high ſtation declared he had rather ſee a *Turk's turban* there than a *Cardinal's cap*—one really ſhuts the book, almoſt ready, with Charlotte Smith, to write an Ode to *Deſpair*.

As to Lindſey, as a writer, he is a poor creeping ſoul. I think I ſhall put down ſome ſtrictures; but the worſt is, one ſhall be involved by degrees in ſo many different controverſies—nature and degree of *inſpiration*, doctrine of *ſatisfaction*, our own *eſtabliſhment*, *ſubſcription* to articles, &c. *liturgy*, *epiſcopacy*, &c. (for they are all lugged in—) and now, beſides the caſe of the *demoniacs*, the exiſtence of any *devil* or *Satan* at all, which Lindſey denies. Another difficulty is that of obviating the ſayings and examples of many latitudinarian proteſtants, thrown in our teeth, men otherwiſe of great note, and univerſally almoſt eſteemed—ſome of our own church, that were or are Biſhops, who have wiſhed for a change of forms, &c. But however, the bold ſtrokes of Prieſtley, Lindſey, &c. will let them ſee every day, more and more, the danger of innovation, and cure them, perhaps, of their diſorder.

Copy

Copy of Mrs. Salmon's Letter to her Siſter, on the Death of Biſhop Horne.

[Referred to p. 174.]

My dear Siſter,

17th Jan. 1792.

THIS morning, at 20 minutes paſt two o'clock, our dear *lord* departed this life. He died, as he lived, a ſaint indeed! He had not been able for ſome days to expreſs himſelf clearly; but yeſterday, when Mr. Selby read prayers, he joined with him, and repeated the Lord's prayer with as much compoſure as ever he did in his life. After that he received the ſacrament with my miſtreſs and the ladies, Mr. Millard, Mr. Selby, Gilbert, and myſelf. And, when that was over, he ſaid, "*Now I am bleſſed indeed!*"—All was peace and joy and comfort within. He bleſſed us all ſeverally, and thanked us for all we had done. Had you ſeen him bolſtered up, bleſſing his children, and ſpeaking comfort to his wife, in the hope and truſt of their meeting again, you would never have forgot it. I am ſure I never ſhall; nor do I wiſh it. We have reaſon to think that he did not ſuffer at laſt, as he went off without a groan, and has ſtill a ſmile upon his face, as if he was alive. He is to be buried at Eltham. I can write no more, though I have more to ſay. Your good Maſter may like to hear how he departed. I hope you will read this to him, though it is ſcarcely to be underſtood. I cannot ſay more.

Yours affectionately,

E. Salmon.

CAUTIONS

TO THE

READERS of Mr. LAW,

(And, with very few Variations, to the Readers of BARON SWEDENBORG.*)*

[Referred to p. 75 and 162.]

FIRST. Either J. Behmen's ſcheme is a new revelation, or an explanation of the old. If the latter, why is it wrapt up in ſuch myſtic jargon, never heard of in the Chriſtian church before, and not given us in Scripture language, which is the only explainer of itſelf?—If the former, it is an impoſture and deluſion; for extraordinary inſpirations are not to be credited, unleſs vouched by miracles, which God always ſent to atteſt his extraordinary commiſſions: and if they are pretended to come from him, and do not, then it is a demonſtration that they come from the devil, "*transformed into an angel of light.*" To equal the imaginations of men to the holy Scriptures of God, and think them as much the inſpiration of God, as what was dictated as ſuch to the holy Prophets and Apoſtles, is ſtrictly and properly enthuſiaſm. This Mr. Law has done; for he ſays, he looks upon the writings of J. Behmen to be no more human than St. John's Revelation.

II. Mr. Law by creation will have nothing farther meant than the formation of the world out of preexiſtent matter; contrary to the ſenſe always put upon it by the Chriſtian church. The formation is deſcribed

described ſtep by ſtep; but the creation in Gen. i. verſe 1. muſt relate to the production of, or giving being to, the matter, in its dark and *inform* ſtate. The conſequence of Mr. Law's opinion muſt be, either that matter, though diſtinct from, is co-eternal with, God, which cannot be; or elſe, that it is an emanation, generated from his ſubſtance or eſſence, which is the abomination of Platoniſm brought into Chriſtianity. The confounding God and created nature together is the eſſence of Paganiſm, and the foundation of all the errors in the Heathen and Chriſtian world. The Scriptures are conſtantly guarding againſt it, and diſtinguiſhing Jehovah from what is only the work of his hands. Eternal nature is a blaſphemous contradiction; for God only is eternal; he only has being in himſelf, and gives it to every thing elſe. Nature may be a manifeſtation, or repreſentation of God, as a picture is of a man; but has no more connexion with his ſubſtance or eſſence, than that hath with its original, or the painter that drew it.

III. Mr. Law denies the wrath of God againſt ſin. Now, that wrath in God is the ſame weak and infirm paſſion that is in man, no body will ſuppoſe. But that it produces effects, which the image of wrath executed by man is taken to give us an idea of, is a truth the Scriptures are full of from Geneſis to Revelation. And it is deſcribed under all the images that are dreadful in nature; chiefly by that moſt dreadful of all, fire. "*Our God is a conſuming fire.*" No one will ſuppoſe from this text, that God is really material fire;

fire; but that his juſtice, vengeance, wrath, or whatever you pleaſe to call it, will have an effect upon ſinners, that is pictured by the effects of fire upon natural bodies.

Nor can all the wit and invention of man get rid of thoſe innumerable Scriptures that ſpeak of the wrath of God to be executed upon a ſinful world, under the lively figure and repreſentation of it, fire; as any one may ſee, that will turn to the Concordance. Sure I am, that if theſe can be conſtrued to mean, a *dark, fiery, whirling anguiſh riſing up and opening its birth in the inward depth and ground of the ſoul,* there can be no certainty in words. The lake of fire or hell is not within but without the ſinner; for he is to be caſt into it. That inward remorſe, anguiſh and deſpair make a part there is no queſtion; but they are not the whole.

IV. But there is a conſequence that follows this notion of no wrath of God againſt ſin, and ſtrongly inſiſted upon by Mr. Law, which ſhakes the foundation of Chriſtianity; viz. that Chriſt did not die to propitiate or appeaſe that wrath: that he did not die as a ſacrifice in our ſtead. This demoliſhes the doctrine of a vicarious ſatisfaction for ſin, made outwardly upon the croſs, by the blood of him, who, being God, could give it infinite merit, to ſatisfy infinite juſtice; and, being man, could make the ſatisfaction in the ſame nature in which the ſin that required it was committed.

Mr. Law ſays, God is love. True. But is he not

juſtice

justice and truth as well as love? Had not Truth said, "The soul that sinneth, it shall die?" And did not Justice require the execution of that sentence? God is not only just, but justice itself; and justice cannot remit the least farthing; else it were not justice. God's attributes must not fight with or conquer and subdue one another. On the contrary, they magnify and exalt one another. Thus his justice is magnified, in that it exacts full and adequate satisfaction; his wisdom is magnified, in finding out such means to make it; his mercy and love, in affording those means and fulfilling all his promises in him, in whom mercy and truth thus met together, righteousness and peace kissed each other. The inward application of this satisfaction made outwardly by the blood of Christ, shed upon the cross, to the heart of every believer, by the hand of faith for its justification, with the sanctification that accompanies it, by the water flowing with the blood, to a new birth and life of righteousness from the death of sin, is doubtless the great end and intent of Christianity; as much as taking a medicine is the end and intent of its being given. But the Gospel preached and read, and the sacraments administered in the Church, are the instruments appointed to work all this, by the power of the spirit that goes with them as channels into the heart of every believer. But if, before he has received the grace of Christ by these which are the only appointed means of receiving it; or if, instead of going on with humility and diligence in searching the

Scriptures

Scriptures of God, a perſon is to ſhut himſelf up and ſearch the inward depth and ground of his heart, what will he find there but the devil, ready to take advantage of his having left his only guide, and *transforming himſelf into an angel of light*, under the diſguiſe of great flights of devotion and illumination, to inſtil his diabolical ſuggeſtions, and lead the deluded ſoul, blindfold, and thinking herſelf ſafe in the hands of the ſpirit of God, to deny and write againſt the ſatisfaction and atonement made for her ſins by the blood of her Redeemer? For by theſe very means have we ſeen one of the brighteſt ſtars in the firmament of the Church (Oh! lamentable and heart-breaking ſight!) falling from the heaven of Chriſtianity into the ſink and complication of Paganiſm, Quakeriſm, and Socinianiſm, mixed up with chymiſtry and aſtrology, by a *poſſeſt cobler*; and alas! when a man comes to forſake the Bible, and write againſt its doctrines, what matters it whether it is done by the light of nature, the light within, or the inſpoken word? *Believe not*, therefore, good people, *every ſpirit*, whiſpering to your ſoul in a fit of quietiſm, but *try the ſpirits*, by the Bible, *whether they are of God*. Keep to *that*, and let your faith, hope, love and devotion riſe as high as they will. The higher the better.

V. As to the *angelical world*, *glaſſy ſea*, &c. it is a mere romance, without the leaſt countenance from holy Scripture; nor does he, I think, produce above a text or two, by way of proof. The holy Scriptures

tell

tell us, the world was good at the finiſhing of it, but by the devil came ſin, the parent of all evil, natural and ſpiritual—that Chriſt came to redeem us from it all, to ſatisfy for our ſins, to raiſe our ſouls to righteouſneſs, by his ſpirit here, and to glorify us, body and ſoul, hereafter. This ſcheme is complete, without ſearching after the ſtate of the chaos, before it was in being, or fancying this world to be the *ruins of the angelical*, as William Whiſton did it was the tail of a Comet. The ſame is to be ſaid of the notion of Adam caſed up in *ſpiritual materialities*, one over another, like the coats of an onion. How many of theſe he had, Mr. Law does not ſeem ſure, giving different accounts in different books. Inſtead of inventing hypotheſes concerning the nature of paradiſe, let us ſtudy the way that led the penitent thief into it; repentance and faith in a Saviour on the croſs, King of kings, and Lord of lords.

VI. Mr. Law is very lax and latitudinarian with regard to the government and diſcipline of the Church; which though, as he ſays, it will not ſave a man, yet, is abſolutely neceſſary, to preſerve thoſe doctrines, that will. A hedge round a vineyard is, in itſelf, a poor paltry thing; but break it down, and all they that go by, will pluck off her grapes. And no ſin has been puniſhed with heavier puniſhments, for that reaſon, than throwing down fences and making it indifferent, whether a Chriſtian be of any church or none, ſo he be but a Chriſtian, and have the birth of the inſpoken word, which is a Pope in every man's heart. But

if

if Chriſt left a Church upon earth, and ordered ſubmiſſion to the appointed governors of it, ſo far as a man reſiſts or undervalues this ordinance of Chriſt, ſo far he acts not like a Chriſtian, let his inward light be what it will. In the ſame manner, I think, he is injudicious in condemning *all human* writings, commentators, &c. becauſe people are divided through the multiplicity of them. All human learning, that tends not to the knowlege of God, deſerves the cenſure he beſtows in a very maſterly manner. But how are we to underſtand the holy Scriptures, and be able to teach and explain them to others, without a knowlege of the languages in which they are written? And towards this the labours of the faithful ſervants of God, who have gone before us, cannot but be of great ſervice. And therefore, I ſee not why time is not as well ſpent, in the writings of the noble army of ſaints, and martyrs, and confeſſors, as in thoſe of J. Behmen, and much better than in ſearching for truth in the *inward depth* and *ground of the heart*, which is indeed, we ſee, "*deceitful above* "*all things. Who can know it?*"

Copy

Copy of a Letter to a Lady on the subject of Jacob Behmen's Writings.

[See p. 74.]

Madam, April 8th, 1758.

THOUGH your letter did not give me all the satisfaction I had hoped for, yet I find in it several hints, for which you are much to be honoured; and, to say the truth, I never met with a person, who, after diving into those matters with which you are at present engaged, did yet possess such a spirit of humility, and remain so open to conviction. Being therefore persuaded you have no disposition to reject the truth, provided I can make it appear to you, and I have no temptation, God is my witness, to offer you any thing else instead of it, I have resolved to address myself more closely to the subject in question; for, till we descend to particulars, but little good can be expected from general objections, easily obviated by as general answers; and perhaps, after all, the real merits of the cause have not been brought into consideration.

I am ready to join issue with you, that if J. Behmen was not inspired, he must either have been a hypocrite or a madman; and that his writings are utterly to be rejected by every sober Christian. You have shewn your judgment, Madam, in thus bringing the whole matter to a single point: for now there is only one question to be settled; and, as you suspect me of taking up with false reports of your author, I shall not

not be content with any report at all; but ſet down his own words or refer to their place where I have occaſion to ſpeak of his doctrines.

You argue for the probability of his inſpiration from thoſe words of St. Peter, Acts ii. 17. which, if you examine the place, will appear to have been applied, not to any future inſpirations at ſome diſtance of time, near to the diſſolution of the world; but to the preſent event then brought to paſs: "THESE, ſays he, "are not drunken, as ye ſuppoſe; but THIS IS "*that which was ſpoken by the prophet Joel; it ſhall* "*come to paſs in the laſt days,*" &c. where it is plain St. Peter applies theſe words of the Prophet to the miraculous gifts of the ſpirit at the time then preſent. He does not indeed confine the gifts of the ſpirit to that time and ſeaſon only; yet his words give us no ground to expect any extraordinary effuſions towards the concluſion of the world. How this affair is, and what we are really to look for, muſt be learnt from ſome other paſſages.

The error, I preſume, ariſes from a miſunderſtanding of that phraſe, *the laſt days*, which are taken for theſe days and this age, when things are drawing apace to their latter end. But, Madam, the Scripture has divided the ages of the world into three grand periods; the firſt of which is called *the Beginning*, whoſe date begins at the creation, and takes in all the generations till the eſtabliſhment of the law of Moſes: as where Chriſt ſays, "From the beginning it was not ſo." Matt. xix. 8. Mark, x. 6. The ſecond is called the

Old

Old Time, or the Time of the *Law*, when the people of GOD were under the elements of the world, and the *oldneſs* of the letter. The third and laſt period is the time of the *Meſſiah*, when the law was fulfilled, and *all things became new:* and this period, from its firſt commencement to its concluſion, is meant by the *latter days*, the *laſt time*, &c.

After this rule the bleſſed Apoſtle thus expreſſeth himſelf, Heb. ix. 26. "*But now once in the* END *of the* "*world hath He* (Chriſt) *appeared to put away ſin by the* "*ſacrifice of himſelf.*" If we ſhould here attend only to the ſound of an expreſſion, without comparing the Scripture with itſelf to attain its ſenſe, we might as well expect that Chriſt ſhould appear again in theſe days to put away ſin, as to expect another miraculous effuſion of the Spirit from thoſe words alleged by St. Peter, wherein the *laſt days* are ſpoken of: for, as it is here ſaid, "In the *end* of the world he *hath* ap- "peared," ſo is it in the other place—"He *hath* ſhed "forth this which ye ſee and hear." And this abundant confirms what I have advanced, that the words in queſtion belonged to an event not now to be expected, but then accompliſhed.

If we are deſirous to know in what poſture the Chriſtian Church ſhould be toward the end of the world, (in the ſenſe in which we commonly underſtand that phraſe) that is, toward the ſecond advent of Chriſt, we ſhall diſcover a face of things very different from what thoſe words of the prophet Joel have deſcribed to us: for theſe days, Madam, are not to be distinguished by the wisdom or holiness of those who live in them, but, on the contrary, by their abominable ignorance and wickedness. The light of God is to be almost extinguished and his lamp going out in the Temple at that midnight wherein the bridegroom cometh; and false delusive lights are to rise up instead of it. Why else is it said, 2 Thess. ii. 3. "*That day shall not come, except there come* a falling "away *first?*" And again, that "*when the Son of Man* "*cometh*, he *should not find faith on earth*;" for that "*false Christs* and *false Prophets*," called in another place (1 Tim. iv. 1.) "*seducing spirits, speaking lies in* "*hypocrisy*," should arise with such seeming pretensions as should be sufficient almost to "*deceive the very* "*elect*:" and that these deceivers should multiply so abundantly, that, for the sake of some few, God in mercy would cut short the days, lest a total corruption should take place?

Our blessed Saviour is particularly earnest with us on this subject, bidding us beware, for that he has *told us before*, that some should be enticing us into the fields and deserts, others into the *secret chambers*, &c. so that ignorance cannot be our excuse if we are "*led away with the error of the wicked*, and *fall from* "*our own steadfastness*."

So little encouragement is there to expect new lights and revelations in these times, that, on the contrary, if any man now pretend to be *some great one*, sent from God to enlighten the world, we are to suspect him for one of these impostors: and as J. Beh-

men

men has aſſumed ſuch a character, the probability lies ſtrongly againſt him, even before we examine his credentials.

There is another thing you will readily grant: that, ſuppoſing any ſuch deceiver ſhould ariſe, with his books written at the inſtigation of *Satan*; I ſay *ſuppoſing* ſuch a thing, there would be all the reaſon in the world to expect a conſiderable mixture of ſanctity, temperance, humility, abſtraction from the world, and other the like virtues: his writings would elſe ſtand no chance to *deceive the elect*; who are not to be enſnared by open vice and bare-faced immorality, but only with high pretences to the contrary. Hence it is, that the miniſters of Satan never appear with their proper colours, but *transformed as the miniſters of* RIGHTEOUSNESS, (2 Cor. xi. 15.) even as their maſter himſelf was into an *Angel of light*; and in this ſhape, as a great and good man has obſerved, the *Devil is moſt a Devil, becauſe he can moſt deceive.* The fact has always been as I am repreſenting it; for, if any Heretic ſtarted up in the Primitive Church, it was ever with ſome pretences to ſuperior holineſs, mortification, giftedneſs, ſpirituality, &c. that his perſonal character might raiſe the admiration of unwary men, and ſo make way for the moſt pernicious and diabolical errors in points of faith. The Scriptures give us ſome inſtances, ſuch as *abſtaining from meats*, and *forbidding to marry*; to which others might be added from eccleſiaſtical hiſtory. The impoſtor is never content either with the ordinary

 knowlege

knowlege, or the ordinary *fruits* of the Gofpel; but would far exceed them, and outftrip the practical attainments of all other Chriftians; the beft of whom he will condemn, as *Sodomites, fatted Swine, Shepherds of Babel, Mouth Apes*, which, with innumerable others of the fame caft, are the lamb-like phrafes of Jacob Behmen. So that if you fhould find a contempt for the vanity of the world, humility, charity, and other great and fhining virtues ftrongly recommended, this is by no means to be allowed as a teft either of the divinity of his commiffion, or the truth of his preaching. For thefe are the *feigned* words (2 Pet. ii. 3.) with which he makes merchandize of unftable fouls, turning their ears from the truth, that they may be turned unto fables: and if many were led away with fuch devices, even in thofe early days, when the *love* of Chriftians did even aftonifh infidels; when a fpirit of martyrdom flourifhed, and the preaching of the apoftles yet founded in the Church; what wonder is it, if many fhould be enfnared by them in thefe dregs of time, when the love of many is waxed cold, and the truth of God is in general *evil fpoken of* throughout the world?

Thefe reflections I have fet down as preliminaries: they are intended as a fprinkling of water to lay any little duft that may have been raifed for the deceiving your eye-fight; and they are offered to a perfon whofe good fenfe and difcernment will immediately fee, and, I have reafon to think, as readily acknowlege, the truth of them.

The

The probability then, it ſeems, as to the affair of inſpiration, is againſt the writings of J. B. Such things are not *now* to be expected, but the contrary. How the fact is in itſelf, we are in the next place to conſider; and there is but one method of doing it to any purpoſe, which is this: There is a word of revelation before us, and we all agree that it was *given by inſpiration of* GOD. Whatever therefore is falſe, *this* muſt be true; *ſo* true, that it is the teſt and ſtandard of all truth upon earth. Every thing that oppoſes this word of truth muſt be a *lie*; and he that delivers it a *liar*. If he pretend to have received it of GOD, it is ſo much the worſe; for then it is not only a lie, but a *blaſphemy*; and he himſelf is a blaſphemer, becauſe he makes the Spirit of truth the author of his lies. What J. B. has written muſt be judged of by this rule, and received or rejected as it ſhall be found to agree with it.

And firſt let us take a view of his ſtyle and method in general, which is not at all like that of the Scripture, but the reverſe of it; for the Scripture is clear and uniform in its language, as coming all of it from the ſame author, and addreſſing itſelf to the capacity of all mankind. Even where it is moſt obſcure, as in the viſions of Ezekiel, and the Revelation of St. John, it borrows ideas from the things that are before us, and takes the viſible objects of the natural creation to expreſs and delineate what is unknown or inviſible: ſo that if you have obtained its meaning in one caſe, you will be able to unriddle it in every other caſe of the ſame ſort: whence ariſes the great uſefulneſs and neceſſity of *comparing ſpiritual things with ſpiritual*, that is, the Bible with itſelf, in order to comprehend them. But how different from all this is the ſtyle of J. B.! His ideas are rarely taken from Nature, but in general from the dark ſcience of Alchymy, in which he had dabbled till his brain was turned: hence it is that we find ſo much about *ether*, *ſpirit*, *matrix*, *genitrix*, *eſſence*, *quinteſſence*, *eſſence of eſſences*, *tinctures*, *extracts*, *harſhneſs*, *ſourneſs*, *bitterneſs*, *attraction*, *fire-breaths*, *ſugar of hell*, *ſalt*, *ſulphur*, *mercury*, and others of the like ſort, ſo abhorrent from the Scripture, that the very ſound of them is ſufficient to frighten any man but a blackſmith out of his ſenſes. If I gueſs right, Paracelſus was the father of this jargon: he held it no crime to deal with the devil for the advancement of medicine and chymiſtry; and the chymical writers of ſucceeding times, after his example, have intermixed with their writings ſome of the higheſt myſteries of the Chriſtian faith, veiled under the occult terms of their own wonderful ſcience, to be underſtood only by adepts, (ſuch as Jacob calls *the children of the lily*) who, they pretended, were to be holy and pure from all ſpot of iniquity: ſo that your author, Madam, with all his myſteries, is very far from being an original; and in his ſtyle and method is ſo oppoſite to ſacred Scripture, that his language muſt not be imputed to the ſame author by any perſon who has rightly conſidered *both*. But you tell me, "*The words are his own, he ſays*: the *ſenſe* only

"was

"was inſpired." And if he ſays this, he is not to be believed any way: for, in the firſt place, his inſpired writings will then be like no other; the prophets and apoſtles having SPOKEN (not *thought* only) *as the Spirit gave them* UTTERANCE: and the whole ſacred Scripture is not called the *ſenſe*, but the WORD of GOD; becauſe Chriſt and the Holy Ghoſt *ſpake* it by the prophets, whoſe uſual introduction is, *Thus* SAITH *the Lord*. Hence it is that the prophet *David*, ſpeaking of his own *inſpiration*, ſays, 2 Sam. xxiii. 2. "*His* word *was in my* tongue;" and again, in the xlvth Pſalm, "*My tongue is the pen of a ready writer*." Whence it is manifeſt, that the inſpiration from the Spirit of GOD did, in fact, always extend to the *tongue*, and the *expreſſions* whether *ſpoken* or *written*: and there are weighty reaſons why it cannot be otherwiſe; but I have no room for them.

Secondly. If Jacob ſays this, he forgets himſelf, and is in two ſtories; for, in his ſecond book, concerning the *three principles*, chap. xxv. 51, he ſays, "We ſpeak *not our own words*, but we *ſpeak* in our "knowlege and driving in the ſpirit that which is "ſhewn us of GOD." Again, chap. xxv. 100, he tells us of "*the ſpirit* that *driveth his pen*:" and his *pen* could not be driven to *thought*, but only to *utterance* or *expreſſion*. So that if what you have obſerved be true, that *the words are his own, he ſays*, then he has contradicted himſelf in terms, and that with regard to the firſt and great point of which he ought to ſatisfy us, viz. the reality of his *inſpiration*, which can receive but little honour from ſuch inconſiſtencies, But the worſt is, that he hath not only contradicted himſelf, but the Scriptures; and that in many more inſtances than I can enumerate within the compaſs of a letter. You ſay, Madam, he has not added to the book, but only explained it; whereas it appears to me (from ſome things which perhaps have not yet fallen in your way) that he contradicts it, and has added many things to it; for he has ſet up doctrines expreſſly condemned by it, and has denied ſeveral of its moſt poſitive aſſertions.

In the piece above mentioned, which is the ſum of all his doctrines, he preaches up "the regiment (rule or dominion) of the *ſtars and elements that driveth the body and ſoul of man*, chap. xviii. 25. But to make the ſoul of man ſubject to be driven by the influence of the ſtars, is no other than Idolatry and Paganiſm: it was this notion that introduced the vain ſcience of aſtrology, and led the Heathen to worſhip the ſtars, as gods endued with the power of over-ruling the affairs of this lower world. But God warned his people againſt this doctrine; Jer. x. 2. *Learn not the way of the Heathen, and be not diſmayed at the ſigns of Heaven:* the ſame is repeated more than once in the law of Moſes. And the contrary is again repeated by Jacob, chap. xx. 87. "*O Cain,* "thy potent kingdom cometh not from God, but hath "its *influence from the ſtarry heaven:*" and again, *ibid.* "The rule and government of this world, ALL ac- "cording to the *influence of the ſtars, not ordained of the* "*Deity.*"

" *Deity.*" Which is doubly falſe: for the government eſtabliſhed in the world is not from the ſtars, as he affirms; but *the powers that be*, whether good or bad, (for this was ſpoken of *Nero*) *are ordained of* God.

" As for his explaining the book, let us take the following inſtance; whence it will follow, that, if he was inſpired, St. John, who wrote the Revelation, certainly was not. The ſeven golden candleſticks, as Chriſt expounded their meaning in viſion to Saint John, did ſignify the ſeven churches of Aſia; and the ſeven ſtars, the angels (that is, the biſhops or chief rulers) of thoſe churches. But Jacob, taking the matter into his hands, expounds them afreſh, and ſays, chap. xx. 42, " The ſeven golden candleſticks " are *his humanity*, the ſeven ſtars are his *deity:*" which two expoſitions, as they can no way be reconciled with each other, we need only compare, to detect the ignorance and impudence of this impoſtor. From another paſſage we ſhall have the ſame concluſion, either againſt *him*, or againſt *Moſes* and St. *Paul.* Chap. xi. 40, he ſays, " Adam looked upon the tree " of knowlege, became infected by luſt, and was *un-* " *done:* and *then*, ſaid the heart of God, *It is not good* " *for him to be alone.*" This throws the temptation of Adam quite into another order, and makes it ariſe from other cauſes than what God hath revealed to us; for Adam gives this as the reaſon of his fall—*The woman whom thou gaveſt to be with me, ſhe gave me of the tree, and I did eat.* Gen. iii. 12. To which St. Paul referring aſſures us (1 Tim. ii. 14.) that

Adam

Adam was not *deceived*; but that *the woman, being deceived, was in the transgression.* This makes the woman to have been *first* in the order of the transgression, and also the immediate cause of Adam's falling after her example. But here Jacob puts in his negative. Adam, according to him, was deceived: and the woman was so far from being first in the order of the transgression, that the angelic man fell and *was undone, before* the woman was taken out of him: so that unless Adam was deceived and *not* deceived, and unless he was both first and last in the order of the transgression, then it must be allowed that Jacob Behmen was not inspired, or that Moses and St. Paul were not; for their doctrines cannot stand together: and here we are to remember, as it was observed above, that if this man was not inspired, and yet affirms that he is, while he is so often giving the lie to the spirit of God, he is not only a liar of the worst sort, but a blasphemer.

You tell me, Madam, he has given no new revelation. So he says, indeed, that he *writes no new thing:* but what is that account of a *limbus*, or *matrix* of pre-existing matter, out of which the world was *generated, born*, and *at length created?* Chap. iv. What is that *heavenly flesh*, that *quinteſſence of the stars*, of which man's *body* was made, chap. x. 10, though God hath revealed to us, that he *formed man of the dust of the ground?* To which also St. Paul alluding says, *The first man is of the earth, earthy.* What, again, but a new revelation, is that strange story, that *Adam should*

ſhould have propagated an angelical hoſt out of his own will, without pain, by awakening in himſelf the paradiſiacal centre? Chap. x. 12. What is this centre? Have Moſes or the prophets ſpoken of it? And are we not told that God ſaid to Adam and Eve in their ſtate of innocence, *Be fruitful and multiply and repleniſh the earth?* Again, where did he learn that Adam had no entrails, ſtomach, or guts? Chap. x. 19. Yet in the perfect ſtate of Adam, God bade him *eat* of the trees of the garden. Therefore, ſays Jacob, he muſt have *taken it into his mouth, and not into the body*. Surely, Madam, this is not to explain the book of God, but to deny it, and to reveal to us ſuch wonderful ſtuff inſtead of it, as is not fit to be repeated or thought of. Yet theſe things, according to the author, are the *root and ground of the depth*; without allowing which he affirms we can know nothing at all. But if there are any depths here, I will be bold to ſay, they are the *depths of Satan*, without fearing any miſchief from that profuſion of threatenings and imprecations which this man hath beſtowed, throughout his works, on all thoſe who dare to gainſay his doctrines.

I might here add ſomething upon his *Light of Nature*; which, as he has deſcribed it at large, is the great myſtery of pagan enthuſiaſm, and the root of modern infidelity.—His abominable pride, where he ſays, *we*, meaning *himſelf* and the *Spirit of* God; with his frequent boaſtings of high and unutterable knowlege, meaning ſuch ſtuff as I have juſt now repeated;—

peated;—the foul venom of his tongue, in railing at the authority of the Church, and all Chriſtian divines from the days of the apoſtles down to his own, without excepting any that I can yet find, unleſs it be ſome of the primitive Heretics, who were juſt ſuch ſaints as himſelf; his ridiculous and anti-ſcriptural interpretation of words; for when the Goſpel hath given us the important ſenſe and interpretation of the name *Jeſus*, "For he ſhall SAVE his people from "their ſins," he goes to his deep language of nature, and declares with much pomp, that "*Je* is his *hum-*"*bling*, and the ſyllable *Sus* preſſeth aloft through all." Chap. xxii. 76.—Theſe and many other things I might expoſe at large: but as I am aſſured from your own words, and am ſatisfied from the whole ſpirit of your writing, that you have humility enough to confeſs an error, when you are convinced of it, I will not weary your patience with any farther obſervations on the writings of Jacob Behmen; but ſhall here conclude them, with heartily recommending you and my own poor endeavours to the grace and bleſſing of Almighty GOD.

You ſeem to take it ill that I *apprehended ſome danger for you*; which indeed I did more than I do at preſent: yet I rejoice, Madam, that any occurrence or any inſtrument, be it who or what it will, has taught you to deſpiſe the world, and ſtirred up in you a thirſt after the wiſdom of GOD. In this, go on and proſper: I heartily bid you GOD ſpeed! and, if you deſire to learn the knowlege of divine myſteries

for

for your edification and cömfort in this vale of misery, there are ways and means, though the *well is deep*, by which, through GOD's blessing on your industry, much *living water* may be drawn out of it; and that without letting down into it the vessel of J. Behmen. If any mysteries of the Scriptures are rightly explained by him, (and it would be hard indeed, if, with all his pretences, he had not hit upon something) the same have also been explained by more sober men, and in a far better manner. An *English* reader need not be at a loss for the interpretation of the Scripture, so long as the writings of Bishop Andrews, Hall, Brownrig, and Mr. Leslie, and many others are current amongst us. These are some of the books I would humbly recommend to your reading. Andrews is a noble and profitable expositor: one of his sermons on the *Passion* is the greatest human composition extant on the subject: his discourses on Repentance and Humiliation, on the necessity of receiving the Holy Spirit, with the Way to distinguish his genuine Fruits, are all admirable. His Devotions breathe a most exalted spirit of piety, while they contain a complete body of the Christian mysteries. There are some English editions: but the best is from a Greek and Latin copy found among his papers after his death, blotted and soiled with his tears. Bishop Brownrig has, among other excellent discourses, eight sermons on the *Transfiguration*, wherein the great mysteries of that part of our Saviour's history are unfolded with equal skilfulness and piety. Leslie, in his History of

Sin

Sin and Heresy, will lay open to you the whole *mystery of iniquity*, traced from the fall of *Lucifer* out of heaven, down to the modern heresies and blasphemies: and, if you would see every false pretence to inspiration detected and exposed beyond a possibility of a reply, you may look into his pieces against the Quakers, with his preface on Antonietta Bourignon. His works are in two volumes in folio, easily to be met with.—For the *spiritual dispositions* no author exceeds Kempis in his Imitation of Jesus Christ. Dr. Cave's Lives of the Primitive Fathers is a book very useful and entertaining, necessary to give some notion of the primitive times, with that knowlege, spirit and discipline, which are now departed from amongst us.

There is one book more which I believe may be very acceptable; and, as you are already in possession of Bishop Hall, it is the last I shall mention;—that is —Quesnel's Moral Reflections on the New Testament. He has a great talent in speaking to the heart, and applying the history of the Gospel, so as to advance us in the spirit and practice of the Christian life. I had almost forgotten Mr. Wogan, the last able expositor which this Church has produced; whose four volumes on the Proper Lessons are in the hands of many pious people, and are greatly recommended by those who make the Bible their study*.

* If this Letter had been of modern date, the writer of it would certainly have added the Commentary on the Psalms: and perhaps he might have added the Lectures on the Figurative Language of the Scripture; and certainly Mr. Waldo's Commentary on the Liturgy of the Church of England.

After

After all that can be ſaid, the Holy Ghoſt himſelf is the beſt interpreter of his own writings; and ſo boundleſs is the treaſure therein contained, that the Scripture compared with itſelf will frequently open ſome things to the faithful enquirer, of which no commentator will inform us. But nevertheleſs, our weakneſs is obliged to call in the help of our brethren on ſeveral occaſions; and, though the Scripture be itſelf the *word of life*, yet it is profitably *held forth* to us by the hand of *man*, and placed on a candleſtick, that they which are in the houſe may ſee the light, and partake of its influences.

That this may ever be the fruit of all *your* reading, and that the light of GOD's Revelation may clear up all your doubts, and guide your feet through the paths of ſound and wholeſome doctrine into the way of eternal peace, is the ſincere wiſh and prayer of,

Madam,

Your moſt obliged, &c. &c. &c.

POEMS.

POEMS.

Having mentioned (p. 6 and 45) Dr. Horne's turn for poetical composition, the Editor thinks the Reader will not be displeased, if a few of his Poems are added for a specimen.

THE FRIEND.

I.

THE fastest friend the world affords
Is quickly from me gone:
Faithless behold him turn his back,
And leave me all alone!

II.

"My friend, sincerely yours *till death*:"
The world no farther goes;
Perhaps, while *earth to earth* is laid,
A tear of pity flows.

III.

Be thou, my *Saviour*, then, my *friend*,
In thee my soul shall trust,
Who false wilt never prove in death,
Nor leave me in the dust.

IV.

Home while my other friends return,
All solemn, silent, sad,
With thee my flesh shall rest in hope,
And all my bones be glad.

THE LEAF.

WE ALL DO FADE AS A LEAF.

Isa. lxiv. 6.

I.

SEE the leaves around us falling,
Dry and wither'd to the ground;
Thus to thoughtless mortals calling,
In a sad and solemn sound;

II.

Sons of Adam, once in Eden
Blighted when like us he fell,
Hear the lecture we are reading,
'Tis, alas! the truth we tell.

III.

Virgins, much, too much, presuming
On your boasted white and red,
View us, late in beauty blooming,
Number'd now among the dead.

IV.

Griping misers, nightly waking,
See the end of all your care;
Fled on wings of our own making,
We have left our owners bare.

V.

Sons of honour, fed on praises,
Flutt'ring high in fancied worth,
Lo! the fickle air, that raises,
Brings us down to parent earth.

VI.

Learned ſophs, in ſyſtems jaded,
  Who for new ones daily call,
Ceaſe, at length, by us perſuaded,
  Ev'ry leaf muſt have its fall!

VII.

Youths, tho' yet no loſſes grieve you,
  Gay in health and manly grace,
Let not cloudleſs ſkies deceive you,
  Summer gives to Autumn place.

VIII.

Venerable ſires, grown hoary,
  Hither turn th'unwilling eye,
Think, amidſt your falling glory,
  Autumn tells a winter nigh.

IX.

Yearly in our courſe returning
  Meſſengers of ſhorteſt ſtay,
Thus we preach this truth concerning,
  "Heav'n and earth ſhall paſs away."

X.

On the Tree of Life eternal,
  Man, let all thy hope be ſtaid,
Which alone, for ever vernal,
  Bears a Leaf that ſhall not fade.

AN ODE.

THE SENTIMENT FROM THE DIVINE HERBERT.

I.

SWEET day, ſo cool, ſo calm, ſo bright,
Bridal of earth and ſky,
The dew ſhall weep thy fall to-night;
For thou, alas! muſt die,

II.

Sweet roſe, in air whoſe odours wave,
And colour charms the eye,
Thy root is ever in its grave,
And thou, alas! muſt die.

III.

Sweet ſpring, of days and roſes made,
Whoſe charms for beauty vie,
Thy days depart, thy roſes fade,
Thou too, alas! muſt die.

IV.

Be wiſe then, Chriſtian, while you may,
For ſwiftly time is flying;
The thoughtleſs man, that laughs to-day,
To-morrow will be dying.

THE FLOWERS.

THE HELIOTROPE.

THROUGH all the changes of the day
  I turn me to the SUN:
In clear or cloudy ſkies I ſay
  Alike—*Thy will be done!*

THE VIOLET.

A LOWLY flow'r, in ſecret bow'r,
  Inviſible I dwell;
For bleſſing made, without parade,
  Known only by my ſmell.

THE LILY.

EMBLEM of him, in whom no ſtain
  The eye of Heav'n could ſee,
In all their glory, monarchs vain
  Are not array'd like me.

THE ROSE.

WITH raviſh'd heart that crimſon hail,
  Which in my boſom glows:
Think how the lily of the vale
  Became like Sharon's roſe.

THE PRIMROSE.

When Time's dark winter shall be o'er,
  His storms and tempests laid,
Like me you'll rise, a fragrant flow'r,
  But not, like me, to fade.

THE GARDEN.

The bow'r of innocence and bliss
  Sin caus'd to disappear:
Repent, and walk in faith and love—
  You'll find an *Eden* here.

A MORNING HYMN ON *EASTER-DAY.*

I.

Hark! the shrill herald of the morn
Begins the sons of men to warn,
  And bids them all arise,
To celebrate his great renown,
Who sends the light refulgent down,
  To bless our longing eyes.

II.

At this the fainting shadows die,
The pow'rs of darkness swiftly fly
  Before the morning star;
Pale trembling murder dares not stay,
And fiends, abash'd at sight of day,
  Back to their den repair.

III.

'Tis this the weary sailor cheers,
Who now no more the tempest hears,
Which morning bids to cease:
O come that day-spring from on high,
When discord shall with darkness fly,
And all be light and peace!

IV.

'Twas this that drew repentant tears
From Peter, led by worldly fears
His master to disown;
Warn'd by the monitor of day,
He cast the works of night away,
And sought th' abjured sun.

V.

Whene'er the bird of dawning crows,
He tells us all how Peter rose,
And mark'd us out the road;
That each disciple might begin,
Awake, like him, from sleep and sin,
To think betimes on God.

VI.

Smote by the eye that looks on all,
Let us, obedient to the call,
Arise to weep and pray;
Till mournful, as on sin we muse,
Faith, like an angel, tells the news,
"The Lord is ris'n to-day!"

ON

DAVID GARRICK's FUNERAL PROCESSION.

THRO' weeping London's crowded ſtreets,
As Garrick's fun'ral paſs'd,
Contending wits and nobles ſtrove,
Who ſhould forſake him laſt.

Not ſo the world behav'd to *him*,
Who came that world to ſave,
By ſolitary Joſeph borne
Unheeded to his grave.

If what is done by mortals here
Departed ſpirits know,
Confus'd and bluſhing, Garrick views
This grand parade of woe.

Tho' much to be admir'd by man,
He had—yet, gracious Heav'n!
Much, very much he had, indeed,
By thee to be forgiv'n.

But thou art good!—And ſince he died
Compos'd, without a groan,
Repentant David, let us hope,
May live through *David's Son.*

WRITTEN AT AN INN.

I.

FROM much-lov'd friends whene'er I part,
A pensive sadness fills my heart;
Past scenes my fancy wanders o'er,
And sighs to think they are no more.

II.

Along the road I musing go,
O'er many a deep and miry slough:
The shrouded moon withdraws her light,
And leaves me to the gloomy night.

III.

An inn receives me, where unknown
I solitary sit me down:
Many I hear, and some I see,
I nought to them, they nought to me.

IV.

Thus in these regions of the dead
A pilgrim's wand'ring life I lead,
And still at every step declare,
I've no abiding city here:

V.

For very far from hence I dwell,
And therefore bid the world farewell,
Finding of all the joys it gives
A sad remembrance only lives.

VI. Rough

VI.

Rough ſtumbling-ſtones my ſteps o'erthrow,
And lay a wand'ring ſinner low;
Yet ſtill my courſe to heav'n I ſteer,
Tho' neither moon nor ſtars appear!

VII.

The world is like an inn; for there
Men call, and ſtorm, and drink, and ſwear;
While undiſturb'd a Chriſtian waits,
And reads, and writes, and meditates.

VIII.

Tho' in the dark oft-times I ſtray,
The Lord ſhall light me on my way,
And to the city of the Sun
Conduct me, when my journey's done.

IX.

There by theſe eyes ſhall He be ſeen,
Who ſojourn'd for me in an inn;
On Sion's hill I thoſe ſhall hail,
From whom I parted in the vale.

X.

Why am I heavy then and ſad,
When thoughts like theſe ſhould make me glad?
Muſe then no more on things below;
Ariſe, my ſoul, and let us go.

THE

THE MONKISH LATIN HYMN,

USED AS A GRACE AFTER MEAT, AT MAGDALEN COLLEGE, OXFORD.

I.

TE Deum patrem colimus,
Te laudibus prosequimur,
Qui corpus cibo reficis,
Cœlesti mentem gratiâ.

II.

Te adoramus, O Jesu,
Te, Fili unigenite,
Te, qui non dedignatus es
Subire claustra virginis.

III.

Actus in crucem factus es
Irato Deo victima;
Per te, Salvator unice,
Vitæ spes nobis rediit.

IV.

Tibi, æterne Spiritus,
Cujus afflatu peperit
Infantem Deum Maria,
Æternum benedicimus.

V.

Triune Deus, hominum
Salutis autor optime,
Immensum hoc mysterium
Ovanti linguâ canimus.

TRANS-

TRANSLATION.

I.

THEE, mighty Father, we adore,
And praiſe thy Name for evermore;
Whoſe bounty feeds all Adam's race,
And cheers the hungry ſoul with grace.

II.

Great co-eternal Son, to thee,
With one conſent, we bow the knee;
For our ſalvation man become,
Thou didſt not ſcorn the virgin's womb.

III.

The Paſchal Lamb, foreſhewn of old,
In thee, ſweet Jeſu! we behold,
And pardon thro' thy blood receive,
While on thy croſs we look and live.

IV.

Thee too, all-hallow'd myſtic Dove,
We ever bleſs, and ever love:
Thy wonders how ſhall we declare?
The Lord was born, the virgin bare!

V.

Almighty everlaſting Three,
No other God we have but thee;
Thy glorious works, immortal King,
In triumph thus we daily ſing.

ESSAYS AND THOUGHTS

ON

VARIOUS SUBJECTS,

AND FROM

VARIOUS AUTHORS, &c.

BY THE RIGHT REVEREND

GEORGE HORNE, D. D.

LATE BISHOP OF NORWICH.

ESSAYS AND THOUGHTS

ON

VARIOUS SUBJECTS, &c.

ABBEY LANDS.

SIR Benjamin Rudyard in a ſpeech (preſerved by Nalſon, ii. 300) mentions it as the *principal parliamentary motive* for ſeizing the abbey lands by Henry VIII. that they would ſo enrich the crown, as that the people ſhould *never be put to pay ſubſidies again;* and an army of 40,000 men for the defence of the kingdom ſhould be maintained with the overplus. How did the matter turn out? Sir Benjamin tells us, "God's part, religion, by his "bleſſing, had been tolerably well preſerved; but it "hath been ſaved *as by fire*; for the reſt is conſumed "and vaniſhed. The people have paid ſubſidies ever "ſince, and we are now in no very good caſe to pay "an army." [A more exact account of this deſign and its conſequences may be found in Sir Henry Spelman's Hiſtory of Sacrilege, chap. vii.]

ABE-

ABELARD.

The bad tendency of Mr. Pope's Eloiſa to Abelard is remarked by Sir John Hawkins, in his Hiſtory of Muſic, vol. ii. page 23, as depreciating matrimony, and juſtifying concubinage. This is founded on a falſe fact; Abelard *was* married. The original letters are finer than even Pope's: they were publiſhed A. D. 1718, by Rawlinſon, from a MS. in the Bodleian library. Sir John Hawkins, ſpeaking of Abelard's ſkill in ſcholaſtical theology, and profligacy of manners, makes the following ſenſible obſervation: "To ſay the truth, the theo-"logy of the ſchools, as taught in Abelard's time, was "merely ſcientific, and had as little tendency to re-"gulate the manners of thoſe who ſtudied it, as geo-"metry, or any other of the mathematical ſciences." —The obſervation may be extended to *other* modes of ſtudying divinity.

ADVERSITY.

The fiery trials of adverſity have the ſame kindly effect on a Chriſtian mind, which Virgil aſcribes to burning land. They purge away the bad properties, and remove obſtructions to the operations of heaven.

——Sive illis omne per ignem
Excoquitur vitium, atque exſudat inutilis humor,

 Seu

Seu plures calor ille vias et cæca relaxat
Spiramenta, novas veniat qua ſuccus in herbas.

GEORG. i. 87.

Or when the latent vice is cur'd by fire,
Redundant humours through the pores expire;
Or that the warmth diſtends the chinks, and makes
New breathings, whence new nouriſhment ſhe takes;
Or that the heat the gaping ground conſtrains,
New knits the ſurface, and new ſtrings the veins.

DRYDEN, 128.

ALCORAN.

EXTRAVAGANT praiſes are beſtowed by Sale and his diſciples on the Koran, which equal the enthuſiaſm of Mahomet and his followers; going every length but that of ſaying, it was dictated by the Spirit of God.—Wonderful and horrible! This not much noticed; not mentioned, I think, in White's lectures, as it ſhould have been, and expoſed. [But if any reader wants ſatisfaction on the ſubject of Mahometiſm, he will find it in Dr. Prideaux's Life of Mahomet.]

AMBITION.

THE ambitious man employs his time, his pains, and his abilities, to climb to a ſummit, on which, at laſt, he ſtands with anxiety and fear, and from which if he fall, it muſt be with infamy and ruin. A man of like turn in the time of Charles II. had, by like unwearied application, attained a like ſituation, on the top of Saliſbury ſpire. Every ſober thinking man will ſay in one caſe what the merry monarch ſaid in the other: "Make the fellow out a patent, "that no one may ſtand there but himſelf."

ANGELS.

Man, a miniſter of Chriſt in particular, ſhould reſemble them in reconciling duty with devotion. They *miniſter to the heirs of ſalvation*; yet *always behold* the *face of their Father in heaven.*

AFRICAN ANTS.

These inſects ſometimes ſet forward in ſuch multitudes, that the whole earth ſeems to be in motion. A corps of them attacked and covered an elephant quietly feeding in a paſture. In eight hours, nothing was to be ſeen on the ſpot, but the ſkeleton of that enormous animal, neatly and completely picked. The buſineſs was done, and the enemy marched on after freſh prey.—Such power have the ſmalleſt creatures acting in concert.

APOPHTHEGMS.

It is ſaid, I think, of Biſhop Sanderſon, that, by frequently converſing with his ſon, and ſcattering ſhort apophthegms, with little pleaſant ſtories, and making uſeful applications of them, the youth was, in his infancy, taught to abhor vanity and vice as monſters.

ASSES.

THERE are wild aſſes in South America. They have three properties which bear a moral application. 1. Though exceedingly ſwiſt, fierce and untractable, after carrying the firſt load, their celerity leaves them, their dangerous ferocity is loſt, and they ſoon contract the ſtupid look and dulneſs of the aſinine ſpecies: one of them becomes like another aſs. 2. If that more noble animal a horſe happens to ſtray into the places where they feed, they all fall upon him; and, without giving him the liberty of flying from them, they bite and kick him till they leave him dead upon the ſpot. 3. They are very troubleſome neighbours, making a moſt horrid noiſe; for, whenever one or two of them begin to bray, they are anſwered in the ſame vociferous manner by all within reach of the ſound, which is greatly increaſed and prolonged by the repercuſſions of the valleys and breaches of the mountains. Ulloa, i. 248. [An Engliſh gentleman, reſident in the Eaſt, kept one of the aſſes of the country for his uſe, who was ſo troubleſome with his noiſe, that he ordered a ſlave to ſtrike him on the noſe with a cane when he began to vociferate; in conſequence of which, the creature in a few days fell from his appetite, and would actually have pined away and died, for want of the liberty of making his own frightful noiſe.]

ATHANASIAN CREED.

The doctrines in the public ſervice (as a noble author has ſuppoſed) are not the true cauſe why people of rank, &c. abſent themſelves; but downright ungodlineſs, amuſements, racing, hunting, gambling, viſiting and intriguing—ſetting out for Newmarket on a Sunday, &c. Would the gentlemen of the turf come the more to church if the Athanaſian Creed were ſtruck out, &c.?

It is not true that theſe doctrines "are acknow-"leged to be ill founded and unſcriptural by every "clergyman of learning and candour;" or that "no "man of ſenſe and learning can maintain them." There have been and are many inſtances both of laity and clergy that hold them to be ſcriptural, and maintain them as ſuch. The abettors of hereſy and infidelity are not the only *men of ſenſe* in the nation, [in *good manners* they certainly do not abound.] Dr. Middleton, when he had apoſtatized, by *men of ſenſe* meant *infidels*. [This article was occaſioned by a pamphlet ſtyled Hints, &c. aſcribed to the D. of G.]

AVARICE.

1. A *canine appetite* inclines perſons to take down their food in ſuch quantities, that they vomit it up again like *dogs*. So Job of the rapacious greedy oppreſſor: "He hath ſwallowed down riches, and he "ſhall

" ſhall vomit them up again." Chap. xx. 15. What is *avarice*, but ſuch an appetite of the mind?

2. He, who flatters himſelf that he reſolves to employ his fortune well, though he ſhould acquire it ill, ought to take this with him, that ſuch a compenſation of evil by good may be allowed after the fact, but is deſervedly condemned in that purpoſe. And it may be obſerved, that a reſolution of this kind, taken beforehand, is ſeldom carried into act afterwards. *Nemo unquam imperium flagitiis quæſitum bonis artibus exercuit.*—Tacit. Hiſt. i.——No one ever exerciſed with virtue power obtained by crimes.

3. The eagerneſs with which ſome men ſeek after gold would lead one to imagine it had the power to remove all uneaſineſs, and make its poſſeſſors completely happy; as the Spaniards pretended to the Mexicans, that it cured them of a pain at the *heart*, to which they were ſubject.

4. Riches will make a man juſt as happy as the emperor of Siam's white elephant, who is ridden by nobody, lives at his eaſe, is ſerved in plate, and treated like a monarch.

5. It is worthy of obſervation, that Perſeus, who loſt the Macedonian empire, was infamous for his avarice; and Paulus Emilius, his conqueror, ſo entirely the reverſe, that he ordered all the gold and ſilver, that was taken, into the public treaſury, without ſeeing it; nor ever was one farthing the richer for his victories, though always generous, of his own, to others.

6. At a time when Perſian bribes were very riſe at Athens, a porter humorouſly propoſed, that twelve of the pooreſt citizens ſhould be annually ſent ambaſſadors to the Perſian court, to be enriched by the king's preſents. Ibid.——Poor men ſhould be made miniſters of ſtate in England, for the ſame purpoſe.

BEARS.

THEIR ſagacity is very great. The Kamtſchadales are obliged to them for what little advancement they have hitherto made, either in the ſciences or the *polite arts*. From them they learned the value of ſimples for internal uſe and external application. They acknowlege the bears likewiſe for their *dancing-maſters*: what they call the *bear-dance* is an exact counterpart of every attitude and geſture peculiar to this animal, through its ſeveral functions: and this is the foundation and ground-work of all their other dances, and what they value themſelves moſt upon. King, iii. 308, chap. v.

BENTLEY.

BENTLEY is a model for polemical preaching, on account of the conciſeneſs, perſpicuity and fairneſs with which objections are ſtated, and the clear, full and regular manner in which they are anſwered.

BIGOTRY.

BIGOTRY.

Arabes artium et literarum omnium adeo rudes erant, ut id imprimis curaſſe putentur, ne Prophetam *ſuum* illiteratum (*uti vulgo audiit Mahommedes*) *ſcientiâ ſuperarent.* Spencer de Leg. Hebræ. lib. ii. cap. 1, ſec. 3.—The Arabians were ſo utterly unſkilled in arts and ſciences of every kind, that they ſeem to have been anxious, above all things, not to ſurpaſs in knowlege their prophet Mahomed, generally allowed to be illiterate.

BLIND MAN.

"I NEVER had the happineſs," ſaid the blind man in the Princeſs Palatine's dream, "to behold the light "and the glories of the firmament, nor can I form "to myſelf the leaſt idea of the tranſcendent beauties "I have often heard mentioned. Such is my ſad con-"dition; and from my ſituation all preſumptuous "beings may learn, that many very excellent and "wonderful things exiſt, which eſcape human know-"lege."—What ineſtimable and divine truths are there not in nature, devoutly to be wiſhed for, though we cannot imagine or comprehend them!—See Boſſuet's Fun. Orat. on this Princeſs.

BLINDNESS OF INFIDELITY.

Josephus tells us, that in the laſt dreadful ruin of his unhappy countrymen, it was familiar with them "to make a jeſt of divine things, and to deride, as ſo "many ſenſeleſs tales, and juggling impoſtures, the "ſacred oracles of their prophets;" though they were then fulfilling before their eyes, and even upon themſelves. Hurd on the Prophecies, p. 434.

BLONDEL.

David Blondel's book is a magazine for the writers againſt Epiſcopacy. It was drawn up at the earneſt requeſt of the Weſtminſter Aſſembly, particularly the Scots. It cloſed with words to this purpoſe: "By all that we have ſaid to aſſert the Rights "of Preſbytery, we do not intend to invalidate the "antient and apoſtolical conſtitution of Epiſcopal pre-"eminence: but we believe that, whereſoever it is "eſtabliſhed conformably to the antient canons, it "muſt be carefully preſerved: and whereſoever, by "ſome heat of contention or otherwiſe, it hath been "put down, or violated, it ought to be reverently re-"ſtored."—This raiſed a great clamour, and the concluſion was ſuppreſſed. On the report getting about, John Blondel, then reſiding in London, wrote to his brother David, who acknowleged that it was true.—See Du Moulin's Letter to Durel, at the end of Bennet on Joint Prayer.

BODY

BODY AND SOUL.

THE reciprocal influence of theſe upon each other is fully and clearly ſet forth in the ſecond volume of a *Philoſophical Eſſay on Man.* Two inferences are to be drawn from this conſideration. Firſt, that we ſhould ſtock the ſoul with ſuch ideas, ſentiments, and affections, as have a benign and ſalutary influence upon the body. Secondly, that we ſhould keep the body, by temperance, exerciſe, &c. in that ſtate which has a like benign and ſalutary influence on the ſoul. The common practice is exactly the reverſe. Men indulge paſſions in the ſoul, which deſtroy the health of the body, and introduce diſtempers into it, which impair the powers of the ſoul. Man being a compound creature, his happineſs is not complete till both parts of the compoſition partake of it. This has been well ſtated by Saurin, diſſ. xxiii. p. 200, where mention is made of a treatiſe of Capellus on the ſtate of the ſoul after death.

BOOKS.

1. IT is with books as with animals: thoſe live longeſt with which their parents go longeſt before they produce them.

2. When we ſtudy the writings of *men,* it is well if after much pains and labour we find ſome few particles of truth amongſt a great deal of error. When we read the *Scriptures,* all we meet with is truth.

In

In the former caſe, we are like the Africans on the Duſt Coaſt, of whom it is ſaid, that they dig pits nigh the water-falls of mountains abounding with gold, and then, with incredible pains and induſtry, waſh off the ſand, till they eſpy at the bottom two or three ſhining grains of the metal, that pays them only as labourers. In the latter caſe, we work in a mine ſufficient to enrich ourſelves and all about us.

3. Of the Spaniſh books, ſays Monteſquieu, the only one good for any thing is that which was written to ſhew that all the reſt were good for nothing.

4. Sir Peter Lely made it a rule, never to look at a bad picture, having found by experience, that, whenever he did ſo, his pencil took a tint from it.—Apply this to bad books and bad company.

5. I have ſaid, and I abide by it, cries Voltaire, that the fault of moſt books is their being too long.—A writer who has reaſon on his ſide will always be conciſe.

6. The books which compoſed the Alexandrian library were employed to heat the baths in that city, then 4000 in number; yet were they ſix months in conſuming. The reaſoning of the Caliph at that time was: Either theſe books are agreeable to the book of God, or they are not. If they are, the Koran is ſufficient without them; if they are not, they ought to be deſtroyed.

7. The greateſt and wiſeſt men have not been proof

proof againſt the errors and ſuperſtitious conceits of the age in which they lived. Auguſtus Cæſar thought the ſkin of a ſea-calf to be a preſervative againſt lightning; and expected ſome grievous calamity to befall him in the courſe of the day, if at riſing he happened to put the left ſhoe upon the right foot:—but we are not therefore to ſay, that Auguſtus Cæſar was a fool. The very learned and able Biſhop Jeremy Taylor, on a certain topic, aſſerts what was rather ſuited to the notions current in his time, than what was philoſophically true; but it does not follow, that the *Holy Living and Dying*, in which this paſſage occurs, is therefore a fooliſh book. He would be indeed a fooliſh man, who ſhould catch at ſuch a paſſage, and make it a reaſon for rejecting all the excellent inſtruction and counſel contained in that golden treatiſe.

8. Boſſuet, before he ſat down to compoſe a ſermon, read a chapter in the prophet Iſaiah, and another in Rodriguez's tract on Chriſtian perfection. The former fired his genius, the latter filled his heart. Dominichino never offered to touch his pencil, till he found a kind of enthuſiaſm or inſpiration upon him.—Biograph. Dict.

9. Patrons are but too apt to reward their authors with compliments, when they want bread. Sorbiere, being treated in this manner by his friend Pope Clement IX., is ſaid to have complained in the following humorous terms:—"Moſt Holy Father,

"ther, you give ruffles to a man who is without a "ſhirt."

10. Valeſius uſed to ſay, he learned more from *borrowed* books than from his own; becauſe, not having the ſame opportunity of reviewing them, he read them with more care.

11. Some books, like ſome fields, afford plenty of proviſion for various creatures—while, as to others,

-- Jejuna quidem clivoſi glarea ruris
Vix humiles *apibus* caſias roremque miniſtrat:
Et tophus ſcaber, et nigris exeſa chelydris
Creta, negant alios æque ſerpentibus agros
Dulcem ferre cibum, et curvas præbere latebras.

Georg. ii. 212.

The coarſe lean gravel, on the mountain ſides,
Scarce dewy bev'rage for the bees provides:
Nor chalk, nor crumbling ſtones, the food of ſnakes,
That work in hollow earth their winding tracks.

Dryden, 293.

12. The Biographia Britannica, a work which, notwithſtanding its ſingular merit, I cannot help calling Vindicatio Britannica, or a defence of *every body*. Royal and Noble Authors, ii. 68.

13. Voltaire's Univerſal Hiſtory, a charming bird's-eye landſcape, where one views the whole in picture ſque confuſion, and imagines the objects more delightful than they are in reality, and when examined ſeparately. Ibid. 87.

14. By the writers of dialogues matters are often contrived, as in the combats of the Emperor Commodus, in his gladiatorial capacity. The antagoniſt

of

of his imperial majesty was allowed only a *leaden* weapon.

15. It is said of Ascham, that "he lost no time in "the perusal of mean and unprofitable books." See the reflection on it in Biog. Br. 2d edit.

16. "Fronti nulla fides" is a just maxim—otherwise, one should be prejudiced against a book with this title—Fog Theologiæ Speculativæ Schema.

17. "To read while eating was always my fancy, "in default of a tête-à-tête. 'Tis the supplement to "society I want. I alternately devour a page and a "piece: 'tis as if my book dined with me." Rousseau, b. 6. vol. ii. p. 137.

18. Genuine knowlege should be diffused. "Quid "magni faceres," said archbishop Warham to Erasmus, "si uno agresti popello predicâris? Nunc libris "tuis omnes doces pastores, fructu longè uberiore." Cooper's Charge, p. 22.—"What great work could "you have wrought, had your preaching been con-"fined to one small and rustic flock? But now, with "much more extensive benefit, your books instruct "the shepherds of all other flocks."

BRACHMANS AND ALEXANDER.

Great indeed was the stateliness of the Brachmans! When Alexander expressed a desire to converse with them, he was told, these philosophers made no visits; if he wanted to see them, he must go to their houses.—The tradition of a fall and restoration was strong among them.

BRIBERY.

The Spartans were the only people that for a while ſeemed to diſdain the love of money; but, the contagion ſtill ſpreading, even they, at laſt, yielded to its allurements; and every man ſought private emoluments, without attending to the good of his country. —"That which has been is that which ſhall be!"

OF BUYING BOOKS.

Young men ſhould not be diſcouraged from buying books. Much may depend on it. It is ſaid of Whiſton, that the accidental purchaſe of Tacquet's Euclid at an auction firſt occaſioned his application to mathematical ſtudies.—Biog. Dict. art. Whiſton, vol. xxi. p. 394.

CATHARINE I. OF RUSSIA.

She was not very brilliant and quick in her underſtanding; but the reaſon why the Czar was ſo fond of her, was her exceeding good temper: ſhe never was ſeen peeviſh or out of humour; obliging and civil to all, and never forgetful of her former condition.—Coxe, i. 568, from Gordon.—Peter was ſubject to occaſional horrors, which at times rendered him gloomy and ſuſpicious, and raiſed his paſſions to ſuch a height, as to produce a temporary madneſs. In theſe dreadful moments Catharine was the only perſon who ventured to approach him; and ſuch was the kind of faſcination ſhe had acquired over him, that her preſence had an inſtantaneous effect,

and

and the firſt ſound of her voice compoſed his mind and calmed his agonies. From theſe circumſtances ſhe ſeemed neceſſary, not only to his comfort, but to his very exiſtence: ſhe became his inſeparable companion on his journies into foreign countries, and even in all his military expeditions.—P. 554.

CHARACTERS AND ACTIONS OF REMARKABLE PERSONS.

1. It will be hereafter with a wicked man, when he is puniſhed for his ſins, as it was with Apollodorus, when he dreamed that he was flayed and boiled by the Scythians, and his *heart* ſpoke to him out of the caldron: "Εγω σοι τȣτων αιτια."—"I am the cauſe "of theſe thy ſufferings."

2. Lyſimachus, for extreme thirſt, offered his kingdom to the Getæ, to quench it. His exclamation, when he had drank, is wonderfully ſtriking—"Ah! "wretched me! who, for ſuch a momentary gratifi- "cation, have loſt ſo great a kingdom! Φευ της εμης "κακιας, ος, δι ηδονην ȣτω βραχειαν, εςερημαι βασιλειας "τηλικαυτης."—How applicable is this to the caſe of him, who, for the *momentary* pleaſures of ſin, parts with the *kingdom* of heaven!

3. Horticulture, as it was the primitive employment of man, ſo it is what great geniuſes, after having paſſed through the buſieſt ſcenes in the political and military world, retire to with pleaſure towards the cloſe of their days.—See Sir W. Temple's Gardens of Epicurus.

4. A

4. A truly great genius doth not think it beneath him to attend to little things. When Paulus Emilius, after his conqueſt of Macedon, entertained the principal men of Greece, he ſhewed that he underſtood the ordering and placing of his gueſts, and how every man ſhould be received according to his rank and quality, to ſuch an exact nicety, that the Greeks were ſurpriſed to find him ſo expert and careful even about trifles, and that a man engaged in ſo many weighty affairs ſhould obſerve a decorum in ſuch little matters. He told them, the ſame ſpirit was required in marſhalling a banquet, as an army. See Plutarch.

5. The ſame Paulus Emilius, when he had followed to the grave two of the beſt of ſons, one a few days before his triumph, the other a few days after it, told a convention of the Romans, that, after ſuch a tide of ſucceſs, he had feared a reverſe of fortune either to them or himſelf; that he now felt his mind perfectly at reſt, as, by the ſtroke falling on him and his family, he looked upon his country to be ſafe.—There is a generoſity and greatneſs of ſoul in this behaviour not eaſy to be paralleled, as it came from a heart, ſays Plutarch, truly ſincere, and free from all artifice.

6. It is finely obſerved by Plutarch, that, "as that "body is moſt ſtrong and healthful, which can beſt "ſupport extreme cold and exceſſive heat, in the "change of ſeaſons; and that mind the ſtrongeſt "and firmeſt, which can beſt bear proſperity and "adver-

"adversity, and the change from one to the other; "so the virtue of Emilius was eminently seen, in that "his countenance and carriage were the same upon "the loss of two beloved sons, as when he had achieved "his greatest victories and triumphs."—How doth this example reproach and shame the weakness and inconstancy of Christians!

7. The old proverb, *Mocking is catching*, was remarkably exemplified in the great Mr. Boyle; who, when young, by imitating stuttering children, acquired himself a habit of stuttering, of which he was never after perfectly cured.

8. Lord Orrery (Dr. Bentley's antagonist) was fond of two sorts of company. He either improved himself by conversing with men of real genius and learning, or else diverted himself with those in whose composition there was a mixture of the odd and ridiculous: the foibles of such he would touch and play off with a delicacy and tenderness that prevented any offence from being taken even by the parties themselves, who enjoyed the humour, and joined in the laugh as heartily as the rest of the company.

9. The day after Charles V. (one of the wisest as well as most fortunate of princes) had resigned all his kingdoms to his son Philip, he introduced, and recommended to his service, his faithful counsellor and secretary, with these remarkable words; "The pre-"sent I make you to day is a far more valuable one "than that I made you yesterday."

10. I am aſhamed to think, that a little buſineſs and few cares ſhould indiſpoſe and hinder me in my religious exerciſes, when I read, that Frederic king of Pruſſia, at a time when all his enemies were upon him, and his affairs ſeemed abſolutely deſperate, found leiſure to write a kind of philoſophical teſtament in French verſe. See Age of Louis XV. ii. 213.

11. Children ſhould be inured as early as poſſible to acts of charity and mercy. Conſtantine, as ſoon as his ſon could write, employed *his* hand in ſigning pardons, and delighted in conveying through *his* mouth all the favours that he granted. A noble introduction to ſovereignty, which is inſtituted for the happineſs of mankind.—Jortin's Remarks on Eccleſiaſtical Hiſtory.

12. Cyrus had taken the wife of Tigranes, and aſked him what he would give, to ſave her from ſervitude? He replied, All that he had in the world, and his own life into the bargain. Cyrus, upon this, very generouſly reſtored her, and pardoned what had paſſed. All were full of his praiſes upon this occaſion, ſome commending the accompliſhments of his mind, others thoſe of his perſon. Tigranes aſked his wife, whether ſhe did not greatly admire him? "I never "looked at him," ſaid ſhe. "Not look at him!" returned he; "upon whom then did you look?" "Up-"on him," replied ſhe, "who offered his own life to "redeem me from ſlavery."—This charming example ſhould be copied into our behaviour in the houſe

of

of God; where we ſhould behold and contemplate the beauties and perfections of that bleſſed perſon alone, who actually did give his life a ranſom for us.—See Xenoph. Cyropæd. iii. 147.

13. When Conſtantine was inſtigated by his courtiers to make examples of the Arians, who had inſulted his ſtatues, he ſilenced them by raiſing his hand to his face, and ſaying, "For mine own part, I do not "feel myſelf hurt."

14. Would you ſee human vanity and miſery at the higheſt? Behold the globe of the world carried in proceſſion before the corpſe of the Emperor Charles VII. who, during the ſhort courſe of his wretched reign, could not keep poſſeſſion of one ſmall unfortunate province.

15. Victor Amadeus, tired of buſineſs and of himſelf, capriciouſly abdicating his crown, and a year afterwards as capriciouſly repenting, and deſiring to have it again, diſplayed fully the weakneſs of human nature, and how difficult it is to gratify the heart, either with or without a throne.

16. Claude Lorrain ſtudied his art in the open fields, where he frequently continued from the riſing to the ſetting ſun. He ſketched whatever he thought beautiful or ſtriking, and marked, in ſimilar colours, every curious tinge of light on all kinds of objects. Theſe were afterwards improved into landſcapes, univerſally allowed to be ſuperior to thoſe of all other artiſts who have painted in the ſame ſtyle. In like manner Shak-

ſpeare and Ben Jonſon travelled and aſſociated with all ſorts of people, to mark different *traits* in the characters and tempers of mankind, which were afterwards worked up into their inimitable plays. Every writer ſhould follow theſe examples, and take down thoughts as they occur in reading or converſing, to be ready for uſe afterwards, when he ſits down to compoſe.

17. To the haſty correctors of the *ſacred* text may be applied what an ingenious author has obſerved, when ſpeaking of the critics on *claſſical* writers.— "The learning of the ancients had been long ago "obliterated, had every man thought himſelf at li- "berty to corrupt the lines which he did not under- "ſtand." Adventurer, vol. ii. p. 189, No. 58.

18. Obſcurity of expreſſion is elegantly called, by Mrs. Montague, "that *miſt* common to the *eve* and "*morn* of literature, which in fact proves it is not at "its high meridian." See Eſſay on Shakſpeare, p. 286.

19. Some make the diſcharge of the Chriſtian miniſtry to conſiſt in aſſerting the rights of the church, and the dignity of their function; others, in a ſtrenuous oppoſition to the prevailing ſectaries, and a zealous attachment to the eſtabliſhed church government; a third ſort, in examining the ſpeculative points and myſtical parts of religion; few, in the mean time, conſidering either in what the true dignity of the miniſterial character conſiſts; or the only

end

end for which church government was at all established; or the practical influence, which can alone make speculative points worth our attention—the reformation of the lives of men, and the promotion of their truest happiness here and hereafter. Gilpin's Life, p. 160.

20. It is observed of King, bishop of London in 1611, that he was so constant in preaching, after he was a bishop, that he never missed a Sunday, when his health permitted. Biograph. Dict. from Fuller.

21. The morning after the massacre of Paris, when the streets were covered with the bodies of slaughtered men, women, and children, before they were thrown into the Seine, the Catholics bethought themselves of a *charitable* device, which was, to strip them naked, in order to distribute their bloody clothes *to the poor!* —Saint Foix, Histoire de l'Ordre du S. Esprit.

22. To the soul confined in this material world, but aspiring to another and a better, apply the following lines:

——————Pent in his cage
Th' imprison'd eagle sits, and beats his bars;
His eye is rais'd to heav'n. Tho' many a moon
Has seen him pine in sad captivity—
——————still he thirsts to dip
His daring pinions in the fount of light.

Poetical Epistle to Anstey, on the English Poets.

23. In treating of the human mind, and the management of it, the two great sources of illustration

 are

are *agriculture* and *medicine.*—Bacon's Advancement of Learning, vii. 3.—Our Saviour therefore so frequently applied to them (as the prophets had done before) for the illustration of his doctrine.

24. Champagne, a celebrated painter, was given to understand, he might have any thing from Cardinal Richelieu, if he would leave the service of the Queen Mother—"Why (said he) if the Cardinal could "make me a better painter, the only thing I am ambitious of, it would be something; but, since that "is impossible, the only honour I beg of his Eminency is the continuance of his good graces."

25. It was a saying of Lord Clarendon's father, that he never knew a man arrive to any degree of reputation in the world, who chose for his friends and companions persons in their qualities inferior, or in their parts not much superior to himself. And Huetius, I think, tells us, that as often as he heard of any one of very eminent character in the republic of letters, he never rested, till, by some means or other, he had obtained an introduction to his acquaintance; and this from his earliest youth.

26. It happened formerly that a Rotterdam produced an Erasmus. And it happened lately, as the General Evening Post (Mar. 14, 1771) informs us, that a goose hatched four-and-twenty Canary birds. But these are events that do not happen every day.

27. When the Mexican Emperor Gatimozin was put upon the rack by the soldiers of Cortes, one of his nobles, who lay in tortures at the same time, complained

complained piteously to his sovereign of the pain he endured. "Do you think, said Gatimozin, that I lie upon "roses?" The nobleman ceased moaning, and expired in silence.—When a Christian thinks his sufferings for sin, in sickness, pain, &c. intolerable, let him remember those of *his* Lord, endured patiently on that bed of sorrow, the *cross*; and he will think so no longer.

28. When Gatimozin, just taken, was brought into the presence of Cortes, he (Cortes) gave strict orders that the Mexican nobleman taken with the Emperor should be secured and strictly looked to, lest they should escape. "Your care, said Gatimozin, is needless; "they will not fly; they are come to die at the feet "of their sovereign!"—Such should be the disposition and resolution of the disciples and soldiers of Christ.

29. Little circumstances convey the most characteristic ideas; but the choice of them may as often paint the genius of the writer, as of the person represented.—Well exemplified in the instance of the Duchess of Marlborough.—See Royal and Noble Authors, vol. ii. 200.

30. Inscription (not perfectly Augustan) on the Earl of Shrewsbury's sword; "Sum Talboti, pro occidere "inimicos."—"I am Talbot's, for to slay his foes."

31. Wraxall, speaking of a cathedral, or abbey, in Livonia, demolished by the Russians, expresses himself thus:—"Posterity will see the standard wave "where the crucifix has stood, and the matin bell "will be succeeded by the trumpet."—P. 278.

32. In former times, when Lord Keeper North applied close to his studies, and spent his days in his chamber, he was subject to the spleen, and apprehensive of many imaginary diseases; and, by way of prevention, he went thick clad, wore leather skull-caps, and inclined much to physic. But now, when he was made attorney-general, and business flowed in upon him, his complaints vanished, and his skull-caps were destined to lie in a drawer, and receive his money.—Life of Lord Keeper North.

33. As men are preferred, their zeal and diligence often remit, instead of increasing. Urban III. thus inscribed a letter to Archbishop Baldwin—"Monacho *ferventissimo*, Abbati *calido*, Episcopo *tepido*, Archiepiscopo *remisso*."—"*Most fervent* as a Monk, *warm* as "an Abbot, *lukewarm* as a Bishop, *cold* as an Arch-"bishop."—Life of Baldwin in Biog. Britan.

34. To *instruct*, and to *govern*, are two things; and a man may do the former well, who does the latter very indifferently. It is part of Dr. Allestry's character, as drawn in his epitaph; "Episcopales infulas eâdem "industriâ evitavit, quâ alii ambiunt; cui rectius "visum Ecclesiam *defendere*, *instruere*, *ornare*, quam "*regere*."—"He shunned the mitre as industriously as "others seek it; he chose rather to *defend*, *edify*, and "*adorn*, than *govern* the Church."—Biog. Brit.

35. Bishop Andrews, when a lad at the University, used every year to visit his friends in London, and to stay a month with them. During that month, he constantly made it a rule to learn, by the help of a

master,

master, some language, or art, to which he was before a stranger. No time was lost.

36. When the same eminent person first became Bishop of Winton, a distant relation, a blacksmith, applied to him to be *made a gentleman*, i. e. to be ordained, and provided with a good benefice. No, said the Bishop, you shall have the best *forge* in the county; but—*every man in his own order and station.*

37. It was a good rule of Dr. Hammond's always to have a subject in hand; in which case he observed, that, whatever course of reading he happened to be in, he never failed of meeting with something to his purpose. For this reason, no sooner had he finished one sermon, or tract, but he immediately put another upon the stocks. Thus he was never idle, and all his studies turned to present account. He never walked out alone without a book, and one always lay open in his chamber, from which his servant read while he dressed or undressed himself. His Life by Fell, though written in a style far from clear and agreeable, is one of the most improving books I ever read.

38. Jordano (Luca) the painter was so engaged in his business, that he worked at it even on holydays. Being reproached for this by a brother artist—"Why," said he, "if I was to let my pencils rest, they would "grow rebellious, and I should not be able to bring "them to order, without trampling on them."—This man had so happy a memory, that he recollected the

manner

manner of all the great masters, and had the art of imitating them so well as to occasion frequent mistakes.

39. Grove, the Presbyterian, published in 1728 a funeral sermon on the Fear of Death. The subject was treated in so masterly a manner, that a person of considerable rank in the learned world declared, that, after reading it, he could have laid down and died, with as much readiness and satisfaction, as he had ever done any thing in his life.—Biog. Dict. art. *Grove.*—The sermon must have been a good one to have wrought such a persuasion: but how the persuasion would have kept its ground, had the person been taken at his word, and ordered to prepare for instant death, is another question.

40. Remarkable is the following passage of Josephus, relative to the wickedness of his countrymen before Jerusalem was besieged by the Romans—"That "time abounded with all manner of iniquity, so that "none was left undone: Yea, though one en"deavoured to invent some new villany, yet could "he invent none that was not then practised."

41. Sauveur, the French mathematician, when he was about to court his mistress, would not see her, till he had been with a notary, to have the conditions on which he intended to insist reduced into a written form; for fear the sight of her should not leave him enough master of himself. Like a true mathematician, he proceeded by rule and line, and made his calculations when his head was cool.

42. Alex-

42. Alexander ſent Phocion 100 talents.—"Why to "me, more than others?"—"Becauſe he looks upon "you as the only juſt and virtuous man."—"Then "let him ſuffer me to continue ſo."—Philip before had offered him a large ſum. He was preſſed to take it, if not for himſelf, yet for his children. "If my "children," cried Phocion, "reſemble me, the little "ſpot of ground, with the produce of which I have "hitherto lived, and which has raiſed me to the "glory you mention, will be ſufficient to maintain "them. If it will not, I do not intend to leave "them wealth, merely to ſtimulate and heighten "their luxury."

CHARITY.

1. In the world, no man liveth or worketh for himſelf alone; but every tradeſman, mechanic, huſbandman, &c, contributeth his labour and his ſkill towards ſupplying the different exigencies of the public, and rendering ſociety comfortable. So ought it to be among Chriſtians in the church, which is a body compoſed of many members, and requireth that each member ſhould perform its proper office for the benefit of the whole.

2. Among the ancient Romans there was a law kept inviolably, that no man ſhould make a public feaſt, except he had before provided for all the poor of his neighbourhood.—So the Goſpel—"Thou, when "thou makeſt a feaſt, call the poor," &c.—See Rule of Life, 166.

3. Let

3. Let him, who has not leisure or ability to penetrate the mysteries of the SS. take comfort in this saying of Austin: "Ille tenet et quod patet et quod latet "in divinis sermonibus, qui charitatem tenet in mori-"bus."—"He is master of all that is plain, and all that "is mysterious in the Scriptures, who is possest of the "virtue of charity."

4. The end of knowlege is charity, or the communication of it for the benefit of others. This truth may be finely illustrated by a passage in Milton. P. L. viii. 90 & seq.

——————Consider first, that great
Or bright infers not excellence: the earth,
Though, in comparison of heav'n, so small,
Nor glist'ring, may of solid good contain
More plenty than the sun that barren shines;
Whose virtue on itself works no effect,
But in the fruitful earth; there first receiv'd
His beams, unactive else, their vigour find.

5. It is very remarkable, that Chesterfield, that man of the world, that man of pleasure, places charity to the distressed at the head of rational pleasures.—See the Letter on Expenses, vol. ii. 800.

6. There is no state of life, which does not furnish employment for care and industry: the mean must serve the great out of necessity; and the great are equally bound to serve the mean out of justice and charity.—Heylyn, ii. 325.

7. At man's first creation, charity was the divine principle implanted in his heart by his Maker. The adversary,

adverſary, by temptation, diſplaced it, and left ſelf-love in its room, which was cheriſhed by man, to the deſtruction of himſelf and his poſterity. Thus a certain miſchievous bird repairs to the neſt of one that is harmleſs, and having devoured the eggs of the little innocent owner, lays one of her own in their place: this the fond fooliſh bird hatches with great aſſiduity, and, when excluded, finds no difference in the great ill-looking changeling from her own. To ſupply this voracious creature, the credulous nurſe toils with unuſual labour, no way ſenſible that ſhe is feeding an enemy to her race, and one of the moſt deſtructive robbers of her future progeny.—See Goldſmith, v. 264.

8. It is not eaſy to conceive, how much ſin and ſcandal is occaſioned by a ſevere quarrelſome temper in the diſciples of Chriſt. It ſtirs up the corruptions of thoſe with whom they contend; and leads others to think meanly of a profeſſion which has ſo little efficacy to ſoften and ſweeten the tempers of thoſe who maintain it.—Doddridge, Fam. Expoſ. ii. 186.

9. Bees never work ſingly, but always in companies, that they may aſſiſt each other.—An uſeful hint to Scholars and Chriſtians.

10. An abbé, remarkable for his parſimony, happened to be in company where a charitable ſubſcription was going round. The plate was brought to him, and he contributed his louis-d'or. The collector, not obſerving it, came to him a ſecond time. *I have put in*, ſaid he. *If you ſay ſo, I will believe you*, returned

the

the collector, *though I did not see it.—I did see it*, cried old Fontenelle, who was present, *but did not believe it.*

11. There are many deceptions concerning charity. 1. It may be practised on false motives; interest, custom, fear, shame, vanity, popularity, &c. 2. It is a mistake to imagine it will atone for a want of other virtues, or for a life of vice and dissipation.—See Dupré, Serm. iii. Crit. Review, April 1782, p. 260.—Mr. Law's character of *Negotius*. Voltaire says, "the effect "is the same, whatever be the motive." But surely the worth of every action must be estimated by the motive on which it is performed. He who attends me when I am sick, with a view to the making of my will, and getting my estate, is a very different man from him who does it only because he loves me. Yet the effect may be the same: I may be equally taken care of in either case. We are to be judged by one who knows the thoughts of our hearts, and will judge us accordingly. Charity made consistent with vice—Brown's Sermons, 278.——See Charity well described under the idea of Generosity, Fitzosborne's Letters, 123.

12. Mickle, the translator of the Lusiad, inserted in his poem an angry note against Garrick, who, as he thought, had used him ill, by rejecting a tragedy of his. Some time afterward, the poet, who had never seen Garrick play, was asked by a friend in town to go to King Lear. He went, and, during the first three acts, said not a word. In a fine passage of the fourth,

fourth, he fetched a deep ſigh, and, turning to his friend, "I wiſh," ſaid he, "the *note* was out of my "book!"—How often, alas, do we ſay and write bitter things of a man, on a partial and intereſted view of his character, which, if we knew it throughout, we ſhould wiſh unſaid or unwritten!

CHINESE.

1. It is an odd circumſtance, that when a man dies, among the Chineſe, the relations and friends wait *three days*, to ſee whether he will riſe again, before they put the corpſe into the coffin. Voyages and Travels, iv. 92, from Navarette. We are told, from the ſame author, that many in that country, in their life-time, get their coffin made, and give a treat to their acquaintance on the day it comes home. It is cuſtomary for the Emperor, in particular, to have his coffin ſome time with him in the palace. Many keep it in ſight for ſeveral years, and now and then go into it. Ibid.

2. It ſhould be in an Univerſity, as in the Empire of China, where "no huſbandman is ever idle, and "no land ever lies fallow." Ibid. 121.

3. Accompliſhments of every kind are acquired and preſerved by uſe and practice; and the Scholar and Chriſtian would do well to reflect upon a piece of diſcipline in the Chineſe armies, by which a ſoldier who ſuffers his arms to contract the leaſt *ruſt* is puniſhed on the ſpot with thirty or forty blows of the batoon.

batoon, Ibid. 286, from Le Compte, and Duhalde— 313, 261.

——Sulco attritus ſplendeſcere vomer.
GEORG. i. 46.

Worn in the furrow ſhines the burniſh'd ſhare.
DRYDEN.

4. In China, the aſpirants, in the literary way, are examined by the eminent men, for their degrees. The Emperor Kang Hi, finding matters did not go on as they ſhould do, took it into his head, one day, to examine the examiners, and ſent ſeveral of the old Dons packing into the provinces, for inſufficiency. "The dread of ſuch another examination," ſays our author, "keeps thoſe chiefs of the literati cloſe to "their ſtudies."

CHRISTIANITY.

1. WITH difficulty men are induced to give up their favourite opinions: ſtill harder is the taſk to draw them from their favourite vices.—Could a religion be leſs than divine, which cauſed the Heathen world to quit both?

2. "Religion," ſay ſome, "was invented by prieſts "and politicians, to keep the world in order." It is a good thing, then, for that purpoſe at leaſt. But the misfortune is, none of the ſuppoſed impoſtors of this kind have ever been named, who lived till *after* the general principles of religion were found diſſeminated among mankind, as the learned Stillingfleet ſhews

ſhews at large (Orig. Sac. b. i. chap. 1.) even from the teſtimonies of the Egyptians and Greeks themſelves.

3. The differences among Chriſtians, about leſſer matters, prove the truth of thoſe great and fundamental points in which they all agree.

4. The little effect which Chriſtianity hath on the lives of its profeſſors is frequently made an argument againſt it. So with regard to philoſophy, the ſame objection is thus put and anſwered in Cicero's Tuſc. Queſt. lib. ii. ſect. 5.—A. *Nonne verendum eſt igitur, ne philoſophiam falſâ gloriâ exornes? Quod eſt enim majus argumentum, nihil eam prodeſſe, quam quoſdam perfectos philoſophos turpiter vivere?* M. *Nullum verò id quidem argumentum eſt. Nam ut agri non omnes frugiferi ſunt qui coluntur, ſic animi non omnes culti fructum ferunt. Atque ut ager quamvis fertilis ſine culturâ fructuoſus eſſe non* poteſt, *ſic ſine doctrinâ animus: ita eſt utraque res ſine alterâ debilis.* See Lactant. De falſ. Sap. vol. iv. 226.

A. Is it not then to be feared, that you aſcribe to philoſophy a glory that does not belong to it? For what can afford a ſtronger argument of its inefficacy, than the vicious lives of ſome of its moſt learned profeſſors? *M.* That argument is not concluſive. For as agriculture cannot render all ſoils fruitful, ſo neither are all minds equally improved by inſtruction. Yet neither can any ſoil, nor any mind, bring forth good fruits by the unaſſiſted force of its natural fertility; but both muſt remain unproductive without the aid of cultivation.

5. In Conſtantinople behold the judgments of God on apoſtates from true religion, and corrupters of it: ſee Jews and Chriſtians perpetrating on each other the moſt enormous villanies, as the price of obtaining the favour of the Turks! At the ſame time behold the Greek prelates, even while groaning under the yoke of the oppreſſor, employing their time, their wealth, and their intereſt, in over-reaching and ſupplanting each other for a metropolitan ſee, or a patriarchate, at the court of that oppreſſor!

6. Chriſtianity has, in every age, produced good effects on thouſands and tens of thouſands, whoſe lives are not recorded in eccleſiaſtical hiſtory; which, like other hiſtory, is for the moſt part a regiſter of the vices, the follies, and the quarrels of thoſe who made a figure and a noiſe in the world. Socrates, in the cloſe of his work, obſerves, that, if men were honeſt and peaceable, hiſtorians would be undone for want of materials.—Jortin's Remarks, b. ii. ad fin.

7. Theft was unknown among the Caribbees, till Europeans came among them. When they loſt any thing, they ſaid innocently—"The Chriſtians have "been here!"

CHURCH.

1. THE enemies of the Church are encouraged to proceed in their attacks, by the timidity of her friends; as Lyſander, at the ſiege of Corinth, bade his men be of good courage, when he ſaw a hare run along upon the walls.

2. Learned

2. Learned and good men are often deterred from engaging the adverſaries of religion, more through fear of their ribaldry than their arguments; as Antipater's elephants, which beheld the apparatus of war unmoved, ran away at the grunting of the Megarenſian hogs.

3. To admit all the jarring ſects and opinions into the church by a *comprehenſion*, would be, as one well obſerves, to jumble together an indigeſted heap of contrarieties into the ſame maſs, and to make the *old chaos* the plan of a *new reformation*.

4. Thoſe clergymen, who betray the cauſe of their maſter, in order to be promoted in his church, are guilty of the worſt kind of ſimony, and pay their ſouls for the purchaſe of their preferments.

5. Hereſies ſeem, like comets, to have their periodical returns.

6. Some think variety of religions as pleaſing to God as variety of flowers. Now there can be but one religion which is true; and the God of truth cannot be pleaſed with falſehood, for the ſake of variety.

7. Nothing is more common than for a religious or political ſect to diſclaim a principle, and then reſume it under another form: as the *Circoncelliones* uſed no *ſwords*, becauſe God had forbidden the uſe of one to St. Peter; but they were armed with clubs, which they called the clubs of Iſrael, and with which they could break all the bones in a man's ſkin. See Le Beau, i. 170. See Jortin's Remarks on Eccl. Hiſt. iv. 388.

8. The heat and acrimony with which ſome men write againſt revelation remind one of the cruelties practiſed by the abovementioned fanatics, who covered the eyes of the Catholics that fell into their hands with *lime* diluted with *vinegar*. Ibid.

9. Apply to quarrels among Chriſtians the following lines, addreſſed by Adam to Eve, after their mutual accuſations and upbraidings:

> But riſe: let us no more contend, nor blame
> Each other, blam'd enough elſewhere; but ſtrive,
> In offices of love, how we may lighten
> Each other's burden in our ſhare of woe.

10. Upon viewing many of our places of worſhip in the country, one would be tempted to think the Church of England had adopted the maxim laid down in a neighbouring kingdom, "That cleanli-"neſs is not eſſential to devotion." A church of England lady once offered to attend the kirk there, if ſhe might be permitted to have the pew ſwept and lined. "The pew ſwept and lined!" ſaid Meſs John's wife, "my huſband would think it down-"right popery!"

11. If the intended reformation of our liturgy goes on, the reformers may hereafter bring us in a bill like that of the Cirenceſter painter:

Mr. Charles Terebee to Joſeph Cook, debtor.

	l.	*s.*	*d.*
To mending the Commandments, altering the Belief, and making a new Lord's Prayer, -	1	1	0

12. It is a principle advanced by Preſident Monteſquieu, that, where the magiſtrate is ſatisfied with the eſtabliſhed

established religion, he ought to repress the direct attempts towards innovation, and only grant a toleration to other sects.—B. xxv. ch. 10.—See Hume, vol. vii. p. 40. and 41.

13. Sir Matthew Hale used to say, "Those of the "separation were good men, but they had narrow "souls, or they would not break the peace of the "Church about such inconsiderable matters, as the "points in difference were."

14. Lord Clarendon, somewhere in his Life, makes this severe reflection—"That clergymen understand "the least, and take the worst measure of human af- "fairs, of all mankind that can read and write." Cited by Temple, in his Essay on the Clergy, p. 22. See his last chapter, On the service clergymen may do their country in matters civil and temporal.—The reason of the abovementioned circumstance it might be curious to investigate.

15. The person presiding over a church should diligently mark the very first starting of an error, or heresy, and employ a proper hand immediately to check and extinguish it; as, by order of the New River Company in London, a watchman is nightly fixed at such a height, near the river head, as to be able to overlook the whole town, and, on the momentary appearance of any conflagration, to turn the water full on the mains leading to the respective quarter, however remote the situation: by which wise and commendable measure, the water generally arrives at the place of destination before the

fleeteſt meſſenger.—Morning Chronicle, Jan. 27, 1781.

16. "As I do not check any ſuſpicions in my own "mind, I ſhall not eaſily be reſtrained from utter-"ing them; becauſe *I know not how I ſhall benefit "my country, or aſſiſt her counſels, by ſilent medita-"tions.*"—Pulteney, in Johnſon's Debates, vol. i. p. 5. A friend of the *church*, who is able to write or ſpeak, in theſe days, ſhould make the ſame reflections.

17. A right good man may be a very unfit magiſtrate: and, for diſcharge of a biſhop's office, to be well minded is not enough; no, not to be well learned alſo. Skill to inſtruct is a thing neceſſary, ſkill to govern much more neceſſary in a biſhop. It is not ſafe for the church of Chriſt, when biſhops learn what belongeth unto government as empirics learn phyſic, by killing of the ſick. Biſhops were wont to be men of great learning in the laws both civil and of the church; and while they were ſo, the wiſeſt men in the land for counſel and government were biſhops."—Hooker, vii. 24, p. 398.

COLLINS. (ANTHONY)

THIS perſon, on his death-bed, was under great anxiety, and, juſt before he expired, with a deep ſigh pronounced the following words—*Locke has ruined me!* His niece, who attended him at the time, related this circumſtance to Mr. Wogan, the pious author of an Eſſay on the Proper Leſſons; as he aſſured a friend

friend of mine, the Rev. Dr. Merrick of St. Ann's, Soho.

COMPOSITION.

1. Distension in the bowels is a ſign of a bad digeſtion. In an author it is a ſymptom of the ſame infirmity.

2. If a man's ſtudies are dry, his compoſitions will be inſipid. Diſtil a bone, and you will have a quantity of water.

3. He, that would write well in any tongue, muſt follow this counſel of Ariſtotle;—to think with the learned, but ſpeak with the common people, that theſe may underſtand, and thoſe approve him.—Aſcham, p. 57.

4. Aptneſs, knowlege, and uſe make all things perfect; but they muſt join forces, or nothing will be well done. The firſt is the gift of God; the ſecond we muſt have from others; the third we attain by our own diligence and labour.—p. 117.

5. The ſame arguments are quite different in their effects, when drawn up and urged by a man of genius. They go farther, and pierce deeper, like the ſhafts of Hercules, which, Heſiod tells us, were winged with eagles' feathers.

6. He, who would excel in any thing (oratory *e. g.*) muſt not ſerviſely copy any one orator throughout, but from different perſons ſelect the accompliſhments for which they are ſeverally eminent.

7. It was Cicero's opinion, that he, who would ſpeak well, muſt write much:

Caput autem est, quod (ut verè dicam) minime facimus, (est enim magni laboris, quem plerique fugimus) quàm plurimùm scribere.—De Orat.—But the principal point is one from which most of us shrink, on account of the labour that attends it; I mean frequent and much composition.

8. Depth of sentiment, illustrated by a bright imagination, is like the sea when the sun shines upon it and turns it into an ocean of light.

9. Illustrations are peculiarly beautiful, where they are fetched from something near akin to the subject which they are employed to adorn: as *e.g.* Sprat's observations on the age of learning among the Arabians—" Methinks that small spot of civil arts, " compared to their long course of ignorance before " and after, bears some resemblance with the coun- " try itself; where there are some few little vallies, " and wells, and pleasant shades of palm trees; but " those lying in the midst of deserts and unpassable " tracts of sand." Hist. of Roy. Soc. p. 45.

10. Zeuxis, the famous painter, before he sat down to a picture, used to animate his fancy by reading some passage in Homer relative to his subject.—A good hint to those who are about to compose in prose and verse.

11. Every man has a certain manner and character in writing and speaking, which he spoils and loses by a too close and servile imitation of another; as Bishop Felton, an imitator of Bishop Andrews, observed—" I had almost marred my own natural " trot,

"trot, by endeavouring to imitate his artificial am-"ble."—Wanley, 647.

12. It was a rule with Archbiſhop Williams, to give himſelf ſome recreation before he ſat down to compoſe, and that in proportion to the importance of the compoſition.—See his life in Lloyd's Worthies, p. 379.—Dr. H. More, after finiſhing one of his moſt laborious and painful works, exclaimed—"Now, for theſe three months, I will neither think "a wiſe thought, nor ſpeak a wiſe word, nor do "an ill thing."—Life in the Biog. Dict.

13. In an oration, one would wiſh that the whole ſhould be well compoſed, and ſuitable to the dignity of the ſubject. But let the progreſs to what is great and brilliant be gentle and gradual. Such is the rule and method of Nature in all her works. At the firſt dawning of the brighteſt day that ever ſhone, light and darkneſs were ſcarcely diſtinguiſhable. Lawſon, 380.

14. In compoſitions, young writers produce the moſt, but old ones the beſt, as Lord Bacon obſerves of grapes.—"The vine beareth more grapes when it "is young; but grapes that make better wine when "it is old; for that the juice is better concocted."

15. Style ſhould reſemble the atmoſphere of Italy, which "embelliſhes all objects by ſhewing them "with clearneſs; for which reaſon, its gulfs, its "woods, its caſcades, and its meads, have a grace "unknown beneath other ſkies." M. Sherlock's Letters, p. 21.

 16. The

16. The author of Hudibras had a common-place-book, in which he had reposited, not such events or precepts as are gathered by reading; but such remarks, similitudes, allusions, assemblages, or inferences, as occasion prompted, or meditation produced; those thoughts that were generated in his own mind, and might be usefully applied to some future purpose. Such is the labour of those who write for immortality. Johnson, i. 288.

17. Augustus loved correctness and accuracy in all his compositions, and never delivered his mind on any serious matter, even in his own family, without memorials or written notes. Ferguson, Rom. Hist.—A method practised and recommended by Bolingbroke and Chesterfield, to attain a habit of correctness in speaking.—So Bishop Atterbury of *writing*, "Let nothing, "though of a trifling nature, pass through your pen "negligently." Letters, i. 118.

CONSCIENCE.

1. A MAN reproached with a crime of which he knows himself to be innocent, should feel no more uneasiness than if he was said to be ill when he felt himself in perfect health.

2. When Cleomenes was on the point of taking a bribe from Aristagoras, his virtue was preserved by his daughter, a child of *nine years old*, who exclaimed, "Fly, father, or this stranger will corrupt "you."—Conscience would often perform this office for us, if we would attend to its admonitions.

3. The

3. The ſame power (conſcience) ſhould do for us, reſpecting our paſſions and appetites, what an attendant was ordered every day at dinner to do for Darius, after the burning of Sardis, reſpecting his enemies—cry out, *Remember the Athenians.*

CONTENTMENT.

1. WHEN Chriſt bade us limit our cares to the day that is paſſing over us, he conſulted our natural quiet no leſs than our ſpiritual welfare; ſince the chief ſources of moſt men's uneaſineſs are chagrin at what is paſt, and forebodings of what is to come. Whereas, "what is paſt ought to give us no un-"eaſineſs, except that of repentance for our faults; "and what is to come ought much leſs to affect us, "becauſe, with regard to us and our concerns, it is "not, and perhaps never will be."

2. Plutarch, ſpeaking of that inviolable friendſhip which ſubſiſted between Pelopidas and Epaminondas, ſays, "The true and only cauſe of this excellent "conduct was their virtue, which kept them, in "all their actions, from aiming at *wealth* and "*glory*, which fatal contentions are always attended "with *envy*; but being both equally inflamed with "a divine ardour to make their country proſperous "and happy by their adminiſtration, they looked "upon each other's ſucceſs as their own."

3. In general, as he obſerves, among the Grecians, the perſonal enmity borne by great men of the ſame city to each other, exceeded that which they bore

bore to the enemies of their country.—The ſame paſſions have operated in the ſame manner among Chriſtians; of which we have a remarkable inſtance at the ſiege of Conſtantinople by Mahomet II. when ſuch was the animoſity ſubſiſting between the Greeks and Latins, within the city, that one of the former declared, he had rather ſee a Turk's turban in Conſtantinople than a Cardinal's cap.

4. When old Diocleſian was called from his retreat, and invited to reſume the purple, which he had laid down ſome years before, "Ah! (ſaid he) if you "could ſee thoſe fruits and herbs at Salona, which "I cultivate with my own hands, you would never "talk to me of empire."

CONVERSATION AND COMPANY.

1. DR. ARBUTHNOT, in his book upon Aliment, tells us, (p. 7.) that, "in general, whatever be the "ſtate of the *tongue*, the ſame is that of the inward "coat of the *ſtomach*." For which reaſon phyſicians look at one to diſcover the foulneſs of the other. What propriety is there in that axiom of our Lord, "Out of the abundance of the *heart* the *mouth* "ſpeaketh!"

2. A man's *countenance* ſhould be well watched by him who would know his mind; for, in ſpite of all endeavours, one will very often be the index of the other. See Collier on the Aſpect: Eſſays, ii. 121.

3. A man's real ſentiments often diſcover themſelves

ſelves by *words* ſpoken on a ſudden, in drink, in anger, in pride, in grief.

4. The deepeſt deſigns are ſometimes made manifeſt by *deeds* of kindneſs done, without a viſible cauſe, to a man or to his dependents, ſecretly to gain him or them from him.

5. Wiſe and reſerved men are beſt expounded by knowing the *ends* they have in view, as ſuch work uniformly on a preconcerted plan; but weak and ſimple perſons by their *natures*, becauſe they do many things abſurdly, and without reaſon; as one, who had been a Pope's nuncio in a certain kingdom, when, upon his return, his opinion was aſked with regard to a ſucceſſor, gave his advice, "That in any "caſe his Holineſs ſhould *not* ſend one too wiſe; "becauſe," ſaid he, "no wiſe man would ever "imagine what they in that country were like to "do."

6. You will beſt learn a man's weakneſſes and faults from his enemies, his virtues and abilities from his friends, his hours and cuſtoms from his ſervants, his ſentiments and opinions from his confidents.

7. It is expedient to have an acquaintance with thoſe who have looked into the world, who know men, underſtand buſineſs, and can give good intelligence and good advice when they are wanted.

8. Knowlege is to be obtained from ſome men by being free and talkative, which provokes them to be ſo too; from others by reſervedneſs and taciturnity, which induce them to truſt and depoſit their ſecrets with us.

9. In

9. In all conferences and negotiations a watchful and preſent wit is neceſſary, to promote the main matter, and yet obſerve incidental circumſtances; as Epictetus gives it in precept, that every philoſopher ſhould ſay to himſelf, "I will do this alſo, and yet "go on in my courſe."

10. Of other men's affairs it may be ſometimes uſeful to know much, but it is always neceſſary to ſay little.—The emptieſt of all characters is a buſy-body:

Της πολυπραγμοσυνης ουδεν κενεωτερον αλλο.

11. It is difficult to account for the choice which ſome men make of their companions. Lycas, the Peripatetic, had a gooſe that lived with him, walked with him, attended him upon all occaſions, and, when it died, was buried as a brother, with burial *philoſophic*.—See Ælian. de Animal. lib. vii. c. 36.

12. Great abilities and fine accompliſhments are often concealed under the moſt unpromiſing appearance; as travellers have obſerved, that the mountains which contain within them mines of gold, ſilver, and precious ſtones, are generally barren.

13. Among the Athenians, the greateſt feſtal pleaſure conſiſted in a flow of learned, ſprightly and polite converſation, as agreeable, in a word, as uſeful and intereſting. The Banquet of Plato and that of Xenophon give us a model of the ordinary table-talk of the Athenians; and it was thus that they prevented the two extremes of licentious mirth and

irkſome

irksome weariness, which preside but too often at most long meals. Goguet, xi. 225.

14. Compliments uttered *pro forma*, by those that hate one, bring to mind the ceremonies used in Spain, where a captain never corrects his soldier without first asking his leave, and the Inquisition never burns a Jew without making an apology to him.

15. A man should be very well established in faith and virtue, who attempts to reclaim a witty and agreeable profligate: otherwise, he may become a convert instead of making one. Chapelle, a person of this character, was met one day in the street by his friend Boileau, who took the opportunity of mentioning to him his habit of drinking, and the consequences of it. Unfortunately, they were just by a tavern. Chapelle only desired they might step in there, and promised he would listen patiently and attentively. Boileau consented; and the event was, that, about one in the morning, they were carried home, dead drunk, and in separate coaches.

16. "I am no niggard according to my ability to "impart what I know; but it is where I find some "appetite: otherwise my most familiar friends, some "of them, are as ignorant of my notions as any "stranger; for, if they discover no stomach, I use "not to examine them, no not to offer them; and "it would be in vain.—Pauci enim inviti discunt. "Few learn against their will."—Mede, 811.—So again, 815—"I am not unwilling to communicate

"to

"to you most of my tow, [material—from *tow* or "*hemp*, for ropes], because I perceive you make some "account of them; for in the university where I "live, I know not a second man that understands "any thing concerning such mysteries, or desires to "be made acquainted with them."

17. I have somewhere met with an observation, that conversation, in the first part of the morning, is like a *dram*; it heats, and hurries, and muddles, and incapacitates for business, which should therefore be entered upon, previously to visiting and chit-chat, with a mind calm, and cool, and undisturbed.—I believe this is true.

18. Never *speak*, but when you have something to *say*—"Wherefore shouldest thou run, seeing thou "hast no tidings?"—See Bishop Butler's excellent Sermon on the *Tongue*.

COUNCIL.

1. WHAT Gregory Nazianzen says of ecclesiastical Synods, in his tract *de Differentiis Vitæ*, is remarkable: "*Mihi certum est deliberatumque, nunquam posthac an-"serum aut gruum temerè inter se pugnantium synodis "interesse.*"—"On this point my resolution is fixed, "never again to be present at synods of geese and "cranes, employed solely in fighting with each other." —And so Procopius, "*Se nullius synodi felicem vidisse "exitum*"—"That he had never seen good conse-"quences result from a synod."

2. Wise men, when they meet together in numbers,

bers, ſometimes make fooliſh determinations. Monteſquieu, in his Perſian Letters, ſpeaking of the quarrel of Ramus, which obliged the legiſlature of France to interpoſe, ſays—" It looks as if the heads of the " greateſt men *idiotized*, when they meet together." Letter cix.—The truth, perhaps, is, that intereſt, baſhfulneſs, indolence, or ſome other cauſe, occaſions men, who could give the beſt opinions, to withhold them, and yield to thoſe of others more forward and domineering.—See Jortin on the Various Motives by which the ſeveral Members of an Eccleſiaſtical Council may happen to be actuated. Remarks on Eccl. Hiſt. ii. 185.

COURAGE OF DIFFERENT SORTS.

WHEN Pelopidas was cited to be tried, that valour, which was haughty and intrepid in fight, forſook him before his judges. His air and diſcourſe, timid and low, denoted a man who was afraid of death. Contrary behaviour of Epaminondas.

CRITICISM LITERAL.

1. " I AM almoſt tired of it," ſaid Mr. Bryant to me, May 21, 1785. " It is often employed in removing " little inequalities on the ſurface, when I want to have " a *ſhaft* ſunk, and the rich *ore* drawn forth from the " mine within." He had been mentioning the new editions of Apollodorus, Virgil, &c. by the Germans, Heyne, &c.—May not the ſame obſervation be applied to *ſome* of the notes by Lowth, Blayney, and

T Newcome,

Newcome, on the SS. and to the *generality* of the various readings amaſſed by Kennicott?

2. Critics, by their ſeverity, infeſt authors, as the African ants do the Negroes; but like them anſwer one good purpoſe, by deſtroying all the carrion.

CUDWORTH.

His Collections for the remaining part of his Intellectual Syſtem, and Daniel's Weeks, in 3 vols. folio, after many adventures and mutilations, were lodged in the Britiſh Muſeum.—See an account of this matter in Crit. Review for May 1783, p. 391. Sold by Lord Maſham, pillaged by Dodd as Locke's, and thrown into a garret by Davis. The fate of poſthumous writings is treated by Johnſon in one of his papers; whence he deduces an argument for a man's working up his materials, and publiſhing them himſelf; not *collecting* in infinitum, and then leaving thoſe collections to be employed by the cook of his executor in ſingeing a gooſe.

DEATH.

1. There is ſomething very affecting in the words ſpoken by the gallant Sir Philip Sidney to his brother, juſt before his death, occaſioned by a wound received in battle—"Love my memory, cheriſh my friends; "but, above all, govern your will and affections by the "will and word of the Creator; in me beholding the "end of this world, with all her vanities."

2. Saint Aldegonde, a proteſtant in the Low Coun-

tries, when imprisoned under the Duke of Alva, tells us, that "for three months together he recommended "himself to God every night, as if that would be his "last; the Duke having twice ordered him to be put "to death in prison." Ought not every man to do this, as no man can be certain he shall awake on the morrow?—Gen. Dict.

3. In the journey of life, as in other journies, it is a pleasing reflection, that we have friends who are thinking of us at home, and who will receive us with joy when our journey is at an end.

4. The learned Grotius, at the approach of death, would gladly have exchanged all his learning and honour for the plain integrity of one Jean Urick, a devout poor man, who spent eight hours of his time in devotion, eight in labour, eight in sleep and other refreshments.—"*Proh! Vitam perdidi operosè nihil* "*agendo!*"—"Alas! I have wasted my time in being "very busy and doing nothing!"—See Doddridge, Fam. Expos. sect. 14.

5. We often indulge a melancholy pleasure, in thinking that we shall be remembered, and regretted, after our death. How little is to be built on such imaginations, we may learn from the example of Queen Elizabeth, who, when she had closed a long and glorious reign with her life, "was in four days' time as "much forgotten, as if she had never existed, by all "the world, and even by her own servants."—See Carte's Hist. iii. 708.

6. When Gesner found his last hour approaching, he

gave orders to be carried into his *ſtudy*, that he might meet death in a place which had been moſt agreeable to him all his life.

7. When Mr. Paſchal obſerved any of his friends to be afflicted at ſeeing the ſickneſs and pain he underwent, he would ſay—" Do not be ſo concerned for " me. Sickneſs is the natural ſtate of a Chriſtian, be- " cauſe by it we are what we ought always to be, " in a ſtate of ſuffering evils, mortified to the pleaſures " of ſenſe, exempt from all thoſe paſſions which work " upon us as long as we live, free from ambition or " avarice, and in a conſtant expectation of death. " And is it not a great happineſs to be by neceſſity " in that ſtate one ought to be in, and to have " nothing elſe to do, but humbly and peaceably to " ſubmit to it ?"—This is a noble, a juſt, a comfortable ſpeculation.

8. It was a ſaying among the Brachmans, that our life ought to be conſidered as a ſtate of *conception*, and death as a *birth* to a true and happy life.—This thought ſeems juſt, and capable, on the Chriſtian plan, of being improved into a curious and uſeful ſpeculation. —See Biograph. Dict. art. *Gymnoſophiſts*.

9. When we riſe freſh and vigorous in the morning, the world ſeems freſh too, and we think we ſhall never be tired of buſineſs or pleaſure. But by that time the evening is come, we find ourſelves heartily ſo; we quit all its enjoyments readily and gladly; we retire willingly into a little cell; we lie down in darkneſs, and reſign ourſelves to the arms of ſleep, with

with perfect ſatisfaction and complacency.—Apply this to youth and old age, life and death.

10. Apply to the death of an afflicted Chriſtian the beautiful lines of the poet, on the heartfelt pleaſure of finding oneſelf at home, after a toilſome journey:

> O quid ſolutis eſt beatius curis?
> Quum mens onus reponit, ac *peregrino*
> Labore feſſi venimus larem ad noſtrum,
> Deſideratoque acquieſcimus lecto.—
> Hoc eſt, quod unum eſt pro laboribus tantis.

11. Young, healthy, and ſtrong as we may now be, yet a little while, and we ſhall become qualified to join the chorus of the Spartan old men;

> Αμμες ποτ' ημεν αλκιμοι νεανιαι.—

12. When ſickneſs and ſorrow come upon a Chriſtian, and order him to prepare for death, he ſhould be able to ſay, in the words of Æneas,

> Nulla mihi nova nunc facies inopinaque ſurgit.
> Omnia præcepi, atque animo mecum ante peregi.
>
> Æn. lib. vi. 104.

> ———No terror to my view,
> No frightful face of danger, can be new.
> Inur'd to ſuffer, and reſolv'd to dare,
> The fates, without my pow'r, ſhall be without my care.
>
> Dryden, 155.

13. Adeon' rem rediiſſe, ut, qui mihi conſultum eſſe optumè velit, PATREM extimeſcam, ubi in mentem ejus. ADVENTI venit? Quod ni fuiſſem incogitans, ita eum expectarem ut par fuit!—Phorm. act. i. ſc. 3.

Is it come to this?
My father, Phædria!—my best friend!— that I
Should tremble, when I think of his return!
When, had I not been inconsiderate,
I, as 'tis meet, might have expected him!

COLMAN.

14. Cum tuba magna sonum dederit, cum venerit hora
Judicii, inter oves da mihi, Christe, locum.
Sis mihi, sis *Jesus*, ne me maledictio tangat;
Dulcis in aure sonet vox, " Benedicte, veni!"

DIETERIC. ii. 581.

15. A Christian may say of death, what Orestes, in Sophocles, says of the report of being dead:

Τι γαρ με λυπει τεθ' οτ' αν λογω θανων,
Εργοισι σωθω, κα' ξενεγκωμαι κλεος;

ELECTRA, 59.

Why should this grieve me, that in words I die,
When I in deeds am saved, and by them rais'd
To glory?

POTTER.

16. They, who have done much, pride themselves in a short epitaph; they, who have done little, in a long one.

17. The different ranks and orders of mankind may be compared to so many streams and rivers of running water. All proceed from an original small and obscure; some spread wider, travel over more countries, and make more noise in their passage, than others; but all tend alike to an ocean, where distinction ceases, and where the largest and most celebrated rivers are equally

equally loſt and abſorbed with the ſmalleſt and moſt unknown ſtreams.

18. Immatura peri; ſed tu felicior annos
Vive tuos, conjux optime, vive meos.

I died untimely; happier doom be thine;
Live out thy years, dear huſband! live out mine.

19. *On viewing the Deanry Houſe, by Dr. Smith, late Dean of Cheſter.*

Within this pile of mould'ring ſtones
The Dean hath laid his wearied bones;
In hope to end his days in quiet,
Exempt from nonſenſe, noiſe, and riot;
And paſs, nor teas'd by fool nor knave,
From this ſtill manſion to his grave.
Such there, like richer men's, his lot
To be in four days' time forgot.

See his Poetic Works and Life.

20. It is an evil diſpoſition in ſome men to revile and publiſh the faults of thoſe who are no longer alive to anſwer for themſelves. It is the diſpoſition of vultures, jackalls and hyænas, who prey upon carcaſſes, and root up the dead.

DESPAIR.

The moſt tremendous circumſtance recorded of that moſt dreadful ſcourge the plague of Athens is, that the inſtant a perſon was ſeized he was ſtruck with deſpair, which quite diſabled him from attempting his cure.

DEVOTION.

1. He, who ſeldom thinks of heaven, is not likely to get thither; as the only way to hit the mark is to keep the eye fixed upon it.

2. The ſoldier, ſaith Xenophon, who firſt ſerves God, and then obeys his captain, may confidently hope to overcome his enemy.—The caſe is the ſame in ſpirituals.

3. The Veſtal Virgins were wont to ſpend ten years in learning their religion, ten years in practiſing it, and ten years in teaching the young Veſtals.

4. He, who hath his thoughts about him, can enjoy no bodily pleaſure while he thinks his ſoul is in danger of hell fire. But the reflection that all is right with reſpect to another world doubles every joy we can taſte in this. As Livy tells us of Paulus Æmilius, who had vanquiſhed Perſeus, but for a while thought he had loſt his ſon Scipio—*Ne ſincero gaudio frueretur, cura de minore filio ſtimulabat.* When his ſon returned alive and well, *Tunc demum, recepto ſoſpite filio, victoriæ tantæ gaudium conſul ſenſit.* Lib. xliv. ſect. 44.—His anxiety reſpecting his youngeſt ſon prevented his ſatisfaction from being complete. But, when his ſon returned alive and well, then at laſt the Conſul opened his mind to the full enjoyment of ſo great a victory.—The pleaſures of ſenſe are pleaſures only to the virtuous, and the Chriſtian, after all, turns out to be the true Epicure.

5. Boer-

5. Boerhaave, through life, consecrated the first hour after he rose in the morning to meditation and prayer; declaring, that from thence he derived vigour and aptitude for business, together with equanimity under provocations, and a perfect conquest over his irascible passions. "The sparks of calumny," he would say, "will be presently extinct of themselves, unless "you blow them—

("*Spreta exolescunt; si irascare, ignita videntur.*)

"and therefore, in return, he chose rather to com-"mend the good qualities of his calumniators (if they "had any) than to dwell upon the bad."—Life, p. 53.

6. To our Saviour and his commands may be applied, with propriety, what Hamlet, in Shakspeare, says of the injunctions of his father's ghost—

——Remember thee!—
Yea, from the table of my memory
I'll wipe away all trivial fond records,
All saws of books, all forms, all pressures past,
That youth and observation copied there;
And thy commandment all alone shall live
Within the book and volume of my brain,
Unmixt with baser matter.——

7. To one who knows much of religion, and practises little, may be applied what Milton says of Satan perched on the tree of life—

————Nor on the virtue thought
Of that life-giving plant, but only us'd
For prospect, what, well us'd, had been the pledge
Of immortality; so little knows

Any,

Any, but God alone, to value right
The good before him, but perverts beſt things
To worſt abuſe, or to their meaneſt uſe.

P. L. iv. 196.

8. Lord Aſtley, before he charged, at the battle of Edgehill, made this ſhort prayer—"O Lord, thou "knoweſt how buſy I muſt be this day. If I forget "thee, do not thou forget me!" There were certainly, ſays Hume, much longer prayers ſaid in the parliamentary army; but I doubt if there was ſo good an one. Vol. vii. p. 65.

9. The divine, who ſpends all his time in ſtudy, and contemplation on objects ever ſo ſublime and glorious, while his people are left uninſtructed, acts the ſame part the eagle would do, that ſhould ſit all day ſtaring at the ſun, while her young ones were ſtarving in the neſt.

10. Dr. Ogden's ſecret for rendering the commandments eaſy is—Love. The ſaying of Madam Chevreuſe is true in the *higheſt* ſenſe. "Without love, "you can never rely on the heart of a perſon at a "minute's warning; you can never inſpire it with "that fervour and vivacity ſo neceſſary in whatever "you wiſh to obtain."

11. Apply to the Bible theſe two lines of Tibullus;

Te ſpectem, ſupremà mihi cum venerit hora,
Te teneam moriens, deficiente manu!

and the following of Pythagoras;

Ταῦτα πονει, ταυτ' εκμελετα, τουτων χρη εραν σε,
Ταυτα σε της θειης αρετης εις ιχνια θησει.

12. Aben

12. Aben Ezra, on Exod. xxxviii. 8. extols the generosity of thofe women who devoted to the conftruction of a holy veffel (the laver) thofe utenfils of felf-love (their brazen mirrors) for which the perfons of their fex have fo great an inclination, and who fhowed, by fuch a facrifice, that they preferred the fervice of God to the pleafures and vanities of the world.—Saurin, Diff. 466.

Thomas Aquinas's Prayer before Study.

Ineffably wife and good Creator, illuftrious original, true fountain of light and wifdom, vouchfafe to infufe into my underftanding fome ray of thy brightnefs, thereby removing that two-fold darknefs, under which I was born, of fin and ignorance.

Thou, that makeft the tongues of infants eloquent, inftruct, I pray thee, my tongue likewife; and pour upon my lips the grace of thy benediction.

Give me quicknefs to comprehend, and memory to retain; give me happinefs in expounding, a facility in learning, and a copious eloquence in fpeaking.

Prepare my entrance on the road of fcience, direct me in my journey, and bring me fafely to the end of it, even happinefs and glory, in thine eternal kingdom, through Jefus Chrift our Lord.—See the Latin.

DISPUTATION.

1. Disputation makes us ready and expert in uſing the knowlege we have, but ſufficeth not for the acquiſition of more. It is *exerciſe*, but not *food*.—Hiſt. of R. S. p. 18.

2. It is but too much a cuſtom to give ill names to thoſe who differ from us in opinion. Dr. Hammond mentions, as a humorous inſtance of it, that when a Dutchman's horſe does not go as he would have him, he in great rage calls him an *Arminian*.

DUELLING.

From the Will of Colonel Thomas, dated London, September 3, 1783.

" I am now called upon, and, by the rules of what " is called honour, forced into a perſonal interview " with Col. Gordon. God only can know the event; " and into his hands I commit my ſoul, conſcious " only of having done my duty. In the firſt place I " commit my ſoul to Almighty God, in hopes of his " mercy and pardon for the irreligious ſtep I now (in " compliance with the unwarrantable cuſtoms of this " wicked world) put myſelf under the neceſſity of " taking."

ECCLE-

ECCLESIASTICUS.

The late Sir Edward Dering used to say, "He "did not pretend to underſtand much of the Bible, "but he was ſure the gentleman who wrote that book "knew the world as well as any man that ever lived "in it." Sept. 29, 1782. There is more good ſenſe, and are better precepts for the conduct of life, than in all the morality of the heathen. Dr. Campbell, Biog. Brit. iii.215.—It is pity but a ſmall and fair edition of the Greek were printed for the uſe of ſcholars and preachers.

ECSTASIES.

There is a ſet of Mahometan heretics, who excuſe themſelves from going the pilgrimage to Mecca, affirming, that the purity of their ſouls, their ſublime contemplations, &c. ſhew them Mecca and Mahomet's tomb, without ſtirring out of their cells.—They are called Ebrbuharites.

EDUCATION.

1. So important a concern did the right education of children appear to Auguſtus Cæſar, that, when maſter of the world, he himſelf attended to that of his grandchildren. *Nepotes et literas, et alia rudimenta, per ſe plerumque docuit: ac nihil æque laboravit quam ut imitarentur chirographum ſuum. Neque cænavit*

cœnavit una, nisi ut imo lecto assiderent: neque iter fecit, nisi ut vehiculo anteirent, aut circa adequitarent. Sueton. August. 64. Ernest.—He himself instructed his grandsons in the rudiments of literature and science, and was peculiarly assiduous to teach them to imitate his own hand-writing. They always supped in his company, and were placed on the lowest couch; and on all his journies they either preceded him in another carriage, or rode on horseback by his side.

So in the same place, with respect to the girls—*Filiam & neptes ita instituit, ut etiam lanificio assuefaceret, vetaretque loqui aut agere quidquam, nisi propalam, & quod in diurnos commentarios referretur.*—His daughter and grand-daughters by his direction were carefully taught to spin; and they were habituated to speak and act on all occasions so openly, that every word and deed might be entered in a journal.

2. The Neapolitan jockies break in their colts with so rough a hand, and such want of temper, that the animal's spirit is quite beaten down: I once saw one thrown down by a brutal fellow, and almost strangled.—Travels in the Sicilies.

3. Such is the force of education and habit, that there is hardly a quaker to be found, young or old, who has not the command of the irascible passions. Why can it not be so with others?

4. "In the schools of philosophy anciently," says Goldsmith (i. 339.) "were taught the great maxims

"of

"of true policy; the rules of every kind of duty; the "motives for a true discharge of them; what we owe "to our country; the right use of authority; wherein "true courage consists; in a word, the qualities that "form the good citizen, statesman, and great cap-"tain; and in all these Epaminondas excelled."—See his character there drawn, for eloquence, knowlege, modesty: he knew not what it was to be ostentatious. Spintherus said of him, "he had never met "with a man, who knew more or spoke less."—O that our young statesmen and officers would copy him!—Agesilaus, himself a great commander, seeing him passing at the head of his infantry, after having attentively considered and followed him with his eyes a long time, could not help crying out, in admiration of him, *O the wonder-working man!*

5. Indulgence, when shown in too great a degree by parents to children, generally meets with a bad return. It seems to awaken a strange malignity in human nature towards those who have thus *displayed* an injudicious fondness. Children delight in vexing such parents. There may be two reasons—1. It makes them feel foolish, to be so *cockered* and teased with kindness.—2. It discovers a weakness, over which they can insult and triumph. But whatever may be the cause, it furnishes an argument to parents, why they should never practise this behaviour towards their children.—The present miseries of France arose under the government of a kind and indulgent monarch.

6. We

6. We are all in a ſtate of education for the kingdom of heaven, *in ſtatu pupillari*, upon earth: the education of our immortal ſpirits is our ſole buſineſs. For this we are formed in the womb, and paſs through the ſeveral ſtages of infancy, youth, and manhood. Studies of the ſchool fit us for manhood; ſo manhood, and the ſeveral occupations conſequent upon it, is a ſtate of preparation for ſomething elſe. Faith and practice are the end of wiſdom and knowlege, and prepare us for the converſation, ſociety and intercourſe of angels, as wiſdom and knowlege prepare us for the converſation of men.

7. Milton's plan of education has more of ſhow than value. He does not recommend thoſe ſtudies to boys, which, as Cicero ſays, *adoleſcentiam alunt*. Inſtead of laying a ſtreſs on ſuch authors as open and enlarge a young underſtanding, he preſcribes an early acquaintance with geometry and phyſics: but theſe will teach no generous ſentiments, nor inculcate ſuch knowlege as is of uſe at all times and on all occaſions. Mathematics and aſtronomy do not enter into the proper improvement and general buſineſs of the mind—ſuch ſciences do not apply to the manners, nor operate upon the character. They are extraneous and technical. They are uſeful; but uſeful as the knowlege of his art is to the artificer. An excellent writer obſerves, we are perpetually moraliſts, but we are geometricians only by chance. Our intercourſe with intellectual nature is neceſſary; our ſpecula-

tions

tions upon matter are voluntary and at leiſure. Phyſical knowlege is of ſuch rare emergence, that one man may know another half his life, without being able to eſtimate his ſkill in hydroſtatics or aſtronomy: but his moral and prudential character immediately appears. Thoſe authors therefore are to be read at ſchools, that ſupply moſt axioms of prudence, moſt principles of moral truth, and moſt materials for converſation; and theſe purpoſes are beſt ſerved by poets, orators, and hiſtorians. (Warton, 117.)—Milton afterwards reaſoned better on this ſubject, P. L. viii. 191.

EIDER.

THIS is a bird in Iceland. It lays moſt eggs in rainy weather: as ſoon as the young ones are out of the egg, the mother leads them to the ſhore: when they come to the water ſide, ſhe takes them upon her back, and ſwims with them for the ſpace of a few yards, when ſhe dives; and the young ones, who are left floating on the water, are obliged to take care of themſelves. So the parent carries children into the world, *dives*, and leaves them to combat with its waves.—Van Troil's Letters.

ELOQUENCE.

FOR the difference between Cicero's eloquence and that of ſome who ſtyled themſelves *Attic*, dealing in ſhort ſentences and turns, like Pliny afterwards, ſee Middleton's Life of Cicero, iii, 332.—Is there not at this time a ſimilar decline in England from the true, nervous flowing eloquence—particularly of the pulpit? Dr. *Blair* is the *Pliny*.

EMPLOYMENT.

1. Employment is the beſt cure for *grief*; as Tacitus tells us of Agricola, that, when he had loſt his ſon, *in luctu bellum inter remedia erat*—he reſorted to war as a remedy againſt grief. In. Vitâ, ſect. 28.

2. Cheerfulneſs is the daughter of *employment*; and I have known a man come home in high ſpirits from a funeral, merely becauſe he had had the management of it.

3. Anxiety and melancholy are beſt diſpelled and kept at a diſtance by *employment*. On the day before the battle of Pharſalia, Plutarch tells us, when dinner was ended in the camp, while others either went to ſleep, or were diſquieting their minds with apprehenſions concerning the approaching battle, Brutus employed himſelf in writing till the evening, compoſing an epitome of Polybius.

ENEMIES.

The uſe to be made of their revilings, &c. is thus ſet forth by biſhop Taylor: "Our enemies "perform accidentally the office of friends: they tell "us "us our faults, with all their deformities and aggra-"vations: they offer us affronts, which exercise our "patience, and restrain us from scandalous crimes, "lest we become a *scorn and reproof to them that hate "us*. And it is not the least of God's mercies, that "he permits enmities among men, by means of which "our failings are reproved more sharply, and cor-"rected with more severity and simplicity than they "would otherwise be. The gentle hand of a friend "is more apt to bind our wounds up, than to probe "them and make them smart."—See Life of Christ, fol. p. 541.

ENVY.

Envy pines at the applauses which virtue receives; as Plutarch tells us, that when Titus Flaminius, by conquering Philip, had restored the Grecian cities to their freedom, the acclamations of the people assembled at the celebration of the Isthmian games caused the crows, as they were flying over the stage, to drop down dead upon it.—In Vitâ Flamin.

EPAMINONDAS.

HIS HUMILITY AND PATRIOTISM.

His enemies, jealous of his glory, with a design to affront him, caused him to be elected the city scavenger. He accepted the place with thanks, and declared, that, instead of deriving honour from his office, he would give it dignity in his turn.—I dare ſay kennels never were ſo well ſcoured before.

EVIL.

ORIGIN OF IT.

1. The philoſophers of old ſaw the world overflowed by a torrent of corruption, as the Egyptians beheld their country every year deluged by the Nile. Both were equally to ſeek for the ſpring-head and cauſe of theſe effects.

2. The ancient philoſophers ſpeak of man's degeneracy, with its conſequences, in a much better way than many, who pretend to be friends to reaſon and to Chriſt, but are ſo to neither, while they make it their buſineſs to extenuate the fall of man, and the corruption introduced thereby into human nature. See ſome wonderful citations in Orig. Sacr. iii. 3.

EULER.

Euler lived at Peterſburgh during the adminiſtration of Biron, one of the moſt tyrannical miniſters that ever breathed. On the philoſopher's coming to Berlin, after the tyrant's death, the late Queen of Pruſſia, who could hardly get a word out of him, aſked him the reaſon of his ſilence.—"Becauſe," ſaid he, "I come from a place where if a man ſays a word "he is hanged."

EURI-

EURIPIDES.

Many of the Athenians, during their captivity at Syracuſe, owed the good uſage they met with to the ſcenes of Euripides, which they repeated to their captors, who were extremely fond of them. On their return they went and ſaluted that poet as their deliverer, and informed him of the admirable effects wrought in their favour by his verſes. Scarce any circumſtance could be more pleaſing and flattering than this teſtimony.

EXERCISE.

The moſt common cauſe of fatneſs is too great a quantity of food, and too ſmall a quantity of motion; in plain Engliſh, gluttony and lazineſs. I am of opinion, that ſpare diet and labour will keep conſtitutions, where this diſpoſition is ſtrongeſt, from being fat. You may ſee in an army forty thouſand foot ſoldiers without a fat man amongſt them: and I dare affirm, that by plenty and reſt twenty of the forty ſhall grow fat.—Arbuthnot.

FACTION.

While a faction entertain their old principles, it is folly to ſuppoſe they will not, when opportunity ſerves, return to their old practices. *Quæro, quid facturi fuiſſetis? Quanquam quid facturi fueritis non*

 dubitem,

dubitem, cum videam quid feceritis. Cic. pro Ligario. The fine lady will be the *cat* ſhe was, when a *mouſe* runs before her.

FAITH.

1. In the affairs of this world, as huſbandry, trade, &c. men *know* little and *believe* much. In the affairs of another world, they would know every thing, and believe nothing.

2. If we are rationally led, upon clear principles and good evidence, to believe a point, it is no objection that the point is myſterious and difficult to be accounted for. A man in his ſenſes will not deny the phænomenon of the harveſt moon, becauſe he cannot ſolve it.

3. When the Jews attribute the miracles of our Saviour to the power of magic, they prove the facts, without diſproving the cauſe to which we aſcribe them.

4. Enthuſiaſts require *aſſurance*, and philoſophers will be content with nothing leſs than *demonſtration*. But how is it in the affairs of common life? The ſoldier does not aſk a demonſtration, whether, in the day of battle, he ſhall be crowned with victory, or covered with diſgrace; but, fearing the worſt, and hoping the beſt, he minds his duty: the merchant does not want a demonſtration concerning the returns of his trade: the huſbandman cannot promiſe himſelf a plentiful crop, proportioned to his labour and induſtry.

duſtry. No man can aſſure himſelf that he ſhall ſee another day: but every one minds his buſineſs as if he knew for certain that he ſhould: and he would be thought a downright madman that acted otherwiſe.

5. Faith is reckoned for a virtue, and rewarded as ſuch, becauſe, though it be an aſſent of the underſtanding upon proper evidence, the will hath a great ſhare in facilitating or withholding ſuch aſſent. For the ſtrongeſt evidence will be nothing to him who does not enquire diligently after it, judge honeſtly and impartially of it without paſſion or prejudice, and frequently conſider and reflect upon it from time to time through life, that it may produce its fruits, and be a principle of action. *Theſe* are acts of the will, in a man's power to perform or not to perform, and therefore rewardable. On the performance or non-performance of theſe, not on the evidence, which is always the ſame, it depends, whether a man ſhall believe, or not: and here we muſt look for the true reaſons why one man is a Chriſtian, and another an Infidel.

6. Rational evidence may ſatisfy men's minds of the truth of a doctrine, but it is grace which muſt bring them to obey and adhere to it, by convincing them of its excellence, by ſubduing the deſires and affections that militate againſt it, and ſo improving an *hiſtorical* into a *ſaving* faith.

7. "Experience (ſaith Mr. Hume) is our only guide

"in matters of fact?" Doth he mean our own experience or that of others? If our own, we are to believe nothing but what we ourſelves have ſeen parallel inſtances of; if that of others, we depend for that upon *teſtimony*, which alone informs us, there has been in paſt ages an eſtabliſhed order and courſe of nature, and at certain times a violation or ſuſpenſion of them.

8. There are many people who cannot ſee; there are more, perhaps, who will not. It is remarked of the elder Scaliger, that, in his confutation of Cardan, he would not read the ſecond edition of the book *de Subtilitate*, in which were made a great number of corrections, leſt he ſhould be deprived of many occaſions of triumphing over his adverſary. Gen. Dict. Scaliger.—See another inſtance in Jones's Eſſay, p. 191.

9. Infidelity is often puniſhed with credulity. The prediction of a mad life-guard-man was attended to in London by thoſe who never heeded the prophecies of Iſaiah, or Jeremiah; and an impudent mountebank ſold a large cargo of pills, which, as he told the people, were *excellent againſt earthquakes*.

10. The deiſt will not believe in Revelation till every difficulty can be ſolved. The atheiſt will not believe in the being of a God, but upon the ſame terms. They muſt both die in their unbelief. They ſhould believe upon ſufficient evidence, and truſt God for the reſt. The atheiſt *e. g.* cannot reconcile

cile the notion of a God with the exiſtence of evil. But there is ſufficient evidence for the exiſtence of both. Here let us reſt: God has his reaſons for permitting evil, or he would not have permitted it. If he has been pleaſed to diſcover them in his word, or if we can diſcover them by a view of things, well: if not, ſtill, reaſons there are; and, what we cannot know now, we ſhall know hereafter.

11. No *cloud* can overſhadow a true Chriſtian, but his faith will diſcern a *rainbow* in it.

12. Firſt Tim. iv. 6. *Nouriſhed up in the words of faith.*—"It is one thing for a man to enlighten "his underſtanding, to fill his imagination, and to load "his memory; and another to nouriſh his heart with "it. A man nouriſhes himſelf with it, if he live upon "it; and he lives upon it, if he change it into his "own ſubſtance, if he practiſe it himſelf, if he render "it proper and familiar unto himſelf, ſo as to make it "the food and nouriſhment with which he ought to "feed others."—Queſnel in loc.

FALSE LEARNING.

1. Some people rate the modern improvements in religious knowlege by the volumes of metaphyſical ſubtilties written upon the ſubject; as the Emperor Heliogabalus formed an eſtimate of the greatneſs of Rome, from ten thouſand pounds' weight of cobwebs which had been found in that city.

2. Two

2. Two learned phyſicians and a plain honeſt countryman, happening to meet at an inn, ſat down to dinner together. A diſpute preſently aroſe between the two doctors, on the nature of aliment, which proceeded to ſuch a height, and was carried on with ſo much fury, that it ſpoiled their meal, and they parted extremely indiſpoſed. The countryman, in the mean time, who underſtood not the cauſe, though he heard the quarrel, fell heartily to his meat, gave God thanks, digeſted it well, returned in the ſtrength of it to his honeſt labour, and at evening received his wages. Is there not ſometimes as much difference between the *polemical* and *practical* Chriſtian?

3. Ariſtotle, in his Metaphyſics, diſputes againſt certain philoſophers, who, it ſeems, held that a thing might *be*, and *not be*, at the ſame time.

4. Many parts of what is called *learning* reſemble the man's horſe, which had but two faults; he was hard to catch, and good for nothing when he was caught. —See Warton's Preface to Theocritus, p. 17.

————Fools ſhall be pull'd
From wiſdom's ſeat; thoſe baleful unclean birds,
Thoſe lazy owls, who, perch'd near fortune's top,
Sit only watchful with their heavy wings
To cuff down new-fledg'd virtues, that would riſe
To nobler heights, and make the grove harmonious.

Pierre, of lazy Senators, in Venice Preſerved.

5. The ſcience called Metaphyſics ſeems never to have been of ſervice to true religion, but only to have obſcured

obſcured and darkened its truths, which, under that cover, have often been ſtolen away by its enemies. May it not be compared to the *miſt*, or *fog*, deſcribed by Homer, as ſpread on the tops of the hills?

Ποιμεσιν ȣτι φιλην, κλεπτῃ δε τε νυκτος αμεινω.—Il. γ. 11.

Swift-gliding miſts the duſky fields invade,
To thieves more grateful than the midnight ſhade.
POPE's Il. b. iii. v. 17.

6. Superſtition often leads to Atheiſm. Many Turks are Epicureans; and in countries where Popery prevails, the *philoſophers*, as they affect to call themſelves, are running apace into Materialiſm. When a man has been cheated by a rogue pretending to honeſty, he is apt too haſtily to conclude, there is no ſuch thing as honeſty in the world.

7. Magic was originally nothing more than the application of natural philoſophy to the production of ſurpriſing but yet natural effects. Chemiſts had opportunities of being beſt acquainted with the elements and their operations, and were the greateſt magicians, and reputed conjurers.

8. Sir Henry Wotton ordered the following inſcription to be put on his monument—

Diſputandi pruritus eccleſiarum ſcabies.

The itch of diſputation is the bane of the church.

9. The ſame perſon being aſked, if he thought a Papiſt could be ſaved? "You may be ſaved," replied he,

he, "without knowing that."—An excellent anſwer to the queſtions of impertinent curioſity in religious matters.

10. Many perſons ſpend ſo much time in criticiſing and diſputing about the Goſpel, that they have none left for practiſing it. As if two ſick men ſhould quarrel about the phraſeology of their phyſician's preſcription, and forget to take the medicine.

11. "Geo. Trapezuntius had a good portion of the "ſpirit which prevailed among the learned of his times: "proud, conceited, dogmatical, impatient of contra- "diction, and quarrelſome, he contributed, as much "as any one, to falſify the maxim of Ovid—*Ingenuas "didiciſſe*, &c." Biog. Dict.—See inſtance of Laurentius Valle, Valeſius, Scioppius, Scaliger, Cardan, and others.

12. Never (ſay the moderns) were the SS. ſo much ſtudied, and ſo thoroughly explained, as at preſent. So, probably, ſaid the Phariſees, and doctors of the law, when they crucified Chriſt. Refined criticiſms on the ſacred writings made the moſt faſhionable branch of learning among the Jews, in compariſon of which, profane literature was held in great contempt, and indeed, by many of their zealots, in great abhorrence—See Joſeph. Antiq. lib. xx. cap. ult. § ult. Doddridge i. 317.—Our Lord "received not "glory from men;" he never ſoothed the vanity of great and learned men, in order to obtain their favour. The Jews *ſearched the SS.* but it was in order to find in them their own fond fancies concerning

concerning temporal greatneſs, wealth and dominion.

13. Apply to the contraſt between the ſalutary doctrines and beautiful imagery of Scripture on the one hand, and the noxious tenets and barren ſpeculations of metaphyſical ſcepticiſm on the other, the following lines of Collins in his Oriental Eclogues—

> Here, where no ſprings in murmurs break away,
> Or moſs-crown'd fountains mitigate the day,
> In vain ye hope the dear delights to know,
> Which plains more bleſt, or verdant vales beſtow;
> Here rocks alone, and taſteleſs ſands are found,
> And faint and ſickly winds for ever howl around.

Ecl. ii. Haſſan's addreſs to his camels travelling through the burning deſerts of the Eaſt.

14. Apply to the caſe of a Chriſtian what Pacatius ſays of Theodoſius, and the treatment he received from Fortune—*Quem ſceptro et ſolio deſtinaverat, nunquam indulgenter habuit: ſed ut ſeveri patres his quos diligunt triſtiores ſunt, ita illa te plurimis et difficillimis reipublicæ temporibus exercuit, dum aptat imperio.*—Fortune did not treat with kindneſs the man whom ſhe had deſtined for the ſceptre and the throne: but as ſevere parents are moſt harſh to the children whom moſt they love, ſo ſhe prepared him for empire by the trials which ſhe obliged him to ſuſtain in the moſt difficult ſeaſon of the republic.

15. Saurin, after mentioning ſome inſignificant criticiſm upon which the commentators enlarge, makes the following very pertinent obſervation—" Such is the

" ſpirit

" ſpirit of mankind, that they often conſider ſlightly " thoſe great truths of the SS. upon which our whole " religion is founded, expatiating into diſcuſſions " upon matters of no relation either to our duty or " our happineſs." Diſſ. xxi. p. 181.—So again— " It is amazing to find learned men, who would bluſh " to employ but a few minutes in ſtudying the or- " naments that are moſt in faſhion in their own time, " and who have yet the patience to devour immenſe " volumes, to learn with great exactneſs thoſe of the " remoteſt age." xx. 194.—See Law's Chriſt. Perfect. on this ſubject. See Saurin, 504.

16. Metaphyſical ſpeculations are lofty, but frigid; as Lunardi, after aſcending to an immenſe height in the atmoſphere, came down covered with icicles.

17. Many fine books of religion and morality are already written. We are eager for more. But if we duly attended to the Goſpel, ſhould we want them? A ſingle ſhort direction from God himſelf is authoritative and deciſive. A text would ſave us the trouble of reading many diſſertations; and the time which we thus ſpend in learning, or rather, perhaps, pretending to learn, our duty, might be ſpent in practiſing it.

FAME.

PLACES in the Temple of Fame are a tenure, againſt which, of all others, *quo warrantos* are ſure to be iſſued.

FLOWERS

FLOWERS PROSCRIBED.

When the Dutch patriots were rampant in 1787, flowers of an orange colour were profcribed; and the officers of juftice were for fome time employed in removing anemones and ranunculufes from the Hague. Their reftoration was foon after effected by the Pruffian troops.—See Bowdler's Letters, p. 43.

FORTITUDE.

1. Frederic the famous Duke of Saxony was playing at chefs in his tent with his coufin and fellow-prifoner the Landgrave of Lithenberg, when a writ was brought him, figned by the Emperor, for his execution the next morning, in the fight of his wife and children, and the whole city of Wittemberg. Having carefully perufed it, he laid it down as a paper of no concern, and faying to the Landgrave, "Coufin, take good heed to your game," returned to his play, and gave him a check-mate.

2. It is a noble character which Afcham gives of the above mentioned Duke—"He thinketh nothing "which he dare not fpeak, and fpeaketh nothing "which he will not do."

3. Polybius relates, that when the battle was begun, which was to decide the fate of the Macedonian empire, Perfeus bafely withdrew to the city Pydne, under pretence of facrificing to Hercules; "a god," fays Plutarch, "that is not wont to regard the of-

"ferings of cowards, or grant ſuch requeſts as are "unjuſt; it not being reaſonable, that he, who never "ſhoots, ſhould carry away the prize; that he ſhould "triumph, who ſneaks from the battle; or he, who "takes no pains, ſhould meet with ſucceſs. To "Emilius's petition the god liſtened; for he prayed "for victory with his ſword in his hand, and was "fighting at the ſame time that he implored the di-"vine aſſiſtance."—An excellent hint for the Chriſtian ſoldier to obſerve and improve upon.

4. "To ſtand in fear of the people's cenſure or "common talk may argue a harmleſs and peaceable "mind, but never a brave and truly heroic ſoul." Plutarch, 94.

5. The body's weakneſs often proves to be the ſoul's ſtrength, and men are better Chriſtians in ſickneſs than in health: like the ſoldier in Antigonus's army; who, being naturally weak and ſickly, was a very hero, till, out of regard for him, the king put him under the care of his phyſicians, who made a cure of him; after which, he never appeared ſo fond of danger, or daring in battle, being delivered from that miſery which made life a burden.—Plut. in Vit. Pelop.

6. A general in time of peace, a pilot in a calm, and a clergyman when people are in health, are of very little account. War, ſtorm, and ſickneſs cauſe them all to be ſought to and confided in.

7. A Chriſtian is a warrior by his profeſſion, and has, through life, a ſucceſſion of enemies to encounter. Luſt

Luſt attacks him in the days of his youth, ambition diſquiets his riper years, and avarice infeſts his old age. His condition reminds one of that obſervation of Plutarch concerning the Romans of the firſt ages, that "if ever God deſigned that men ſhould ſpend "their lives in war, they were the men. In their "infancy they had the Carthaginians to contend "with for Sicily; in their middle age the Gauls for "Italy itſelf; and in their old age they were obliged "again to contend with the Carthaginians and Han-"nibal."—Vit. Marcell. ad init.

8. When a Chriſtian beholds ſickneſs (his laſt more eſpecially) coming towards him, he ſhould addreſs it, as St. Andrew did the Croſs, as that which he had long expected, and which would convey him to his bleſſed Maſter, by whoſe ſufferings it had been ſanctified. Let us alſo bear in mind, that even on the croſs St. Andrew ceaſed not to inſtruct and admoniſh thoſe around him. The words of a preacher, in ſuch circumſtances, never fail to make a deep and laſting impreſſion.—*Ille verò, cum Crucem eminus intueretur, eam ſalutavit, hortatuſque eſt, ut diſcipulum ejus, qui ei ſuffixus fuiſſet, exciperet; eam dedicatam et conſecratam eſſe Chriſti corpori, ejuſque membris, quaſi margaritis, ornatam; diu eam defatigari ipſum expectando, quemadmodum Chriſtum magiſtrum expectâſſet; lætum ſe ad illam venire, cujus deſiderio jam diu teneretur: itaque orare, ut ſe exciperet, ac magiſtro redderet; ut per illam ipſum Chriſtus reciperet, qui per eam ipſum redemiſſet. Cumque ventum eſſet ad Crucem, primùm Chriſtum oravit,*

vit, deinde populum hortatus est, ut in eâ fide et religione, quam tradidisset, *permaneret. In Cruce verò biduum vixit, cum interea nullum finem docendi populi fecit.*— Perionius de Gestis Apostolorum.

He saluted the Cross when he beheld it afar off, and entreated it to receive him as the disciple of that Master who had himself been nailed upon it. He declared that it was dedicated and consecrated to the body of Christ, and was more adorned with his limbs than if inlaid with pearls; that it had long expected him, as it had expected his Master Christ before him; that he had long looked forward to it with impatience, and was now arrived at it with pleasure: wherefore he besought it to receive him, and restore him to his Master; that the same Cross, by which he had been redeemed, might be the instrument of conveying him to his Redeemer. When come to the foot of the Cross, he first prayed to Christ, and then exhorted the people to remain steadfast in the faith which he had delivered to them. He lived two days upon the Cross, and during all that time never ceased to admonish and instruct the people.

FRETFULNESS.

The argument urged against it by the Psalmist deserves to be well fixed in our minds; and indeed, if it were so, we should need no other. "Fret not "thyself against the ungodly, &c. FOR they shall soon "be cut down like the grass," &c. Who could envy

envy a flower, though ever ſo gay and beautiful in its colours, when he ſaw that the next ſtroke of the mower would ſweep it away for ever?

GREATNESS.

A MAN wiſhes for it, and cannot be eaſy without it: no ſooner has he attained his wiſh, but you hear him lamenting his hard lot, complaining of cares, and troubles, and viſits: he has no peace, not an hour to himſelf; his expenditure is greater than his income, &c. &c. All this is wrong; he only expoſes his own weakneſs. He wanted honour and exaltation: he has got them, and muſt take their neceſſary appendages with them. If he thinks proper to receive the pay, he ſhould not find fault with the duty. The troubles of a ſtation are deſigned as an antidote to the poiſon of its temptations. They humble the poſſeſſor, and ſhew him to himſelf. They ſhould be borne with meekneſs and patience, and made this uſe of. See what Fenelon has ſaid on the *Croſs of Proſperity*, ii. 143. 155. Alſo a ſermon in Maſſillon's *Petit Carême*, where he ſhews a *court* to be the beſt ſchool for learning mortification and ſelf-denial.

GRIEF.

GRIEF is fruitleſs and unavailable in every caſe but one, viz. *ſin*. We take to it kindly in every inſtance but that.

HAPPINESS,

ON FIFTY-SIX POUNDS PER ANNUM.

A CLERGYMAN applied to the Dean of Christchurch for the little vicarage of Blenddington, then vacant, value, *de claro*, about 40l. per ann. "Sir," said he, "I maintain a wife and six children on "56l. per ann.—Not that I should regard the matter, "were the income certain: but when a man considers it may be taken from him any day of the week, "he cannot be quite so easy."—"I will get the living "for you, if I can," answered the Dean; "but I "would not have you raise your expectations too high; "because, if any member of the college will take it, "by our rules he must have it."—"O Sir," replied the divine, "it would make me the happiest man in the "world!—but if I miss it, I shall not be unhappy. "—I never knew what it was to be unhappy for one "hour in my whole life."

HIGH CHURCH.

A NAME invented, according to Mr. Leslie, under which the Church of England might be abused with greater security. Such are declared by Steele, in his Crisis, to be worse than Papists, and the very opposite to Protestants. Leslie, in his Letter from Barle-duc, speaks of rods and tests prepared for the Church of England by the Whigs, &c. had they succeeded in Sacheverel's

Sacheverel's trial; the intention of which was to make her *ſwallow her own dung*, as they ſaid, and abjure her doctrines.

HISTORY.

1. HISTORY, in general, is an account of what men have done to make each other unhappy. In the hiſtory of the preſent age, it is a ſtriking circumſtance, that the hiſtorian, amidſt a ſeries of murders and calamities, is glad to relieve himſelf and his reader, by dwelling on ſo minute an incident, of a different kind, as that of the ſeeds ſown by Anſon on the deſert iſle of Fernandes, which the Spaniards afterwards found to be grown up; and the goats, with their ears cut, which ſerved to verify the adventures of Selkirk, who, being left upon the iſland, had lived there ſeveral years.—See Age of Louis XIV. ii. 109.

2. Lord Cheſterfield gives a good direction in reading hiſtory, viz. to read ſome ſhort general hiſtory of a country; to mark the curious and intereſting periods, ſuch as revolutions in the government, religion, laws, &c.; then to conſult the larger hiſtories for full information as to *them*.

3. It is well obſerved by Hume, that, in reading hiſtory, trivial incidents, which ſhew the manners of the age, are often more inſtructive as well as entertaining, than the great tranſactions of wars and negocia-

tions, which are nearly similar in all periods, and in all countries of the world. Vol. v. 56.

4. History, while it instructs us, flatters our pride by the manner in which that instruction is conveyed. For what we learn by *precept*, we are indebted to the wisdom and authority of another. The learning obtained from *example* is obtained by deductions and applications of our own.

HOBBES.

"Let us do justice," says Bishop Warburton, "to that great man's memory, at a time his writings seem entirely neglected; whom with all his errors, and those of the most dangerous nature, we must allow to be one of the first men of his age, for a bright wit, a deep penetration, and a cultivated understanding: several of whose uncommon speculations, while they remained with him, lay unregarded; but, when taken up by others, of whom we deservedly have a better opinion, received their due applause and approbation. —— Mr. Locke borrowed and improved many—*e. g.* that liberty belongs not to the will—the finest and most intricate dissertation in his Essay, as he confesses to Limborch." Warburton's Miscell. Translations in Prose and Verse, p. 124, printed 1724, for Barker, with a Latin dedication to Sir Robert Sutton.—[Hobbes was a great favourite with Voltaire: "Vir-

"tuous citizen! enterprising spirit—the forerunner "of Spinosa and of Locke!"—It is said in thy law of nature, "that every man having a right to all things, "every one has a right over the life of his fellow-"creatures." Is not power here confounded with right?"—See Voltaire's Ignorant Philosopher, p. 53.]

HONESTY.

"Honesty," saith Dr. Rees, in his Dictionary, "is a plant supposed to be possessed of eminent me-"dical virtues; but it hath not the fortune to be "received into the *shops*."—The Doctor is perfectly grave, but the words admit of a humorous sense.

HOPE.

When the soul grows weary in her Christian course, and is ready to faint by the way, she should be refreshed and invigorated by a view of those heavenly joys, which are to reward her labours. For so, when the Carthaginian soldiers were well nigh overcome with the difficulty and danger of the passage over the Alps, their wise general, from the top of those stupendous mountains, whence there was a prospect of all Italy, showed them the fruitful plains watered by the river Po, to which they were almost come; and therefore, that they had but one effort more to make, before they arrived at them. He represented to them, that a battle or two would put a glorious period to their toils, and enrich them for ever, by giving them poſſeſſion of the capital of the Roman empire. This ſpeech, filled with ſuch pleaſing hopes, and enforced by the ſight of Italy, inſpired the dejected ſoldiers with freſh vigour and alacrity to purſue their march.

HUMAN FRAME.

1. Chyle is an *emulſion*, in making which from the food we take in, the teeth and jaws act as the peſtle and mortar; the ſpittle, bile, pancreatic juice, &c. are the menſtruum, inſtead of the water which the chymiſt employs; the ſtomach and inteſtines are the preſs; and the lacteal veſſels the ſtrainers to ſeparate the pure *emulſion* from its fæces. Arbuthnot on Aliment, p. 67.

2. What mechaniſm is that, which can attenuate a fluid compounded of the ingredients of human aliment, as oil, ſalts, earth, and water, ſo as to make it flow freely through the lymphatic veſſels, though ſome of them are a hundred times ſmaller than the arterial capillaries, ten of which are not equal to one hair! What mechaniſm is that, which from one uniform juice can extract all the variety of vegetable juices to be found in plants; which from ſuch variety of food as enters the ſtomach of an animal, can make a fluid very nearly uniform, viz. blood; and again from that uniform fluid can produce the variety of juices in the animal's body! Yet all theſe operations

operations are as mechanically and regularly performed as corn is ground in a mill, or cyder made from apples in a preſs.

3. The lacteal veſſels are the *roots* of an animal, whereby it draws its nouriſhment from the food in the inteſtines, as a vegetable does from the mould in which it is ſet; only a vegetable has its root planted without, and an animal within itſelf. A fœtus in the womb is nouriſhed like a plant, but afterwards by a root planted within itſelf.— p. 74.

4. Some inſects have their wind-pipes on the ſurface of their bodies, and are therefore killed by the contact of oil, not as a poiſon, but as it excludes the air.—Arbuthnot on Air, p. 115.

IDLENESS.

1. An indolent, idle man is a *carcaſs*; and, if he does not take care, the *birds of prey* (the miniſters of vengeance) will be at him. In Romney Marſh, when the ravens, hovering on high, and keeping a ſharp look-out, ſee a ſheep turned on his back, ſo fat and unwieldy that he cannot recover himſelf, they inſtantly ſouſe down upon him, pick out his eyes, and then devour the body, carrying it away piecemeal, as they are able. Perſons are then ſet to watch on purpoſe to prevent this cataſtrophe.—*Watch YE!* King's Morſels of Criticiſm.

2. Adam worked in Paradiſe; afterwards in the world. "My Father worketh hitherto" (ſays our Lord) "and I work." There is probably no abſolute

lute idleneſs, but in hell, and in the reſemblances of hell.—Ditto, p. 126.

3. The buſy man, ſay the Turks, is troubled with one devil, but the idle man is tormented with a thouſand.

4. Idleneſs is the moſt painful ſituation of the mind, as *ſtanding ſtill*, according to Galen, is of the body.—See Brown's Vulgar Errors, iii. 1.

5. The irkſomeneſs of being idle is humorouſly hit off by Voltaire's old woman in Candide, who puts it to the philoſophers,—Which is worſt; to experience all the miſeries through which every one of us hath paſſed, or, TO REMAIN HERE DOING NOTHING ?"

6. Biſhop Cumberland being told by ſome of his friends, that he would wear himſelf out by intenſe application, replied,—" It is better to *wear* out than " to *ruſt* out."

7. It was an obſervation of Swift, that he never knew any man come to greatneſs and eminence, who lay a-bed in a morning.

8. The moſt ſluggiſh of creatures, called the Potto, or Sloth, is alſo the moſt horrible for its uglineſs—to ſhow the deformity of *idleneſs*, and, if poſſible, to frighten us from it.

9. In the mind, as well as the body natural and politic, ſtagnation is followed by putrefaction. A want of proper motion does not breed reſt and ſtability, but a motion of another kind; a motion unſeen and inteſtine, which does not preſerve, but deſtroy.

10. Sloth

10. Sloth proceeds from want of *faith* or *courage*, or *love*, 2d Peter, i. 8.—*Add to faith virtue*, &c.—*These things make you, that you be* ουκ αργους—not idle and unprofitable.—See Whitby in loc.

11. The following is an admirable observation of Rousseau, in his *Confessions*, b. v. vol. ii. p. 89.—"In my opinion, idleness is no less the pest of "*society*, than of solitude. Nothing contracts the "mind, nothing engenders trifles, tales, backbiting, "slander and falsities, so much as being shut up in "a room, opposite each other, reduced to no other "occupation than the necessity of continual chatter-"ing. When every one is employed, they speak "only when they have something to say; but, if you "are doing nothing, you must absolutely talk in-"cessantly; and this, of all constraints, is the most "troublesome, and the most dangerous. I dare go "even farther, and maintain, that, to render a circle "truly agreeable, every one must be not only doing "something, but something which requires a little "attention."

JEWS.

Lord Chesterfield once told Lady Fanny Shirley, in a serious discourse they had on the Evidences of Christianity, that there was *one*, which he thought to be invincible, not to be got over by the wit of man; viz. *the present state of the Jews*—a fact to be accounted for on no human principle.—This anec-

dote

dote was related to me by a perſon who had it from Lady Fanny herſelf.

INTENTION.

INTENTION is the ſame in the inner man, as the eye is in the outer. While the eye is clear, it illuminates the whole body; each member is perfectly enlightened for the performance of its functions as if itſelf were an eye. If any humours ſuffuſe the eye, the whole body is inſtantly overwhelmed with darkneſs. So the ſyſtem of a man's conduct by a pure or vitiated *intention*. The intention is the *view* in which the action is performed, the *aim*, as we ſay, taken before the performance of it. If the light be darkneſs, if that which ought to direct the action be itſelf perverted and depraved, how great muſt be that depravity!

KINGS.

1. "BEFORE an opera is to be performed at Turin, the king himſelf takes the pains to read it over, and to eraſe every line that can admit of an indecent or double meaning. This attention is particularly paid to the theatre, on account of the morals of the Royal family." Mrs. Miller's Letters from Italy, i. 200.

2. Kings honour human nature, when they diſtinguiſh and reward thoſe who do moſt honour to it, and while they

they give encouragement to those superior geniuses, who employ themselves in perfecting our knowlege, and who devote themselves to the worship of truth. Happy are the sovereigns who themselves cultivate the sciences; who think with Cicero, that Roman consul, the deliverer of his country and father of eloquence; "Literature is the accomplishment of "youth, and the charm of old age. It gives a lustre "to prosperity, and a comfort to adversity; at home "and abroad, in travel and in retirement, at all times "and in all places, it is the delight of life."—A king, guided by justice, has the universe for his temple, and good men are the priests that sacrifice to him.—Critical Essay on Mac.

3. Though the mask of dissimulation should for some time cover the natural deformity of a prince, he cannot always keep it on. He must take it off sometimes in order to breathe; and one single opportunity is sufficient to satisfy the curious. Artifice, then, shall seat itself in vain on the lips of a prince. We do not form a judgment of men from their words, but by comparing their actions with them, and with each other. Falsehood and dissimulation can never stand this test. A man can act well no part but his own; and, to appear to advantage, must appear in his proper character.—Ibid.

4. Be not thou, then, wicked with the wicked, but be thou virtuous and intrepid among them. Thou wilt make thy people virtuous as thyself; thy neighbours will imitate thee, and the wicked tremble.—Ibid.

5. In-

5. Inundations which lay countries waſte, lightnings which reduce cities to aſhes, the poiſon of the plague which diſpeoples provinces, are not ſo fatal to the world, as the dangerous morals and unruly paſſions of kings. Calamities from heaven endure but for a time; they deſtroy but ſome countries; and thoſe loſſes, though grievous, are retrievable: but the crimes of kings cauſe whole nations to ſuffer, from generation to generation.—Ibid.

LANGUAGE (FIGURATIVE) OF THE SS.

RESPECTING the figurative language of the Scriptures, there is this curious and important queſtion to be determined—Whether God adopted it, becauſe it was the ſtyle of the eaſtern nations; or it became the ſtyle of the eaſtern nations, becauſe God originally conſtituted and employed it?

LAWS.

THE obſervation, made by a great caſuiſt on human laws, holds much ſtronger with regard to divine ones—"The obedience of that man is much too delicate, "who inſiſts upon knowing the *reaſon* of all laws, before "he will obey them. The lawgiver muſt be ſuppoſed "to have given his ſanction to the law from the reaſon "of the thing; but, where we cannot diſcover the rea-"ſon of it, the *ſanction* is to be the only reaſon of our "obedience."—Bp. Taylor's Duct. Dub. b. iii. c. vi. rule 3.

LEARN-

LEARNING.

1. There is no kind of knowlege which, in the hands of the diligent and ſkilful, will not turn to account. Honey exudes from all flowers, the bitter not excepted; and the bee knows how to extract it.

2. Cicero's apology for the great men of Rome who employed their leiſure hours in philoſophical diſquiſitions is worthy notice: ſome, it ſeems, thought ſuch employment unworthy of them.— "*Quaſi verò clarorum virorum aut tacitos congreſſus* "*eſſe oporteat, aut* ludicros *ſermones, aut rerum col-* "*loquia* leviorum. - - - - *Nec quidquam aliud vi-* "*dendum eſt nobis, quos populus Romanus hoc in* "*gradu collocavit, niſi ne quid privatis ſtudiis de operâ* "*publicâ detrahamus.—Quod ſi, quum fungi munere* "*debeamus, operam noſtram nunquam a populari cætu re-* "*movemus, quis reprehendet noſtrum otium, qui in eo non* "*modò noſmetipſos hebeſcere et languere nolumus, ſed etiam* "*ut plurimis proſimus enitimur?*"—Acad. Lucull. ſect. 6. —As if it were proper for eminent men to remain mute in company, or to confine their converſation to drollery and trifles. Placed as we are by the Roman people in this elevated ſtation, our only concern is to take care, that private ſtudy never withdraws us from a due attention to the public ſervice. But if we are ever ready to perform every duty that we owe to our country,

country, who ſhall grudge us an application of our leiſure, by which we not only reſcue ourſelves from indolence, but endeavour to produce fruits advantageous to others?

3. There are ſome who have too mean an opinion of their own abilities, and by fancying themſelves to be uſeleſs, become ſo, and dare not attempt many things, in which they are capable of ſucceeding, and which they ought to perform. This behaviour ariſes more from INDOLENCE OR MELANCHOLY, than from humility.—Jortin's Sermons, iv. 24.

4. Inventors and projectors, however wild and viſionary, often afford matter, which a wiſe man will know how to qualify and turn to uſe, though they did not.—See Account of Settlement in America, i. 65.

5. Mr. Locke always uſed to ſay, "I like your "*builders*; for, whether they ſucceed or not in con-"ſtructing the edifice, they bring together mate-"rials very valuable to a more ſkilful architect."—See Sublime and Beautiful, 92.

6. An original genius reſembles the eagle, who diſdains to ſhare the plunder of another bird; and will take up with no prey, but that which he has acquired by his own purſuit.

7. "I pity unlearned gentlemen in a rainy day!" was the uſual ſaying of Lord Falkland.

LIGHT AND LOVE.

Light is the great ſource of bleſſing in the natural world, *love* in the moral. The excellencies of both are united in the Divine Nature: *God is light*, and *God is love*. A ſlaviſh and ſuperſtitious fear of God proceeds, therefore, from a miſapprehenſion of him; as when the diſciples ſaw Jeſus walking upon the ſea, and knew not who it was, they were ſcared with the appearance; and therefore our Lord, to take off their fear, only made himſelf better known to them: *It is I*, ſays he, *be not afraid*.—See Norris's Sermons, xi. 194.

LOCKMAN.

1. The famous oriental philoſopher Lockman, while a ſlave, being preſented by his maſter with a bitter melon, immediately ate it all. How was it poſſible, ſaid his maſter, for you to eat ſo nauſeous a fruit? Lockman replied, "I have received ſo many favours "from you, that it is no wonder I ſhould once in my "life eat a bitter melon from your hand." This generous anſwer of the ſlave ſtruck the maſter to ſuch a degree, that he immediately gave him his liberty.—With ſuch ſentiments ſhould man receive his portion of ſufferings at the hand of God.

2. The ſame Lockman, being informed by angels (as the legend goes) that God would make him a mon-

arch,

arch, replied—" If he would grant me liberty to " choose my condition of life, I had rather continue " in my present state, and be kept from offending " him: otherwise all the grandeur and splendour of " the world would be troublesome to me."

" Speak the truth;" (said the same philosopher)— " keep your word;—and intermeddle not in affairs which do not concern you."

" Be a learned man, a disciple of the learned, " or an auditor of the learned; at least be a lover of " knowlege, and desirous of improvement."

LYNCH. (Dean)

He was a constant preacher through life, either at the cathedral, one of his livings, or at Grove, his family estate; in short, wherever he happened to be. Of his charities a judgment may be formed from the following circumstance. His son was sent for by the citizens of Canterbury, and chosen burgess, without a shilling expense. " Sir," (said the poorer freemen, sitting sober in their houses when he went round to thank them) " you had a right to " command our votes; *your father fed us*, and *your* " *mother clothed us*." Communicated to me by Dr. Beauvoir, who went round with him. The Dean never forgot any thing once treasured up in his memory.

MAC-

MACDONALD. (Hugh)

The world tempts and disappoints; it excites desires after happiness, but satisfies them not. The case of its votaries too much resembles that of the perfidious rebel, Hugh Macdonald, mentioned by Dr. Johnson in his Journey to the Hebrides, p. 167, who was served with a plentiful meal of salt meat; and, when thirst made him clamorous for drink, a cup was let down to him in the dungeon, which, on lifting the cover, he found to be empty!

MACHIAVEL's OBSERVATION.

It is observable, that Machiavel employs a whole chapter designedly, to prove, that revolutions in states are often presaged by *prodigies*, the causes of which he professeth himself unable to assign; unless they may be attributed to some spirits and intelligences in the air, which give the world notice of such things to come. See Machiav. Disput. l. i. c. 56.

MAHOMET viewing DAMASCUS.

The Arabian false prophet, viewing the delicious and pleasurable situation of Damascus, would not enter that city, but turned away from it with this exclamation; "There is but one paradise for man; and I "am determined to have mine in the other world." *Mutatis mutandis*, how becoming this for a Christian in time of temptation!—See Maundrell, p. 121.

MARRIAGE.

1. Vincent le Blanc, in his Travels, p. 386, tells us, that in three inſtances, within his own knowlege, an emerald diſcovered the incontinency of its wearer, by breaking, when worn in a ring upon the finger. "Such (ſays he) is the virtue of this ſtone, if it be "good and fine, and of the old mine."—It is a pity but that there was an emerald of *the old mine* in every wedding-ring.

2. When the ſubject of *catechiſing* was before the ſynod of Dort, one of the Swiſs deputies told the ſynod, that the cuſtom in his country was, for all parties intending matrimony to appear before their miniſter, who examined them as to their proficiency in their catechiſm, having power to defer the marriage till it was ſuch as he could approve. "I was much af-"fected to this courſe (ſays Hales) when I heard it; "and the ſynod ſhall be ill adviſed, if they make no "uſe of it." Letters to Sir D. Carleton, p. 11.

MEMORY.

One conſiderable ſtep towards remembering things worth remembrance is to forget things which are not ſo.

METHODISTS.

1. A friend of mine having aſked a lady of piety and judgment her opinion of a Methodiſt teacher; "He

"He will ſoon (ſaid ſhe) by great *humility* become the "head of a ſect, and damn all the reſt of the world "in the very ſpirit of charity."

2. The Scriptures mention an *aſſurance of faith*, which our church, in her homilies, calls "a ſure truſt "and confidence that our ſins are forgiven," &c. The methodiſtical aſſurance is an internal feeling, an aſſurance of *ſenſe*. Now *faith* and *ſenſe* are quite different things. In the one caſe, the aſſurance is an inference drawn from the divine promiſes applied to ourſelves; in the other, it is an immediate operation of the ſpirit, a kind of revelation made nobody knows how, and of which we have no evidence but the perſon's own aſſertion.

3. An ingenious French author (Bourſault) ſpeaking of the humility of Friars, and the manner in which it is made to ſerve their intereſt, ſays, they are like pitchers, which *ſtoop* only in order to get *filled*.

MIDDLETON. (Dr.)

"My attention to the claſſics (ſays Middleton) has "made me very ſqueamiſh in my Chriſtian ſtudies." The Doctor ſeems to have been in the caſe of the comet mentioned by Dr. Zach, p. 6. of a paper delivered to the Univerſity of Oxford, when he was admitted to a degree there, in Feb. 1786. "The retardation of "the comet, compared to its period, may clearly be "put to the account of the attraction and perturba- "tion he has undergone in the region of Jupiter and "Saturn."

Middleton and Hoadley.

There was a very ſcarce book ſuppoſed to be written with force againſt miracles. Middleton had long ſearched for it in vain. Hoadley was in poſſeſſion of a copy, and furniſhed him with it. "You "are a wicked man (ſaid he) and will make a bad "uſe of it. Perhaps *I* ought not to give it you. But— "there—take it, and do your worſt."—This anecdote is in the Bodleian library, as I have been informed by a friend.

MINISTRY.

1. "I hope my younger brethren in the miniſtry "will pardon me," ſays Dr. Doddridge, "if I entreat "their particular attention to this admonition—not to "give the main part of their time to the *curioſities* of "learning, and only a few fragments of it to their great "work, the *cure of ſouls*; leſt they ſee cauſe, in their "laſt moments, to adopt the words of dying Grotius, "perhaps with much greater propriety than he could "uſe them—*Proh! vitam perdidi operosè nihil agendo!*" Fam. Expoſ. ſect. 14. The Doctor does not refer to his authority for this anecdote: but his admonition is moſt excellent. See the *whole Improvement*: See alſo Fam. Exp. vol. 1, ſec. 14, where another anecdote is mentioned of Grotius; but the author, from whom I took it, did not cite his authority. On the ſubject of the above admonition of Doddridge, ſee Norris's Conduct of Human Life.—See Doddridge's Sermons and

Tracts, i. 264.—Quesnel on Tit. iii. 9. a proper *text* for a sermon on the subject.

2. It often happens to the teachers of philosophy and religion, as it did to Dr. Solander on the mountain. "You must keep moving," (says the Doctor) "at all events. Whoever sits down will sleep, and "whoever sleeps will wake no more." Yet he himself was the first who found the inclination, against which he had warned others, to be irresistible, and insisted upon being suffered to take a nap, though he had just told the company, that to sleep was to perish.—See Hawkesworth, i 48.

3. "Reason *ought* to direct us (says Lord C.), "but it seldom *does*. And he who addresses himself "singly to another man's reason, without endeavour-"ing to engage his heart in his interest also, is no "more likely to succeed, than a man who should ap-"ply only to a king's *nominal* minister, and neglect "his *favourite*."—The illustration is just and beautiful; and the observation deserves the notice of every one, whose employment it is to win men to faith and righteousness. Dry reasoning, though ever so solid, will not do alone.—See Letters, II. 54. cxxix.

4. Apply to a faithful and vigilant clergy

---- Nunquam, custodibus illis,
Nocturnum stabulis furem, incursusque luporum,
Aut impacatos a tergo horrebis Iberos.

GEORG. iii. 406.

- - - - Who for the fold's relief
Will profecute with cries the nightly thief,
Repulfe the prowling wolf, and hold at bay
The mountain robbers rufhing to the prey.

DRYDEN, 616.

5. Original corruption appears in as many different fhapes as the fabulous Proteus of the ancients, while it exerts itfelf in the different paffions of finful men, transforming them, for the time, into various kinds of beafts.——

Tum variæ illudent fpecies atque ora ferarum,
Fiet enim fubitò fus horridus, atraque tigris,
Squamofufque draco, et fulvâ cervice leæna;
Sed quantò ille magis formas fe vertet in omnes,
Tantò, nate, magis contende tenacia vincla.

—Various forms affume, to cheat thy fight,
And with vain images of beafts affright,
With foamy tufks will feem a briftly boar,
Or imitate the lion's angry roar;
But thou, the more he varies forms, beware
To ftrain his fetters with a ftricter care.

DRYDEN, 587.

So fpeaks Wifdom to *her* children, as well as Cyrene to her fon Ariftcus, Georg. iv. 411.——To accomplifh this work happily, celeftial influences are neceffary, which are conferred in one cafe, no lefs than in the other:——

Hæc ait, et liquidum ambrofiæ diffundit odorem,
Quo totum nati corpus perduxit; at illi
Dulcis compofitis fpiravit crinibus aura,
Atque habilis membris venit vigor.—

This

This said, with nectar she her son anoints,
Infusing vigour through his mortal joints:
Down from his head the liquid odours ran;
He breath'd of heav'n, and look'd above a man.

DRYDEN, 599.

6. With regard to men's principles, we should always put the best construction on dubious cases, and treat those as *friends* to Christianity, who are not avowed and declared *enemies*. By so doing, we may perhaps save a person from really apostatising; his doubts and prejudices may be overcome; and what was wanting in him may be perfected. But, if we suppose and treat him as an enemy, we take a ready way to make him one, though he were not such before. Besides that the addition of a new name, especially if it be a name of eminence, to the catalogue of infidels strengthens that party, and weakens the faith of many, who build it on authority. "He, that is not against us, is on our part." Mark ix. 40.—See Doddridge in loc: and see Life of Sir Thomas Brown, by Johnson, ad fin.

7. Happy the minister, whose days are spent in teaching heavenly truths; his nights in acquiring the knowlege of them, by study and devotion!—

Et quantùm longis carpent armenta diebus,
Exiguâ tantùm gelidus ros noctе reponit.

GEORG. ii. 201.

8. The necessity of a kind and gentle manner, in him who instructs or reproves another, and the sad effect of a contrary temper, are well set forth by

Jerome—

Jerome—*Nihil est fædius præceptore furioso, qui, cum debeat esse mansuetus et humilis ad omnes, diverso torvo vultu, trementibus labiis, effrenatis convitiis, clamore perstrepitat: errantes non tam ad bonum retrahit, quam ad malum suâ sævitiâ præcipitat.* Cited by Dieterich, i. 33.—Nothing is more unseemly than a passionate instructor; who, when he ought to be an example of gentleness and humility to all, is distinguished on the contrary by fierce looks, trembling lips, intemperate noise, and unbridled revilings. Such a man does not by persuasion recal to righteousness those who wander, but by harshness precipitates them into evil.

9. A Christian (a minister especially) should live and act with that disposition for which George Grenville is celebrated by E. Burke.—"He took "public business, not as a duty which he was to "fulfil, but as a pleasure he was to enjoy; and "he seemed to have no delight out of this house, "except in such things as some way related to the "business that was to be done within it." Speech, 25. The sentence preceding is—"With a masculine "understanding and a stout and resolute heart, he had "an application undissipated and unwearied."

10. Mrs. Siddons, the famous actress, receiving many invitations to the houses of the great and opulent, excused herself from accepting any of them, because her time was due to the public, that she might prepare herself in the most perfect manner to appear before them, for their entertainment.—When a clergyman

man is invited to ſpend his hours at card-playing or chit-chat meetings, has he not an apology to make of the ſame kind, but of a more important and intereſting nature? and, if he be deficient in the duties of *his* profeſſion for want of ſo excuſing himſelf, will not Mrs. Siddons riſe up in judgment againſt him, and condemn him?

MOULTING.

The heathen philoſophers allowed human nature to be fallen from original rectitude, and ſunk into a weak, drooping, and ſickly ſtate, which they called πτερορρυησις, the *moulting* of the ſoul's wings.—A juſt and beautiful image: the old feathers drop off, to make way for a new plumage.

MUSIC.

When Agamemnon ſet out for Troy, Homer tells us, he committed his wife to the care of a *muſician*, as the beſt of guardians and preceptors. Nor could the adulterer Ægyſthus ſeduce her, till he had taken off the muſician, whoſe inſtruction, while he lived, kept the princeſs in the path of virtue.—Odyſſ. iii. 267.—How different, in thoſe days, muſt the character of a muſician, and the uſe of muſic have been, from their character and uſe at preſent!

NATURE.

1. Mary Magdalene, like the Heliotrope, followed the *ſun* of righteouſneſs in his diurnal courſe. She

She attended him to his evening retreat, and met his rising lustre in the morning.

> But one, the lofty follower of the sun,
> Sad, when he sets, shuts up her yellow leaves,
> Drooping all night; and, when he warm returns,
> Points her enamour'd bosom to his ray.
>
> THOMSON*.

2. The mind, that has been subject to the fires of wantonness, becomes, like wood burnt to charcoal, apt upon every occasion to kindle and burn again.

3. A bone that is calcined so as the least force will crumble it, being immersed in oil, will grow firm again. Thus, in the figurative language of Scripture, the bones which by sorrow and affliction for sin are "burnt up as it were a firebrand," by pardon and grace are restored to their strength, "flourish, and are made fat."

4. Some persons, who have a great deal of sharp and pungent satire in their tempers, do not discover it unless they are highly provoked; as in the evaporation of human blood by a gentle fire the *salt* will not rise.

5. Eels, for want of exercise, are fat and slimy. For this reason, perhaps, fish without fins and scales were forbidden the Israelites; and the necessity of exercise, both for the body and the mind, might be the moral intended.

* See Evelyn's *Sylva*, p. 37. which suggested the thought.

 6. Stall-

6. Stall-fed oxen, crammed fowls, and high-feeding Christians, are often diseased in their livers. No animal can be wholesome food, that does not use exercise.—See Buchan.

7. The rule which physicians lay down for nurses had been a good one for the fanatical holders-forth in the last century, viz. never to give suck after fasting: the milk, in such case, having an acescency very prejudicial to the constitution of the recipient.

8. Had man persevered in innocence, none of the creatures would have hurt him, and it is possible all might have ministered to him in one way or other; as, upon occasion, the ravens were made to do to the prophet.

9. It was the saying of a great general, that there should be some time between a soldier's dismission and his death; and it has been observed of the most furious polemical writers, as Bellarmine, and others, that they have spent the latter part of their lives in pious meditation. Thus huntsmen tell us, that a fox, when escaped from the dogs, after a hard chace, always walks himself cool, before he earths.—See Floyer and Baynard on Cold Baths, p. 328.

10. Providence hath afforded us an unusual and special instance of the brevity of life in the Ephemeron, whose duration is from six in the evening till eleven. At the beginning of its life it sheds its coat, and spends the rest of its short time in frisking

over

over the waters, on which the female drops her eggs, and the male his sperm to impregnate them. Having thus served their generation, and provided for the continuance of the species, they die and are turned again to their dust: and all this in five or six hours.—

--- Here, fond man,
Behold thy pictur'd life!

Vide SWAMMERDAM, Ephem. Vit.

11. Noxious creatures, in proportion as they are so, teach us care, diligence and wit: weasels, kites, &c. induce us to watchfulness; thistles and moles, to good husbandry; lice oblige us to cleanliness in our bodies; spiders, in our houses; and the moth, in our clothes. Things often become hurtful, not of necessity, but by accident, through our own negligence or mistake. Let this be applied, in the moral world, to the concerns of our souls, and of the church.

12. There are men whom nothing but hell fire flashing in their faces can rouse from sin and sensuality; as I have seen a fellow driving a fat boar, with a lantern and a bundle of straw, to burn a wisp under his nose, as often as he lay down in the mire: when he feels his beard singed, he gets up, and goes forward.

13. After having composed and delivered a sermon, I have often thought of, and repeated, the following lines of Thomson——

Be

Be gracious, Heav'n! for now laborious man
Has done his part. Ye foſt'ring breezes, blow!
Ye ſoft'ning dews, ye tender ſhow'rs, deſcend!
And temper all, thou world-reviving ſun,
Into the perfect year! SPRING, ver. 48.

14. A faithful paſtor, when leaving a flock, of whom he had long had the care, might exclaim in theſe words of Eve in Milton, ſpoken on being told that ſhe muſt quit Eden——

- - - - - - O flow'rs,
My early viſitation and my laſt
At ev'n, which I bred up with tender hand
From the firſt op'ning bud, and gave you names;
Who now ſhall rear you to the ſun, or rank
Your tribes, and water from th' ambroſial fount?

15. The reproaches of an enemy often ſerve to quicken a man in his Chriſtian courſe, as in Siberia they join a large dog to a rein-deer in their ſledges, that the latter may be urged on by the bark of the former.—See Travels of the Jeſuits, by Lockman, ii. p. 155.

16. The manner in which man reſembles his Maker is thus deſcribed by an ancient Bramin: "Figure to yourſelf a million of large veſſels quite "filled with water, on which the ſun darts his lumi-"nous rays. This beautiful planet, though ſingle in "its kind, multiplies itſelf in ſome meaſure, and paints "itſelf totally, in a moment, on each of theſe veſſels, "ſo that a very perfect reſemblance of it is ſeen in "them all. Now our bodies are theſe veſſels filled "with water; the ſun is the image of the Supreme "Being;

" Being; and the figure of the ſun, painted on each " of theſe veſſels, is a natural repreſentation enough " of the human ſoul, created after the image of God " himſelf." Ibid. p. 248.

17. The paſſions, when in the moſt violent agitation, may be allayed by the conſideration of hell torments; as wine, when it ferments, ready to burſt the hoops of its veſſel, is calmed and quieted at once by the application of a match dipped in *ſulphur*.

18. The Chineſe phyſicians never preſcribe bleeding, but allay the heat of the blood by abſtinence, diet, and cooling herbs; ſaying, that, if the pot boil too faſt, it is better to ſubduct the fuel, than lade out the water.

19. Perſecution is contrary to the very nature and deſign of religion, which is to effect the converſion of the ſoul without hurting the body; as lightning injures not the ſcabbard, when it melts the ſword.

20. Vicious examples are moſt noxious when ſet off and recommended by the charms of oratory, or poetry; as ſome poiſonous plants growing on a mountain in China are ſaid to kill only when they are in *flower*.

21. Naturaliſts tell us of harts and hinds, that, in croſſing a piece of water, the hart, as the ſtrongeſt, ſwimmeth firſt, to break the force of the ſtream, and the hind, as being weaker, followeth reclining her head on his back. Woman is the weaker veſſel,

and ſtandeth in need of man to be her conductor through life; that, under his guidance, ſhe may ſtem the torrent of the world, and reach, in ſafety, the ſhore of eternity. "Let her be as the loving "hind, and pleaſant roe;" and let her welfare and ſecurity be equally attended to by her huſband.

22. Huſbandmen are careful continually to ſtir and looſen the earth about the roots of plants. Otherwiſe it grows dry and hard, and miniſters no nutriment. The mind will do the ſame unleſs exercifed, and will ſtarve the virtuous principles planted in it. Our Lord applies this, in the parable of the fig-tree—"I will *dig* about it."

Eſt etiam ille labor curandis vitibus alter,
Cui nunquam exhauſti ſatis eſt. Namque omne quotannis
Terque quaterque ſolum ſcindendum, glebaque verſis
Æternùm frangenda bidentibus. GEORG. ii. 397.

To dreſs thy vines new labour is requir'd,
Nor muſt the painful huſbandman be tir'd:
For thrice, at leaſt, in compaſs of the year,
Thy vineyard muſt employ the ſturdy ſteer
To turn the glebe; beſides thy daily pain,
To break the clods, and make the ſurface plain.
DRYDEN, 548

23. How fine an application do the following lines of the ſame poet admit of, to the benefits of *adverſity*, and the manner in which the divine huſbandman "*purges* every fruitful branch in his VINE, "that it may bring forth more fruit!"

Ac jam olim ſeras poſuit cum vinea frondes,
Frigidus et ſylvis Aquilo decuſſit honorem,

Jam tum acer curas venientem extendit in annum
Rusticus, et curvo Saturni dente relictam
Persequitur vitem attondens, fingitque putando.

GEORG. ii. 403.

Ev'n in the lowest months, when storms have shed
From vines the hairy honours of their head;
Not then the drudging hind his labour ends,
But to the coming year his care extends:
Ev'n then the naked vine he persecutes;
His pruning knife at once reforms and cuts.

DRYDEN, 558.

So again, a few lines after, the care and diligence necessary to be employed with unremitting assiduity, to the last hour, till the grapes are gathered, and the vintage finally secured—

Jam vinctæ vites; jam falcem arbusta reponunt:
Jam canit extremos effœtus vinitor antes:
Sollicitanda tamen tellus pulvisque movendus,
Et jam maturis metuendus Jupiter uvis. GEORG. ii. 416.

The vines, now ty'd with many a strength'ning band,
No more the culture of the knife demand;
Glad for his labour past and long employ,
At the last rank the dresser sings for joy:
Yet still he must subdue, still turn the mould,
And his ripe grapes still fear rough storms or piercing cold.

WARTON, 499.

Again, the tenderness with which young shoots are to be treated and encouraged—

Ac dum prima novis adolescit frondibus ætas,
Parcendum teneris; et dum se lætus ad auras
Palmes agit, laxis per purum immissus habenis,
Ipsa acies nondum falcis tentanda. GEORG. ii. 362.

But

But in their tender non-age, while they ſpread
Their ſpringing leaves and lift their infant head,
And upward while they ſhoot in open air,
Indulge their ohildhood, and the nurſeling ſpare:
Nor exerciſe they rage on new-born life,
But let thy hand ſupply the pruning knife.

DRYDEN, 497.

24. The deſcription of the growth of plants in the ſpring to young and virtuous minds—

Inque novos ſoles audent ſe gramina tutò
Credere; nec metuit ſurgentes pampinus auſtros,
Aut actum cœlo magnis aquilonibus imbrem:
Sed trudit gemmas, et frondes explicat omnes.

GEORG. ii. 332.

The ſpringing graſs to truſt this ſeaſon dares;
No tender vine the gath'ring tempeſt fears.
By the black north or roaring auſter roll'd,
But ſpreads her leaves, and bids her gems unfold.

WARTON, 404.

25. In the work of ſalvation, as in that of huſbandry, man muſt do his part, and God will not fail to do his.

Multum adeo raſtris glebas qui frangit inertes,
Vimineaſque trahit crates, juvat arva, neque illum
Flava Ceres alto nequicquam ſpectat Olympo;
Et qui proſciſſo quæ ſuſcitat æquore terga
Rurſus in obliquum verſo perrumpit aratro,
Exercetque frequens tellurem, atque imperat arvis.

GEORG. i. 94.

Much too he helps his labour'd lands, who breaks
The crumbling clods with harrows, drags and rakes;
Who ploughs acroſs, and back, with ceaſeleſs toil,
Subdues to duſt and triumphs o'er the ſoil;

Z 2 Plenty

Plenty to him, induſtrious ſwain! is giv'n,
And Ceres ſmiles upon his work from heav'n.

WARTON, 114.

26. It is one part of a clergyman's office to deduce, from the ſublime doctrines of the Goſpel, arguments of conſolation, to refreſh and renew the afflicted and weary ſoul. Let the following paſſage be applied to him in theſe circumſtances:

Et cum exuſtus ager morientibus æſtuat herbis,
Ecce ſupercilio clivoſi tramitis undam
Elicit: illa cadens raucum per lævia murmur
Saxa ciet, ſcatebriſque arentia temperat arva.

GEORG. i. 107.

Thus when the fiery ſuns too fiercely play,
And ſhrivell'd herbs on with'ring ſtems decay,
The wary ploughman on the mountain's brow
Undams his wat'ry ſtores; huge torrents flow,
And, rattling down the rocks, large moiſture yield,
Temp'ring the thirſty fever of the field.

DRYDEN, 157.

27. He, who is entruſted with the education of youth, ſhould, above all things, in the firſt place, explore and conſider well the different tempers, diſpoſitions, and abilities of his ſcholars, that they may be trained to the ſeveral profeſſions, or arts, for the ſtudy of which they are reſpectively fitted and qualified by nature. This is the advice given by Virgil to his farmer, that he ſhould find out

Et quid quæque ferat regio, et quod quæque recuſet.
Hic ſegetes, illic veniunt felicius uvæ:
Arborei fœtus alibi, atque injuſſa vireſcunt
Gramina, &c. . . . . . . GEORG. i. 54.

The

The culture ſuited to the ſev'ral kinds
Of ſeeds and plants; and what will thrive and riſe,
And what the genius of the ſoil denies.
This ground with Bacchus, that with Ceres ſuits,
That other loads the trees with golden fruits;
A fourth with graſs unbidden decks the ground.

DRYDEN, 78.

28. When the mind is fatigued with one employment, it may find eaſe and refreſhment by addreſſing itſelf to another of a different nature: as land will receive benefit by change of grain, as much as by lying fallow.——

Sic quoque mutatis *requieſcunt* fœtibus arva.

GEORG. i. 82.

Thus change of ſeeds for meagre ſoils is beſt;
And earth manur'd not idle, tho' at reſt.

DRYDEN, 120.

29. Virgil, ſpeaking of the huſbandman's additional labours occaſioned by noxious animals and plants, makes a fine reflection upon the deſign of Providence in permitting ſuch things.—

——— Pater ipſe colendi
Haud facilem eſſe viam voluit, primuſque per artem
Movit agros, curis acuens mortalia corda;
Nec torpere gravi paſſus ſua regna veterno, &c.

GEORG. i. 121

The ſire of gods and men, with hard decrees,
Forbids our plenty to be bought with eaſe;
And wills that mortal men, inur'd to toil,
Should exerciſe, with pains, the grudging ſoil.

Himſelf invented firſt the ſhining ſhare,
And whetted human induſtry by care.
Himſelf did handicrafts and arts ordain;
Nor ſuffer'd ſloth to ruſt his active reign.

DRYDEN, 183.

30. Civet-cats muſt be fretted and vexed, before the civet is taken out of the bag; for the more the animal is enraged, the muſk is the better.—The only caſe, I think, wherein fretfulneſs and rage turn to account, and improve things.

31. Wit under the influence of paſſion degenerates into malignity, as ſalt expoſed to violent heats will turn *ſour* and *bitter*.

32. Some particulars in natural hiſtory, though confeſſedly fabulous, are univerſally retained and employed as alluſions; for which purpoſe they ſerve as well as if they were true: *e. g.* the phœnix, as a rarity, and as a beautiful ſymbol of the reſurrection; and the notion of a ſwan becoming vocal and melodious juſt before its death. Thus Socrates, as cited by Cicero, —"*Itaque commemorat, ut cygni, qui non ſine cauſâ* "*Apollini dicati ſunt, ſed quod ab eo divinationem* "*habere videantur, quâ* providentes quid in morte "boni ſit, cum cantu et voluptate moriantur; "ſic omnibus bonis et doctis eſſe faciundum." Tuſcul. Diſputat. i. 30.—As ſwans, inſpired by Apollo with a foreſight of the joys of death, die with ſatiſfaction and ſong; ſuch ſhould be the conduct of the wiſe and good.

33. "The

33. "The ſun" (ſaid Mr. Charron) "is my viſi-"ble God, as God is my inviſible ſun."

34. To the converſation of a Chriſtian may be applied what Dr. Cadogan ſays of a child's *breath*—"It is not enough that it be not offenſive; it ſhould "be ſweet and fragrant, like a noſegay of freſh "flowers, or a pail of new milk from a young cow "that feeds upon the ſweeteſt graſs of the ſpring: "and this as well at firſt waking in the morning as "all the day long."—Eſſay on Nurſing Children, p. 46.

35. Riches, honours, and pleaſures are the *ſweets* which deſtroy the mind's appetite for its heavenly food; poverty, diſgrace, and pain are the *bitters* which reſtore it.

36. Young trees in a thick foreſt are found to incline themſelves towards that part through which the *light* penetrates; as plants are obſerved to do in a darkened chamber towards a ſtream of *light* let in through an orifice, and as the ears of corn do towards the *ſouth*. The roots of plants are known to turn away, with a kind of abhorrence, from whatever they meet with, which is hurtful to them; and, deſerting their ordinary direction, to tend, with a kind of natural and irreſiſtible impulſe, towards collections of *water* placed within their reach. The plants called *Heliotropæ* turn daily round with the ſun, and, by conſtantly preſenting their ſurfaces to that luminary, ſeem deſirous of abſorbing a nutriment from its rays. —Surely all theſe afford a leſſon to man.

37. Mr. Temple, at More-park, kept an eagle, into whose cage, among other provision, a living magpie was one day cast. The servants, next morning, were surprised to find the magpie still alive, who lived a great while very comfortably in that state. The eagle seemed much pleased with him, and was often seen to listen very attentively, and not without some degree of admiration, to his chattering.—So kings formerly reckoned it a piece of state to keep a fool.

38. The injunctions given to the Jews, not to eat any creature which died of itself, seem to have a strict regard to health; and ought, on that account, to be observed by Christians as well as Jews.—Buchan's *Domestic Medicine*.—The blood, in these cases, is mixed with the flesh, and soon becomes putrid.

39. To an angry controvertist, endeavouring to puzzle a cause, and to avoid conviction, apply Virgil's description of Cacus—Æn. viii. 252.

Faucibus ingentem fumum (mirabile dictu!)
Evomit, involvitque domum caligine cæcâ,
Prospectum eripiens oculis; glomeratque sub antro
Fumiferam noctem, commistis igne tenebris.

He from his nostrils, and huge mouth, expires
Black clouds of smoke amidst his father's fires;
Gath'ring, with each repeated blast, the night,
To make uncertain aim and erring fight.

Dryden, 335.

40. To the metaphysics of Hume, Le Clerc, and Bolingbroke——

Ibant

Ibant obſcuri ſolâ ſub nocte per umbras,
Perque domos Ditis vacuas, et inania regna.

ÆN. vi. 264.

Obſcure they went, thro' dreary ſhades that led
Along the waſte dominions of the dead.

DRYDEN, 378.

41. To the Arian hereſy——

At ſæva e ſpeculis tempus dea nacta nocendi,
Ardua tecta petit ſtabuli, et de culmine ſummo
Paſtorale canit *ſignum*, cornuque recurvo
Tartaream intendit vocem; quâ protenus omne
Contremuit nemus, et ſylvæ intonuere profundæ.
Audiit et Triviæ longè lacus, audiit amnis,
Sulphureâ Nar albus aquâ, fonteſque Velini:
Et trepidæ matres preſſere ad pectora natos.

ÆN. vii. 511.

And now the goddeſs, exercis'd in ill,
Who watch'd an hour to work her impious will,
Aſcends the roof, and to her crooked horn,
Such as was then by Latian ſhepherds borne,
Adds all her breath: the rocks and woods around
And mountains tremble at th' infernal ſound.
The ſacred lake of Trivia from afar,
The Veline fountains, and ſulphureous Nar
Shake at the baleful blaſt, the ſignal of the war.
Young mothers wildly ſtare, with fear poſſeſt,
And ſtrain their helpleſs infants to their breaſt.

DRYDEN, 713.

42. The eyes of ſwine are turned down towards the earth, ſo that they never behold the heavens, till laid upon their backs; a method ſometimes taken by their keepers, to ſtill their crying.—Apply this

to

to the effects produced by afflictions on worldly-minded men.

43. "April 5, 1772, at midnight, two violent "shocks of an earthquake were felt at Lisbon. "This earthquake was preceded by the *howling of* "*dogs*, and the *melancholy crowing of cocks*. Imme-"diately was heard a subterranean noise, with *howl*-"*ings and whistlings*, as in a great storm: this was "followed by an horizontal shock," &c.—With what unspeakable horror do these circumstances strike the imagination!

44. In the moral, as in the natural world, many trees, after all possible pains have been taken about them, fail in fruit-time. Happy the Christian husbandman, to whom may be applied what Virgil says of his old Corycian gardener;

Quotque in flore novo pomis se fertilis arbos
Induerat, totidem autumno matura tenebat.

GEORG. iv. 142.

For ev'ry bloom his trees in spring afford
An autumn apple was by tale restor'd.

DRYDEN, 211.

45. Apply to repentance, a medicine sharp, but salutary, Virgil's account of the citron—

Media fert *tristes* succos, *tardumque* saporem
Felicis mali; quo non præsentius ullum
Auxilium venit, et membris agit atra venena.

GEORG. ii. 126.

Sharp-tasted citrons Median climes produce,
Bitter the rind, but gen'rous is the juice:
A cordial fruit, a present antidote, &c.

DRYDEN, 175.

46. The

46. The old ſchool maxim, that "the corrup-"tion of one thing is the generation of another," is true in ſpirituals, as well as in phyſics. The death of the old man is the life of the new; and from affections carnal and ſecular, when mortified by the power of religion, ſpring up holy and heavenly ones, vigorous and active in proportion.

Nigra fere, et preſſo pinguis ſub vomere terra,
Et cui *putre* ſolum, *namque hoc imitamur* arando,
Optima frumentis; non ullo ex æquore cernes
Plura domum tardis decedere plauſtra juvencis.

Georg. ii. 203.

Fat crumbling earth is fitter for the plough,
Putrid and looſe above, and black below:
For ploughing is an imitative toil,
Reſembling nature in an eaſy ſoil.
No land for ſeed like this, no fields afford
So large an income to the village lord:
No toiling teams from harveſt labour come
So late at night, ſo heavy laden home.

Dryden, 280.

Therefore, as Virgil goes on, ground where wood has grown, and the leaves, &c. have rotted, though of an unpromiſing appearance, proves fruitful when turned up.——

At rudis enituit, *impulſo vomere* campus.

While ſhines the new-turn'd ſoil beneath th' invading ſhare. Warton, 266.

47. There are *minds*, as well as lands, of ſo harſh and crabbed a diſpoſition that little can be made of them.

Salsa autem tellus, et quæ perhibetur amara,
Frugibus infelix; ea nec mansuescit arando,
Nec Baccho genus, aut pomis sua nomina servat.

GEORG. ii. 238.

Salt earth and bitter are not fit to sow,
Nor will be tam'd or mended with the plough.
Sweet grapes degen'rate there, and fruits declin'd
From their first flav'rous taste, renounce their kind.

DRYDEN, 323.

48. A genius forward, and early ripe, seldom, in the end, answers expectation. Virgil has observed the same thing of land, which throws forth corn too strong at first.——

Ah! nimium ne sit mihi fertilis illa,
Neu se prævalidam primis ostendat aristis!

GEORG. ii. 252.

Let not my land so large a promise boast,
Lest the lank ears in length of stem be lost.

DRYDEN, 341.

49. The character of an universal scholar is apt to dazzle the sight, and to attract ambition. But a greater progress is made in literature, when every man takes his part, and cultivates that part thoroughly, with all his powers.——

- - - - - Laudato ingentia rura;
Exiguum colito.—

GEORG. ii. 412.

To larger vineyards praise and wonder yield;
But cultivate a small and manageable field.

WARTON, 495.

50. Inventors and projectors, however wild and

5 visionary,

visionary, often afford matter, which a wise man will know how to qualify and turn to use, though they did not.—See Account of Settlements in America, i. 65.

51. When an hogshead of sugar is in the highest state of fermentation over the fire, a piece of *butter*, no bigger than a nut, will allay and quiet it in a moment. A tea-spoonful of *oil* quieted the ruffled surface of near half an acre of water in a windy day, and rendered it smooth as a looking-glass.—See Dr. Franklin's account, Phil. Transf. lxiv. part ii.—Like the Divine Spirit, oil acts as a bond of peace to the whole mass which is under its influence.

52. The note of the cuckoo, though uniform, always gives pleasure, because it reminds us that summer is coming. But that pleasure is mixed with melancholy, because we reflect, that what is coming will soon be going again. This is the consideration which embitters every sublunary enjoyment!—Let the delight of my heart then be in thee, O Lord and Creator of all things, with whom alone is no variableness, neither shadow of changing!

53. The world twines itself about the soul, as a serpent doth about an eagle, to hinder its flight upward, and sting it to death.

54. "The affected gaiety of a wicked man is like "the flowery surface of Mount Ætna, beneath which "materials are gathering for an eruption, that will "one day reduce all its beauties to ruin and desola-"tion."—Irene.

55. The

55. The Chriſtian traveller, in his journey through the deſert, like Haſſan, muſt be always *awake*, and upon the *watch*.

At that dead hour the ſilent aſp ſhall creep,
If aught of reſt I find, upon my ſleep;
Or ſome ſwoln ſerpent twiſt his ſcales around,
And wake to anguiſh with a burning wound.

COLLINS's Ecl. ii.

56. So manifold are the diſeaſes to which the body of man is become ſubject, that, in a treatiſe of a Dr. Richard Baniſter, 113 diſeaſes are mentioned, as incident to the *eyes and eyelids* only. See Biog. Brit.—Whether *the mind's eye* be liable to fewer, may be queſtioned.

57. The death and reſurrection of Chriſt repreſent and produce in man a death to ſin, and a reſurrection to righteouſneſs —When the ſun recedes from the autumnal equinox, he brings on the fall of the leaf, with a general withering and ſeeming extinction of the vegetable life during the dead of winter; and, when in his annual motion he riſes again towards our hemiſphere, nature feels a kind of reſurrection.—Heylyn's Lectures, ii. 429.

58. It is with a Chriſtian, as with the Sicilian vines.—"An old proprietor" (ſays Swinburne) "informed me, that the ſtrength of the liquor depended on the cloſe pruning of the vine."—Travels in the Sicilies, ii. 240. ſect. 33.

59. Dr.

59. Dr. Johnſon thus ſpeaks of his ſituation at Rauſay: "Such a ſeat of hoſpitality amidſt the winds "and waters fills the imagination with a delightful "contrariety of images: without is the rough ocean "and the rocky land, the beating billows and the "howling ſtorm: within is plenty and elegance, "beauty and gaiety, the ſong and the dance!"—Apply this to the ſtate of a good man's mind amidſt the troubles of the world, "rejoicing in tribulation."—So ſings a poet, of *conſcience*—

'Tis the warm blaze in the poor herdſman's hut,
That, when the ſtorm howls o'er his humble thatch,
Brightens his clay-built walls, and cheers his ſoul.

COUNT OF NARBONNE, act iv. ſc. 4.

60. It is difficult for a man to ſuppreſs a conceit which tickles his own fancy, though he be ſure to ſuffer by the publication of it. Owen, the epigrammatiſt, had expectations from an uncle, who was a Papiſt; but he could not reſiſt the charm of the following ſatirical diſtich:

An fuerit *Petrus* Romæ, ſub judice lis eſt;
Simonem Romæ nemo fuiſſe negat.

The conſequence was, that the book was put into the *Index Expurgatorius*, and poor Owen put out of his uncle's will.

PARA-

PARADISE.

How beautiful this of Shakſpeare!——

Conſideration, like an angel, came
And whipp'd th' offending Adam out of him;
Leaving his body like a Paradiſe,
T' envelop and contain celeſtial ſpirits.

PARTY.

1. In proſelyting men to a party, one convert is employed to make more from among his old friends and connections; ſomewhat in the manner in which wild gazelles are caught, by ſending into the herd one already *taken* and *tamed*, with a *nooſe* ſo faſtened to his horns, as to entangle the animal that firſt approaches to oppoſe him."—Goldſmith, iii. 86.

2. One is apt ſometimes to wonder, why the characters, ſayings, and writings of ſome men ſtand ſo high in the opinion and eſteem of others. The phænomenon may, perhaps, be partly accounted for by the following obſervation of Dr. Goldſmith:—"It is probable," (ſays he) "there is not in the "creation an animal of more importance to a "*gooſe* than a *gander*."

PATIENCE.

1. A surgeon is never more calm and free from paſſion than when he is about to lance a ſwelling, or

or to perform an amputation. If he were not ſo, he would be likely to miſcarry in the operation, and to kill, inſtead of curing, his patient.—Let this be applied to the caſe of a clergyman reproving, or inflicting eccleſiaſtical cenſures.—*Ut ad urendum et ſecandum, ſic et ad hoc genus caſtigandi rarò invitique veniamus.—Ira procul abſit, cum quâ nihil rectè fieri, nihil conſideratè poteſt.*—Cic. Off. i. ſec. 38.—Like the inciſion knife, and the cauſtic, let this ſpecies of chaſtiſement be rarely and unwillingly reſorted to: in all events let it be inflicted without anger, which in all things is abſolutely inconſiſtent with propriety and deliberation.—See Arnold on Ecclus, xx. 1.

2. The *portraits* of a man of wealth, a man of pleaſure, and a man of power, do not excite our envy. Why then ſhould the *originals*, which are made of as corruptible materials, which paſs away like ſhadows, and laſt not ſo long as their pictures?

3. Afflictions, when accompanied with grace, alter their nature, as wormwood, eaten with bread, will loſe its bitterneſs.—See Arbuthnot on Aliment, p. 15.

4. The bark of a tree contains an oily juice, which, when it is in greater plenty than can be exhaled by the ſun, renders the plant evergreen. Such is the ſtate of the man whoſe virtue is proof againſt the ſcorching heats of temptation and perſecution: he is "like a green olive-tree," in the courts of the temple; "his leaf ſhall not wither."

5. Women are generally ſuppoſed to be in mind, as well as body, of a more delicate frame than men; yet, in the primitive times, they went unhurt through the hotteſt flames of perſecution: as the utmoſt force of boiling water is not able to deſtroy the ſtructure of the tendereſt plant, and the lineaments of a white lily will remain after the ſtrongeſt decoction.

6. An Italian biſhop, who had endured much perſecution with a calm unruffled temper, was aſked by a friend how he attained to ſuch a maſtery of himſelf.—"By making a right uſe of my eyes," ſaid he. "I firſt look up to heaven, as the place whi-
"ther I am going to live for ever: I next look down
"upon the earth, and conſider how ſmall a ſpace of
"it will ſoon be all that I can occupy or want. I
"then look round me, and think how many are far
"more wretched than I am."

7. Regner Lodbrog, impriſoned in a loathſome dungeon, and condemned to be deſtroyed by venomous ſerpents, ſolaced his deſperate ſituation by recollecting and reciting the glorious exploits of his paſt life.—The ſoul, confined in its priſon, the body, and infeſted by deſtructive paſſions, ſhould ſupport and comfort itſelf, by recollecting and celebrating the triumphs of its Redeemer, ſet forth in the Pſalms: ſo Paul and Silas.—See Taylor's Holy Dying, on *Patience*—the caſe of the *Gladiators*.

8. The croſs which is laid upon us muſt be borne: if we are impatient, we loſe the fruit of it; but

if we accept it willingly, and bear it with patience and meek reſignation, it is regarded as equivalent to a puniſhment of our own infliction.

PIETY.

As drawn by Fenelon in a letter to his pupil, the Duke of Burgundy—of whoſe devotion people had ſaid it was "*ſombre, ſcrupuleuſe, & qui* "*n'eſt pas aſſez proportionnée à ſon place.*"—Melancholy, full of ſcruples, not ſufficiently adapted to his ſituation.—"*Si vous voulez faire honneur à votre* "*pieté, vous ne ſauriez trop la rendre douce, ſimple,* "*commode, ſociale.*"—If you wiſh to do honour to your piety, you cannot be too careful to render it ſweet and ſimple, affable and ſocial.—See Maury, 443.

PLEASURE.

1. SURROUNDED with all the gaieties and glories of the court of France, Maintenon and Pompadour both experienced the depredations of melancholy; and declared they were not the happy perſons they ſeemed to be, and that "in all ſtates "of life there was a frightful void." The retreats of St. Cyr and Bellevue were the places in which, (if ever) they taſted happineſs. Ann. Regiſter, 1766. Memoirs of Mad. Pompadour.—See a letter of Lady M. W. Montague, in which ſhe extols the ſuperior

felicity of a milkmaid. These testimonies are curious, and worth noting.

2. A child is eager to have any toy he sees; but throws it away at the sight of another, and is equally eager to have *that*. We are most of us *children*, through life; and only change one *toy* for another, from the cradle to the grave.

3. They, who would enjoy health and strength, should follow the rule prescribed by Constantine, in the education of his sons: Consult in your nourishment only the wants of nature, and seek only in the toils of the body the relaxation of the mind. But most of our amusements now are of the sedentary kind, cards, &c. and journies are performed in the easiest vehicles.

4. People wish for great estates, generally, that they may be enabled by them to live a life of *indulgence*, and follow their *diversions*; which was the very idea formed of this matter by the boy, who said, that if he had the 'squire's estate, he would *eat fat bacon* and *swing all day upon farmer Hobson's gate*.—For the different ideas of people of pleasure, Selden tells of the boy, who said, if he were a lord, he would have a great whip as cried *slash*.

5. The colliers, in the north of England, pass most of their time under ground. When they emerge into day-light, the only thing they take any pleasure in is *cock-fighting*—as if the sun and air had been made for no other purpose.

6. Let

6. Let us think of the moſt exquiſite ſpiritual pleaſures we ever felt on earth, and reflect, that thoſe pleaſures will be eternal in heaven!

> The gentle ſpring, that but ſalutes us here,
> Inhabits *there*, and courts them all the year.

7. We are ſo made as to be always pleaſed with ſomewhat *in proſpect*, however diſtant, or however trivial. Hence the pleaſures of planting, ſowing, building, raiſing a family, educating children, &c. The advancement of our minds, in this world, towards that perfection, of which they are to be poſſeſſed in the next, ſhould be the grand object of our attention.

8. The Spartans wiſhed to their enemies, that they might be ſeized with a humour of building, and keep a race of horſes: the Cretans, that they might be delighted with ſome evil cuſtom.—See Wanley, 137. Becauſe he, whom pleaſure lays hold of, will ſoon be impotent and of no effect.

PLURALITIES.

An ingenious French author (Bourſault) relates the following ſtory.—An Abbé, who had no preferment, exclaiming one day to Boileau againſt pluralities—"Is it poſſible," ſays the eccleſiaſtic, "that the "people you named, who have the reputation of being "very learned men, and are ſuch in reality, ſhould be "miſtaken in their opinion? Unleſs theſe would ab-

" ſolutely oppoſe the doctrine laid down by the apoſtles, " and the directions of councils, muſt they not be " obliged to confeſs, that the holding ſeveral livings at " the ſame time is ſinful? I myſelf am in holy orders, " and, be it ſaid without vanity, of one of the beſt fa- " milies in Touraine. It becomes a man of high birth " to make a figure ſuitable to it, and yet, I proteſt to " you, that if I can get an abbey, the yearly income of " which is only 1000 crowns, my ambition will be " ſatisfied; and be aſſured, that nothing ſhall tempt me " to alter my reſolution."—Some time after, an abbey of 7000 crowns a year being vacant, his brother deſired it for him, and was gratified in his requeſt. The winter following he got another of ſtill greater value; and, a third being vacant, he ſolicited very ſtrongly for this alſo, and obtained it. Boileau, hearing of theſe preferments, went and paid his friend a viſit. " Mr. Abbé," ſays he, " where is now " that ſeaſon of innocence and candour, in which you " declared that pluraliſts hazarded their ſouls greatly?" " Ah! good Boileau," replied the Abbé, " did you but " know how much pluralities contribute towards living " well!"—" I am in no doubt of that," replied Boileau; " but of what ſervice are they, good Abbé, towards " dying well?

POISONOUS PLANTS.

Plants have their atmoſpheres formed of particles emitted from them on all ſides. Theſe atmo- ſpheres

ſpheres have various effects on thoſe who ſtay in them: ſome refreſh the ſpirits, and enliven a man; others bring on a fit of the vapours; and a third ſort lay him aſleep. Thus it is exactly with *men*, and with *books*. It is reported, that in Brazil there are trees, which kill thoſe that ſit under their ſhade in a few hours. Beware of peſtilential authors and their works.

POMFRET.

An old woman, who ſhewed the houſe and pictures at Towceſter, expreſſed herſelf in theſe remarkable words: "That is Sir Robert Farmer: he "lived in the country, took care of his eſtate, built "this houſe, and paid for it; managed well, ſaved "money, and died rich.——*That* is his ſon; he "was made a Lord, took a place at court, ſpent "his eſtate, and died a beggar!"—A very conciſe, but full and ſtriking account.

PREACHING.

1. A church ſtocked with unpreaching divines is like the city of Nibas in the neighbourhood of Theſſalonica in Macedonia, where, Ælian tells us, the cocks were all dumb. Lib. xv. cap. 20.

2. It is as neceſſary for a preacher, in the compoſition of his ſermon, to take into conſideration the paſſions and prejudices of his audience, as it is for

an archer to choose his arrows with an eye to the wind and weather.

3. Preachers would do eminent service to religion; if, instead of labouring to prove plain points, which nobody disputes, such as the obligations of duty, they would employ their powers in stating its measures, discovering the various ways men have of eluding it, and shewing them their conformity or nonconformity to it.

4. The art of *fine speaking* is one thing, that of *persuasion* another. The prudent and affectionate address of a parent or a friend, however plain and unpolished, will do more towards inclining the will, than all the tropes and figures, the logic and rhetoric of the schools.

5. "Scarce any thing," says Dr. Trapp, "has of "late years been more prejudicial to religion, than "the neglect of the *theological* part of it, properly so "called: and it is very greatly to be lamented, that "some writers, even of our own church, out of an un- "due fervour in opposing some erroneous doctrines of "Calvin, have run into the other extreme, and have "too little regarded the necessary doctrines of reli- "gion." Pref. to Preservative, p. 5.

6. To preach *practical* sermons, as they are called, *i. e.* sermons upon virtues and vices, without inculcating those great scripture truths of redemption, grace, &c. which alone can incite and enable us to forsake sin and follow after righteousness, what is it but to put

put together the wheels, and ſet the hands of a watch, forgetting the *ſpring*, which is to make them all go?

7. St. Auſtin did not think himſelf bound to abſtain from all ornaments of ſtyle, becauſe St. Paul ſaid, that he preached the goſpel *not with the enticing words of man's wiſdom. Non prætermitto iſtos numeros clauſularum.*—I do not neglect the muſic of my periods.—He ſtudied to make his language ſweet and harmonious.—See Donne's Sermons, p. 48.

8. Tully's cenſure, paſſed on immoral philoſophers, comes home to the buſineſs and boſoms of wicked clergymen.—*Ut enim, ſi grammaticum ſe profeſſus quiſpiam barbarè loquatur; aut ſi abſurdè canat is, qui ſe haberi velit muſicum, hoc turpior ſit, quod in eo ipſo peccet, cujus profitetur ſcientiam: ſic philoſophus in vitæ ratione peccans, hoc turpior eſt, quod in officio, cujus magiſter eſſe volt, labitur; artemque vitæ profeſſus, delinquit in vitâ.*—See the whole paſſage—*Tuſc. Quæſt.* lib. ii. ſec. 4. non procul ab init. Glaſg. p. 58.—As a grammarian, who ſhould ſpeak barbarous language, or a muſician, who ſhould ſing out of tune, would be the more deſpicable for failing in the very art in which he profeſſed to excel; ſo the philoſopher, whoſe conduct is vicious or immoral, becomes an object of greater diſgrace; ſince, while inculcating the duties of life, he fails in their performance; and, undertaking to reform the lives of others, ſins in the regulation of his own.

9. Terſe

9. Terse moral essays, opposed to the overflowings of ungodliness, remind one of the Chinese, who, in tempestuous weather, throw feathers into the sea, to quiet the storm, and drive away the devil.—See Travels of the Jesuits, by Lockman, ii. 58.

10. It is much to the honour of the Athenians, that they had a law among them, obliging every man, who found a stranger that had lost his way, to direct him into it again. A Christian is under obligation, by the divine law, to do the same in spirituals.

11. At the critical moment of that night, when Count Lestock, in 1741, was going to conduct the Princess Elizabeth to the palace, to dethrone the Regent, and put her in possession of the Russian empire, fear preponderated, and the princess refused to set out. The Count then drew from his pocket two cards, on one of which she was represented under the tonsure in a convent, and himself on a scaffold: on the other, she appeared ascending the throne, amidst the acclamations of the people. He laid both before her, and bade her choose her situation. She chose the throne, and before morning was Empress of all the Russias.—A preacher should take the same method with his people, which the Count took with the Princess. Before the eyes of those who halt between God and the world, through fear or any other motive, should be placed pictures of the joys of heaven, and the pains of

hell.

hell. It remains only for them to choose right, and proceed to action. Success will be the consequence.

12. When the Romans heard Cicero, says Fenelon, they cried out, *O le bel orateur!*—O what a fine orator!—But when the Athenians heard Demosthenes, they called out, *Allons, battons Philippe!*—Come on, down with Philip!—The difference between the eloquence of the Grecian and that of the Roman orator is here expressed in a manner equally judicious and lively: and this is the true criterion of a *sermon*, as well as of an *oration*.—The exclamation of the audience should be, not, *O le bel orateur!* but, *Allons, battons Philippe!*—Let us attack such a *passion*, such an *appetite*, such an *error*; let us oppose the *world*, the *flesh*, and the *devil!* Demosthenes therefore is the author who should be studied and imitated by preachers.

PREDESTINATION.

It is much to be wished, that Christians would apply themselves to obey the gospel, instead of endeavouring to discover the designs of God concerning man before man was created, or the precise manner in which he touches the hearts of those who are converted. Salvation may be obtained without knowlege of this sort: besides, the wit of man may not be able to solve the difficulties that may be ſtarted on every ſide of theſe queſtions; upon which, obſcure and intricate as they are, if deciſions are made and enforced as articles of faith, ſchiſms and factions muſt enſue. But the miſchief is done, and there is no remedy; divines are therefore obliged to explain their own ſentiments, and oppugn thoſe of their adverſaries, reſpectively, as well as they are able. Thus ſtriſes are increaſed, time loſt, and edification neglected.

PRINGLE. (Sir John)

He was particularly fond of Biſhop Pearce's Commentary and Notes. He was brought up in principles of virtue and piety; he was ſeduced to deiſm, but brought back again by an attentive conſideration of the evidence; and *ſettled* by diſcovering that the doctrine of the Trinity made no part of the ſcriptures; that the mercy of God was not confined to a few, excluſive of others, and that future puniſhments were not eternal.—See Kippis's account prefixed to his Speeches.—This is a way of making matters eaſy: a man ſtrikes out of the goſpel what he does not like, and then is graciouſly pleaſed to profeſs himſelf a believer of the reſt. After this faſhion, the religion certainly bids fair to become *univerſal.* "Thus," ſays Kippis, "he added another name to "the catalogue of the *excellent* and *judicious* perſons "who have gloried in being *rational Chriſtians*!"

PRO-

PROSPERITY.

1. Prosperity too often has the ſame effect on a *Chriſtian*, that a calm at ſea hath on a Dutch mariner, who frequently, it is ſaid, in thoſe circumſtances, ties up the rudder, gets drunk, and goes to ſleep.

2. In deſcribing Salluſt, at one time the loud advocate of public ſpirit, and afterwards ſharing in the robberies of Cæſar, Warburton expreſſes this variation of character by the following imagery:

"No ſooner did the warm aſpect of good fortune "ſhine out again, but all thoſe exalted ideas of vir-"tue and honour, raiſed, like a beautiful kind of froſt "work, in the cold ſeaſon of adverſity, diſſolved "and diſappeared."

PROVIDENCE.

1. Sometimes it pleaſeth God to puniſh men for ſmaller ſins in this life; which would not be, unleſs greater puniſhments were prepared for greater ſins in the next. There muſt either be a future day of judgment and retribution, or no God who governs the world.

2. There is a certain part in the great drama, which God intends each of us to act; but we often take a fancy to change it for ſome other, by which means we become miſerable or ridiculous. "It is "an uncontrolled truth," ſays Swift, "that no man "ever

"ever made an ill figure who underſtood his own "talents, nor a good one who miſtook them."—See Aſcham, p. 166.

3. The ſchemes of worldly politicians are ſo many ſpiders' webs, which, when woven with infinite care and pains, are ſwept away at a ſtroke, by Providence, with *the beſom of deſtruction.*

Omnia ſunt hominum tenui pendentia filo;
Et ſubito caſu, quo valuere, ruunt.

OVID.

Hung on a thread, man's periſhable pride
Trembles, and falls as fate and chance decide.

4. What inextricable confuſion muſt the world for ever have been in, but for the variety which we find to obtain in the faces, the voices, and the hand-writings of men! No ſecurity of perſon, no certainty of poſſeſſion, no juſtice between man and man, no diſtinction between good and bad, friends and foes, father and child, huſband and wife, male and female. All would have been expoſed to malice, fraud, forgery, and luſt. But now, every man's face can diſtinguiſh him in the light, his voice in the dark, and his hand-writing can ſpeak for him though abſent, and be his witneſs to all generations. Did this happen by chance, or is it not a manifeſt, as well as an admirable, indication of a divine ſuperintendence?—See Derham, i. 310.

5. When we peruſe the hiſtory of Iſrael in the Scriptures, we behold the working of Providence in every

every event. The hiſtory of other nations would appear in the ſame light, if the ſame perſon were to write it, and unfold in like manner the grounds and reaſons of his proceedings with *them*. At preſent we muſt learn as much as we can, by an application of parallel caſes. So with regard to individuals.

6. We eaſily perſuade ourſelves that a cauſe is good, when its patrons are victorious, and have the diſpoſition of things in their hands. Cicero, pleading before Cæſar, for the life of Ligarius, ſays, that, while the civil war was carrying on, *Cauſa tum dubia, quòd erat aliquid in utrâque parte, quod probari poſſet: nunc melior certè ea judicanda eſt, quam etiam dii adjuverint.*—The cauſe was then doubtful, ſince there was, in each party, ſomething to claim our approbation: but now undoubtedly that cauſe muſt be conſidered as the better, in whoſe favour Heaven itſelf has declared.

7. "Such a reſpect," ſays Plutarch, "had the Romans for religion, that they made all their affairs depend ſolely on the pleaſure of the gods, never ſuffering, no not in their greateſt proſperity, the leaſt neglect or contempt of their ancient rites, or oracles; being fully perſuaded, that it was of much greater importance to the public welfare, that their magiſtrates and generals ſhould reverence and obey the gods, than if they conquered and ſubdued their enemies."—In Vitâ Marcell. iii. 141.

PRO-

PROVOCATIONS

TO BE AVOIDED.

It was well said by Dr. Whichcot—"If I provoke "a man, he is the worse for my company: If I suffer "myself to be provoked by him, I shall be the "worse for his."

RECTITUDE.

Mr. Harris observes, from M. Antoninus, that *rectitude* is ascribed to actions, as denoting the directness of their progression *right-onward*, and quotes from a sonnet of Milton—

Yet I argue not
Against Heav'n's hand or will; nor bate one jot
Of heart or hope; but still bear up, and steer
Right onward.——

Three Discourses, 306.

RELIGION.

"Religion, viewed at a proper point of sight, "hath a very beautiful face. It is innocent, and "very careful not to hurt any body, or, doing it "inadvertently, is uneasy till it hath made him "amends. It always means well, and does as well "as ever it can. If it offends, it wants to be re-"conciled; confesses its faults, prays to be forgiven,

"is

" is desirous to be informed; is less adventurous; " more circumspect; sensible of its own frailty; for- " gives every body; abounds in good will; delights " in good offices; keeps itself clean; is pleased with " itself: looks cheerful; is cheerful! Why, then, " will any one be so indiscreet, as to dress this " lovely form in such a frightful manner, as to ter- " rify the beholder, instead of inviting him to em- " brace it?"—Dr. Newton's Sermon on the Mini- sterial Duty, p. 30.

RETIREMENT.

1. The din of politics in all companies makes one sometimes envy the Carthusian monks, of whom it is said—" They led a life of tranquillity amidst the " general tumults, which distracted the rest of the " world, of which they hardly heard the rumour; " and knew nothing of the mighty sovereigns of the " earth, but by name, when they prayed for them." —Volt. Hist. iv. 128.

2. The following simile of the same writer, upon a subject of the same kind, is extremely just and beautiful.—" The artificers and merchants, whose " humble station had protected them from the am- " bitious fury of the Great, were like ants, who dug " themselves peaceable and secure habitations, while " the eagles and vultures of the world were tearing " one another in pieces." iii. 25.

3. The retired situation of the old solitary saints,

 and

and their moping and musing way of life, threw them frequently into melancholy and enthusiasm, and sometimes into phrensy and madness; and, indeed, there are few heads strong enough to bear perpetual solitude, and a confinement to the same place, the same objects, the same occupations, and the same little circle of action; and when to all this is added want of proper food and proper sleep, it is no wonder if a man lose his senses. Jortin's Sermons, iii. 240.

4. Retirement is necessary at times, to relieve from the cares of life; as the Indians, in some countries, at evening bury themselves in the sand, to escape from the musquettos.—Mosely on Tropical Diseases, p. 20.

N. B. When a man retreats into the country for health, he should go to some distance from the usual scene of business, and cut off the communication with care and anxiety. Ibid. 39.

5. Though retirement is my dear delight, says Melmoth, yet upon some occasions I think I have too much of it; and I agree with Balzac, "*Que la solitude est certainement une belle chose; mais il y a plaisir d'avoir quelqu'un à qui on puisse dire de tems en tems, que la solitude est une belle chose.*" Fitz-osborn, 122.—Solitude is certainly a fine thing; but there is a pleasure in having some one whom we may tell from time to time, that solitude is a fine thing.—It is the disadvantage of retirement and solitude, that men fall into erroneous and fantastical opinions

and

and ſyſtems, for want of ſifting and proving them in converſation and friendly debate. This is well ſtated in Letter lxxiv. p. 365. W. Law was a remarkable inſtance of it.

6. Converſation ſhould certainly be more practiſed than it is, on ſubjects of ſcience, morality, and religion. The leſs a man converſes, the leſs he will be *able* to converſe. Selkirk, who ſpent three years alone in the iſland of Juan Fernandes, had almoſt loſt the uſe of his ſpeech. Thuanus uſed to ſay, reading was not of that uſe to him as converſing with learned men, which he did daily. Why was the ſtyle of Salluſt artificial and dark, when that of Cæſar and Cicero was natural and plain? Becauſe the two latter, by being accuſtomed to harangue ſenates and popular aſſemblies, gave themſelves to uſe ſuch ſpeech as *the meaneſt ſhould well underſtand, and the wiſeſt beſt allow:* whereas Salluſt wrote in his ſtudy, and from books only. Sir John Cheeke, in Aſcham, p. 339.—Cited alſo by Lord Monboddo.

RICH TO ASSIST THE POOR.

Epaminondas, who himſelf had nothing to give, ſent a friend in neceſſity to a rich citizen, with orders to aſk 1000 crowns in his name. His reaſon being demanded by the citizen—"Why," ſaid Epaminondas, "it is becauſe this honeſt man is poor, "and you are rich."—*That* he thought was a ſufficient reaſon.

SAYINGS.

1. ADRIAN, the coadjutor of Ximenes in the government of Castile, was much disturbed at the libels which flew about against them. Ximenes was perfectly easy. "If," said he, "we take the "liberty to act, others will take the liberty to talk, "and write: when they charge us falsely, we may "laugh; when truly, we must amend."

2. Dr. Green of St. John's college, trying to scate, got a terrible fall backwards. "Why, Doctor," said a friend who was with him, "I thought you "had understood the business better." "O," replied the Doctor, "I have the theory perfectly; "I want nothing but the practice."—How many of us, in matters of a much higher and more important nature, come under the doctor's predicament!

3. "You have the word, and we have the sword," said Weston to the reformed divines in Queen Mary's time.

4. Cardinal Wolsey's reflection, made just before he expired, should be laid to heart by every man, when tempted to bestow upon the world, or any thing in it, that affection and service which are due to God.—"Had I but served God as diligently "as I have served the King, HE would not have "given me over in my grey hairs."

5. To those, who would win men to religion by fire and faggot, may be applied the remark of the

Earl

Earl of Huntley, when Protector Somerfet marched into Scotland with 18,000 men, to effect a marriage between the young queen of that kingdom and Edward VI.—" That he difliked not the match, but " hated the manner of wooing."

6. A perfon coming into Melancthon's houfe, found him holding a book with one hand, and rocking a child with the other. Upon his expreffing fome furprife, Melancthon made fuch a pious difcourfe to him, about the duty of a father, and the ftate of grace in which children are with God, that this ftranger went away, fays Bayle, much more edified than he came.

7. Very ftriking is St. Auguftine's reflection, on the effect produced by our Lord's anfwer to thofe who came to apprehend him.—" I am he. Εγω ειμι." *Quid judicaturus faciet, qui judicandus hoc fecit!*—How will he act as a judge, who acted thus as a criminal!

8. Melancthon, when he went to the conferences at Spire, in 1529, made a little journey to Bretten, to fee his mother. The good woman afked him, what fhe muft believe, amidft fo many difputes? and repeated to him her prayers, which contained nothing fuperftitious. " Go on, mother," faid he, " to believe and pray, as you have done, and never " trouble yourfelf about controverfies."—The advice of a wife and a good man.

9. Three or four Englifh gentlemen on their

travels through Italy, happening to be at St. Marino, on a fish day, applied to a butcher, to procure for them, if possible, a joint of veal. The butcher said he would do any thing to oblige them, but could not kill for them, as nobody would buy but themselves. They continued very importunate, and offered to take any quantity. "Well, then, gen-"tlemen," said the fellow, at last, "I will venture to "kill a calf; and, if you will take half of it to day, "I will trust to THE REPUBLIC for the other half to-"morrow."

10. Bajazet, upon the march, at the head of his mighty army, after the capture of his favourite city Sebastia, by the enemy, hearing a poor shepherd playing on his pipe on the side of a hill, exclaimed, —"Happy shepherd, who hast no Sebastia to lose!" —Knolles.

11. Mahomet II. after he had taken Constantinople, being reproached for spending all his time with Irene, a captive Greek, forgetting his intended conquests, and neglecting the concerns of empire, ordered a convention of all his great men; produced Irene before them; asked them, if they could blame him, when they beheld her? and then, to convince them he could master his passions, seizing her by the hair with his left hand, chopped off her head with his right.

12. Very shrewd and sensible observations are often made by persons disordered in their senses. Dr. Heylyn

Heylyn uſed to apply, upon this occaſion, an old Spaniſh proverb, which ſays, that light makes its way into a dark room, through a CRACK.

13. *Nec verò ego*, ſays Sadolet, *aliud medius fidius ſtatuo eſſe ſapientiam, quam meminiſſe unumquemque quid ſui officii et muneris ſit, idque cum fide et cum integritate præſtare.* Epiſt. p. 21.—That, that alone I deem to be wiſdom, which enables a man to keep preſent to his mind a ſenſe of his duty, and with integrity and firmneſs to perform it.

14. Many of thoſe fighting heroes, ſo celebrated in ſtory, may be compared, as Mr. Boyle obſerves, to worthleſs *gnats*, conſiderable only for their *noiſe* and *ſtings* with which they diſturb men's *reſt*.

15. Valeria being aſked, why, after the death of her huſband Servius, ſhe would not marry again? anſwered, "*Ideo hoc facio quia Servius meus, licet aliis mortuus ſit, apud me vivit, vivetque ſemper.*"—This I do, becauſe my Servius, though dead to others, lives, and will ever live, to me.—See Dicterich. ii. 435.

16. Dr. Johnſon being aſked, what he thought of the Scotch univerſities: "Why, Sir," ſaid he, "they are like a beſieged town, where every man "has a mouthful, and no man has a bellyful."

17. The ſame perſon, being aſked by ſome Scotch philoſophers, whether he thought a man would exiſt by choice, or neceſſity? replied—"If an Engliſhman, by choice; if a Scotchman, by neceſſity."

 18. Ro-

18. Rochester said, with astonishment, "That "he did not know how it was, but Lord Dorset "might do any thing, and yet was never to blame." Every body excused whom every body loved for the tenderness of his nature.—Royal and Noble Authors, p. 96.

19. On Lord Dorset's promotion, King Charles, having seen Lord Craven (a proverb for officious whisperers to men in power) pay his usual tribute to him, asked the former, what the latter had been saying? The Earl gravely replied, "Sir, my Lord Craven did "me the honour to whisper, but I did not think it "good manners to listen."—This was exactly in the spirit of Charles's own witticisms. Ibid. p. 97.

20. When the same Lord Dorset was dying, Congreve, who had been to visit him, being asked how he left him, replied, "Faith, he slabbers more wit than other people have in their best health." Ibid. p. 97.

21. Shaftesbury (author of the Characteristics) attempting to speak on the bill for granting counsel to prisoners in cases of high treason, was confounded, and for some time could not proceed; but recovering himself, he said, "What now happened "to him, would serve to fortify the arguments for "the bill—If he, innocent, and pleading for others, "was daunted at the augustness of such an assembly, "what must a man be, who should plead before them "for his life?" Ibid. p. 106.

22. When

22. When the Lieutenant of the Tower offered Strafford a coach, lest he should be torn to pieces by the mob, in passing to execution; he replied, "I "die to please the people, and I will die in their "own way."—Royal and Noble Authors, p. 163.

23. Henry Lord Falkland being brought early into the House of Commons, and a grave senator objecting to his youth, and "to his not looking "as if he had sown his wild oats;" he replied with great quickness, "Then I am come to the properest "place, where are so many geese to pick them up." Ibid. p. 221.

24. "My dear Pouilly," says Bolingbroke, "of "all the men I ever knew in my life, there are but "three fit to take upon them the task of govern-"ing nations—you and I and Pope."—Pope had resigned his understanding to Bolingbroke; who was so pleased with the sacrifice, that he thought Pope, of all the men in the world, qualified to be a *prime minister*. This was most undoubtedly Pope's title; and it is natural for us to suppose, that M. Pouilly de Champeaux held his estate by the same kind of tenure.—The letter containing this very curious passage was lately published in the preface to an edition of the works of Champeaux. On the same principle of vanity, Bolingbroke palmed upon his friends a silly mistress of his for a wit, because she repeated good things which he had said, and pretended to have forgotten. *Ah, la pauvre humanité!*

25. Repentance and renovation consist not in the wish, or purpose, but in the actual operations of a good life. As Dryden observes, that speculative painting, without the assistance of manual operation, can never attain to perfection, but slothfully languishes; for it was not with his tongue that Apelles performed his noble works.

26. The ascent to greatness, however steep and dangerous, may entertain an active spirit with the consciousness and exercise of its own power; but the possession of a throne could never yet afford a lasting satisfaction to an ambitious mind. This melancholy truth was felt and acknowleged by Severus. Fortune and merit had, from an humble station, elevated him to the first place among mankind. "He "had been all things," as he said of himself, "and "all was of little value." *Omnia fuit et nihil expedit.* Distracted with the care, not of acquiring, but of preserving an empire, oppressed with age and infirmities, careless of fame, and satiated with empire, all his prospects of life were closed.—Gibbon, i. 130.

27. "Though I suffer," said Augustine when sick, "yet I am well, because I am as God would "have me to be; for when we will not what he wills, "it is we that are in the fault, and not he, who can "neither do nor permit any thing but what is just." Letter xxxviii. edit. Benedict.

28. "It is incomparably better," says he in the same Letter, "to shut the door of our heart against "just anger, when it offers to come in, than to

"give

"give it entrance; being uncertain, whether it may "not grow too powerful for us to turn it out "again."

29. "*Non est episcopatus artificium transigendæ vitæ* "*fallacis.*—Episcopacy ought not to be looked upon "as an establishment, or a means to procure the "deceitful pleasures of life." Letter lviii.

30. Nectarius, an heathen, interceding with Augustine for some of his fellow-citizens, who had committed some crime, urges this reason to prevail with him: "That it is the duty of a bishop to do "nothing but good to mankind: not to meddle "with their affairs; unless it be to make them bet-"ter, and to intercede with God to pardon their "faults." Letter xc.

SERPENTS.

The effects of their poison are wonderful; as of that called the *Copper-head* in South America. A man stung by one became like a serpent: spots of various colours alternately appeared and vanished on different parts of his body: rage filled his *eyes*, which darted the most menacing looks on all present; he thrust out his *tongue* as the snakes do, and *hissed* through his teeth with inconceivable force.—A striking picture of our great adversary, and the manner in which by his suggestions he acts on the human mind, and fills it with his own temper and disposition. These effects from the bite of a serpent

are

are not more extraordinary, than the foamings and barkings, and difpofition to bite, which have been obferved in cafes of canine madnefs.—See Letters from an American Farmer, by J. Hector St. John, letter x. Crit. Rev. April 1782, p. 267. See in the fame place the account of a battle between two fnakes, a black fnake and a water fnake, each fix feet long, till they both fell into the ditch, where one kept the head of the other under water till he was fuffocated.

SEVERITY PROFITABLE.

CHILDREN are the better for the feverity of their parents; and the reproaches of an enemy ferve often to correct and improve the perfon who is the object of them. The cafe, if we credit Erafmus, is pretty much the fame in the republic of letters.—*Unius Laurentii Vallæ mordacitas non paulo plus conduxit rei literariæ, quam plurimorum ineptus candor, omnia omnium fine delectu mirantium, fibique invicem plaudentium, ac mutuum (quod aiunt) fcabentium.* Epift. iii. 96.—The feverity of Laurentius Valla did more fervice to the caufe of letters, than the abfurd indulgence of thofe, who, giving indifcriminate praife to the works of others, expect the fame for their own, and, to ufe the words of the proverb, agree in fcratching one another.

SHAKSPEARE's

SHAKSPEARE's GENIUS.

Shakspeare was perhaps in ſome inſtances leſs inventive than is commonly imagined. It appears from Dr. Farmer's pamphlet, that there was an aſtoniſhing maſs of materials before him in old tranſlations of the claſſics, of Italian tales, romances, &c. Some of theſe are ſtill extant; but many others, the names of which are preſerved, have periſhed. From the former he is ſeen continually borrowing. The celebrated ſpeech of Volumnia to her ſon is a piece of ſuch remaining proſe, only thrown into blank verſe. In moſt caſes however, though the clay pre-exiſted, he was the Prometheus who animated it.

SHYNESS.

Mr. Loveday uſed to ſtyle *Shyneſs the Engliſh madneſs*. If indulged it may be the cauſe of madneſs, by driving men to ſhun company, and live in ſolitude, which few heads are ſtrong enough to bear—none, if it be joined with idleneſs. Or it may be the *effect* of madneſs, which is miſanthropic and malignant. Some ſay *pride* is always at the bottom. You do not like company, you are uneaſy in it. Why? You are conſcious of ſome infirmity which diſqualifies you from ſhining, and making that figure you wiſh to do. Others excel you in breeding, conver-

verſation,

versation, and the arts of pleasing. You feel self-abasement and vexation at being thus abashed and kept under: you fly from the scene of torment, hating your tormentors, and abusing them either to yourself, or in society of an inferior sort, among those who will join you, having perhaps suffered the same, or worse; and so you relieve and comfort one another. —All this, I am afraid, is too true. An Englishman is upon the reserve, according to Mrs. Piozzi, by way of security, lest he should say something open to the censure and ridicule of others, and so his character should suffer. This is upon the same principle: and so, if he cannot say something fine and witty, and *worthy of himself*, he sits sullen, and says nothing. Thus a whole company, among us, is often silent for a considerable time together, till they wish themselves and one another *farther*. The Italians, it seems, talk freely and easily all that occurs, having no such thoughts and fears. "A "Frenchman," says Ganganelli, "is superficial and "lively; an Englishman profound and gloomy." —Which is best? In a social light, and as a companion, certainly the former.

SLAVERY.

He is a slave, who cannot do that which he wishes to do, and which his sober reason and judgment dictate to be done. When this is to be the case, it is is rather better that the tyrant ſhould be *without*, than *within*; for then he is always at hand to domineer; and he is harder to be vanquiſhed and caſt off.

SOBRIETY.

THE reſidence of wiſdom is ſaid by one of the ancients to be in dry regions, not in bogs and fens. If the temperature of climate and ſoil have a great effect upon the mind, that of the body muſt needs have a far greater; and he, who, by drenching himſelf continually with liquor, puts his body into the ſtate of Holland, may expect to have the genius of a Dutchman for his pains.

SOCIAL DUTY.

1. HE, who laments that he has not leiſure to *purſue his ſtudies*, when he is called upon to perform the duties of life, ſays Epictetus, is like a champion at the Olympic games, who, when he enters the liſts, ſhould fall a crying, becauſe he is not exerciſing without.

2. A neglect of our duty to our friends and families, or to any perſon who may juſtly expect it from us, cannot be excuſed by allotting thoſe hours to meditation, to prayer, to religious ſtudies, which belong properly to ſociety, and to the exerciſe of ſocial virtues. Jortin's Sermons, iii. 238.

SOCI-

SOCINIANS.

THEY projected a league with the churches of Algiers and Morocco, in the time of Charles II. See their propoſal to the ambaſſador, in the works of Leſlie.—Adam Neuſer, who was employed to introduce Socinianiſm into Germany, being diſappointed, went into Turkey, and enliſted among the Janiſaries. Moſheim, iv. 192. 8vo. where ſee an excellent account of the riſe and progreſs of Socinianiſm and its principles. Socinus thought Chriſt was to be worſhipped. (Stillingfleet, 149.) Some of his followers went farther, and denied that article: he tried to reclaim them, but in vain.—See Stillingfleet on the Trinity, preface, p. 59. At p. 62 there is a quotation from a Socinian writer, who ſtyles the Tartars—"the ſhield and ſword of that way of worſhipping God." Paulus Alciatus is there mentioned, who from an Unitarian turned a Mahometan.

SUICIDE.

A SCORPION, when he finds himſelf incloſed, and no way left him to eſcape, will bend his tail round, and ſting himſelf through the head. And it is remarkable, that this is the only animal in the creation, man excepted, that can be made to commit *Suicide.*

SUN.

SUN.

If the ſun were intelligent, he would ſee and know all, even to the intimate ſubſtance of things, as his rays penetrate to and affect every atom of matter. Thus is the Deity intimate to the ſpirits and thoughts of men. Cudworth adduces the inſtance of the ſun, as furniſhing an idea how all things may be viewed and governed by the Deity without pain, labour or fatigue, in anſwer to the objection of the Atheiſts againſt Providence: (Bibl. Choiſ. ix. 64.) and a noble illuſtration it is as was ever conceived by man. A curious paſſage on the ſubject of God's omniſcience is cited by Le Clerc, in the ſame place, from Xenophon's Mem.. c. iv. 17. edit. Oxon. 8vo. God's glory conſiſts in the communication of his goodneſs to his creatures, as the light diffuſed from the ſun is the glory of the celeſtial luminary. Cudworth, B. C. ix. 69.

SUNDAY SCHOOLS.

The different ſects may inſtruct each its own children in a ſchool of its own; but I do not ſee how the children of different ſects can be inſtructed together in one ſchool, as their doctrines, catechiſms, &c. are different, and the children are to be conducted to ſeparate places of worſhip: the parents of one ſort will not approve of their children being carried to the church or meeting-houſe of another. How can you bring them all up in a *catholic way*, unleſs you have one *catholic* i. e. *univerſal*, *general*, *common* religion in which to bring them up? To be of a *catholic ſpirit*, is to unite in that one religion; not to jumble together the errors, inconſiſtencies, and hereſies of all. This muſt end in indifference. It may bring the people of the church nearer to the ſects; but the preſent times do not give us any hope, that it will bring the ſects nearer to the church.—See Bruce, v. i. p. 519—523.

TARTARS,

THEIR CUSTOMS.

1. In Kardan, a province of Tartary, as ſoon as a woman is delivered, ſhe riſes, waſhes, and dreſſes the child. Then the huſband, getting into bed with the infant, keeps it there forty days, and receives viſits *as if he* had lain in.—It ſeemeth not eaſy to account for this cuſtom. Apply this to the caſe of authors who publiſh other people's works as their own, and take the credit to themſelves; or to rectors, who value themſelves on account of the good done by their curates.

2. Various have been the diſputes, in different ages and nations, about the object of adoration. In ſome parts of Tartary, the inhabitants, to make ſhort work of it, worſhip the oldeſt man in the houſe,

houſe, as the being from whom the reſt of the family have received life and all things.—Apply this to thoſe who dote upon antiquity, as ſuch.

TEA.

The Mogul Tartars, Abbé Grozier tells us, who feed on raw fleſh, are ſubject to continual indigeſtions whenever they give over the uſe of tea.—It may be the ſame in ſome degree with all who eat ſo much animal food as we do. It is true, the work of digeſtion is made eaſier by fire, in dreſſing; but then our ſtomachs are weaker than thoſe of the Tartars. Tea ſhould not be drunk, but when there is ſomething for it to feed upon.

TEMPERANCE.

1. Carnivorous animals have more courage, and muſcular ſtrength, and activity, in proportion to their bulk; which is evident by comparing the cat-kind, as lions, tigers, and likewiſe the dog-kind, with herb-eating animals of the ſame bulk. Birds of prey excel granivorous in ſtrength and courage. I know more than one inſtance of iraſcible paſſions being much ſubdued by a vegetable diet.—Arbuthnot.

2. Imitation requires judgment to diſcern when circumſtances are parallel; becauſe, if they are not, it will be abſurd and ridioulous; as a gooſe, that ſees

 another

another goose drink, will do the same though he is not thirsty.—The custom of drinking for company, when drink is disagreeable and prejudicial, seems to be a case of the same kind, and to put a man (feathers only excepted) upon a footing with a goose.

3. The emperor of Abyssinia, at his meals, has always an officer present, whose business it is, as soon as he perceives in his imperial majesty any tendency to intemperance, to tell him of it; upon which he immediately rises from table, and retires.—See Dr. Poncet's Journey into Ethiopia, in the Jesuits' Travels by Lockman, vol. 1.

4. "You Europeans," say the Hottentots, "are "madmen. You build great houses, though your bo-"dies take up but little space: you have so great a "number of wants, in order for clothing and nour-"ishing yourselves, that, not contented with things "sufficient for yourselves in Europe, you come to this "and other countries, in order to dispossess the in-"habitants of their clothes and food. With regard "to ourselves, we want neither money nor wares: "as we neither eat nor dress after your manner, there "is nothing can oblige us to work and disturb our-"selves as you do."

5. Hippocrates and Cornaro did so much honour to physic and temperance, as to insure their bodies from the attack of any disease; nor were they mistaken.

6. Por-

6. Porphyry's comparifon is very juft, that a full meal is like Sifera's banquet, at the end of which there is a nail ftruck into a man's temples.—See Arnold on Ecclus. xxxi. 20.

7. A man who is determined, either by choice or neceffity, to drink rum and water, fhould keep a jealous eye on his *meafure*; that once violated, his palate becomes vitiated; and, if reafon is not exerted to *prevent*, it will feldom be found equal to the tafk of *correcting* a habit formed upon the ruins of fortitude.—Mofely on Tropical Difeafes, p. 55.—An admirable obfervation, deferving well to be regarded by all who drink a mixture of *any fpirit* with water—or even of *wine* and water.

TIME.

1. "No man (faith Lord Bacon) can be fo ftrait-" ened and oppreffed with bufinefs and an active " courfe of life, but he may have many vacant times " of leifure, while he expects the returns and tides " of bufinefs." The queftion is, how thefe fhall be filled up; with ftudy and contemplation, or with fenfuality and pleafure.—A man may be out of his bed for fixteen of the twenty-four hours: what might not be done in that time?" See Rambler, 108. vol. iii. p. 14.

2. " Every day is a year to a filk-worm, and has in " it the four feafons: the morning is fpring, the mid-" dle of the day is fummer, the evening autumn, and

"the night winter."—Voyages and Travels, iv. 193, from Navarette. To man life is a year, and a year is a day.—See the Idler.

3. Past scenes are generally recollected with a solemn sadness, caused by the thought, that the time is gone which will never more return. Our days must be well and profitably spent, if we would remember them with pleasure.

4. In our Christian course, it is but too generally and too truly observed, that, as we grow older, we grow colder; we become more slack, remiss, and weary in well-doing. The reverse ought to be the case, for the reason assigned by the Apostle, when, stirring up his converts to vigour, and zeal, and alacrity, he says—"For now is our salvation nearer than when we believed."—In a *race*, the *push* is made at *last*.

5. What enabled Dr. Birch to go through such a variety of undertakings was his being an early riser. By this method he had executed the business of the morning before numbers of people had begun it. And indeed, it is the peculiar advantage of rising betimes, that it is not in the power of any interruptions, avocations, or engagements whatever, to deprive a man of the hours which have already been well employed, or to rob him of the consolation of reflecting, that he hath not spent the day in vain.—Biog. Brit. ii. 323.

6. There is a traditional anecdote concerning Mr. Boyle,

Boyle, that he uſed ſometimes to have it inſcribed over his door—"Mr. Boyle is not to be ſpoken "with to-day." This was very proper in one who was often engaged in proceſſes of the utmoſt importance, and which required an unremitted attention. Indeed, if literary men, in general, could find a rational method of preventing the interruptions of needleſs morning viſitants, it would be of ſervice to the proſecution of many uſeful deſigns. Ibid. 514.

7. Cardan's motto was, "*Tempus mea poſſeſſio,* "*tempus ager meus.*"—"Time is my eſtate, my land "that I am to cultivate."—Lord, grant me ever to conſider this, and ſo to cultivate it, that it may bring forth fruit to life eternal! *Amen.*

TRIUMPH BEFORE VICTORY.

Nothing can be got, but much may be loſt, by triumphing before a battle. When Charles V. invaded France, he loſt his generals and a great part of his army by famine and diſeaſe; and returned baffled and thoroughly mortified from an enterpriſe, which he began with ſuch confidence of its happy iſſue that he deſired Paul Jovius the hiſtorian to make a large proviſion of paper ſufficient to record the victories which he was going to acquire.

TYPES.

The Mosaic types are like triangular prisms, that must be set in a due light and posture, before they can represent that great variety of spiritual mysteries contained in them. The office of the prophets was to do this, and direct the people to see in these glasses the Son of God fully represented to their view. Still. Orig. Sac. b. ii. c. 5.

VAIN CURIOSITY.

Many people, instead of minding their own business, and securing their souls, amuse themselves with enquiring what will be the fate of Heathens, Jews, Turks, and other Infidels, till they become little better than Infidels themselves—"Lord, "and what shall this man do?" "What is that to "thee? Follow thou me."

UNIVERSITIES.

1. It was a custom with the Gymnosophists, every day, at dinner, to examine their disciples, how they had spent the morning; and every one was obliged to show, that he had discharged some good office, practised some virtue, or improved in some part of learning. If nothing of this appeared, he was sent back without his dinner.—A mighty good institution,

tion, surely! Pity but it could be revived, and practised in college-halls!

2. "For one lost by his own passions," says Maty, "I have known at least forty men ruined by *not* "*being told of their danger.*" He proposes for reformation of universities—

1. Expulsion of those who will not submit to rules and orders, and a state of pupillage.

2. A rigorous exaction of the stated appearances at chapel, and in the hall.

3. To break, by varied hours of lecture, the possibility of long junketings.

4. Some feeling lectures from Plato and Epictetus on the dignity and manliness of the *boni vivere parvo*; the dependence and servility of debt; the *inelegance* and future mischiefs of promiscuous concubinage.

WIT.

1. He, who sacrifices religion to wit, like the people mentioned by Ælian, worships a fly, and offers up an ox to it.

2. Wit, like salt, should excite an appetite, not provoke disgust; cleanse wounds, not create them; be used to recommend and preserve that which is sound, not be thrown away upon that which is already rotten.

3. Wit without wisdom is salt without meat,

and that is but a comfortleſs diſh to ſet a hungry man down to. Wit, employed to diſguiſe and prejudice truth, is ſalt thrown into a man's eyes.

4. Nothing is more abſurd than to divert a man who wants to be comforted; for ſalt, though an excellent reliſher, is a miſerable cordial.

5. Jocularity ſhould not be obtruded upon company when they are not in the humour for it; as a well bred man would no more force ſalt than pepper upon his gueſts, whoſe conſtitutions it might not ſuit.

ON

THE USE OF THE HEBREW LANGUAGE,

IN A

LETTER TO THE HON. L. K.

BY W. J.

LETTER

ON

The Use of the Hebrew Language.

Nayland, Oct. 29th, 1795.

DEAR SIR,

YOU will want little persuasion to the Study of the Hebrew Language, when you know how valuable it is in itself, and what help you will find from the use of it in your other studies: for it will be of service to you as a critic, a mythologist, an antiquarian, a philosopher, and a divine. If the Hebrew were the original language (which, however, is disputed, as all other things are) the different languages of the world must partake of it more or less; and consequently they may be traced up to it. Unless a scholar is able to do this, he will be wanting in a very material part of his business: and, though I would not affront any man of learning, who is an able critic in Greek and Latin, as if he were a person of no knowlege, I am nevertheless very certain he would see much farther, and find great satisfaction, if the Hebrew were added to his other learning.

I must

I muſt leave it to the compiler of the Lexicon to collect the various inſtances in which later languages may be traced up to this original: but I will give you a ſew examples, to ſhow how eaſily it may be done, and to tempt you to find others for yourſelf at a future time.

The word *Aurum*, Gold, is Latin; which can be traced up to no Latin original: but in Hebrew the word אור *Aur* expreſſes a kindred idea; it ſignifies *Light*, to which *Gold* is more nearly allied than any other ſubſtance, from its colour and its ſplendour; and, in the ſymbolical language of the chemiſts, *Gold* ſtands for the *Sun*. When we have once obtained a leading idea in Hebrew, it is pleaſant to ſee how other words in abundance will fall in with it: for hence we have the word *Aurora*, for the light of the morning; *Horus*, a name of the ſun with the Egyptians; *Orion*, the bright conſtellation, the brighteſt in the heavens; ωραι and ωραιος, beautiful; becauſe the light is the moſt beautiful of all things; ουρανος, the heaven; and many others. So ſimple is the Hebrew, and ſo perfect in its conſtruction, that even light itſelf is not an *original* ſenſe; for אור is from אר, a biliteral root, which ſignifies *to flow*; light being in perpetual flux, and the moſt perfect of all fluids; perhaps the only *abſolute* fluid in nature.

Nothing is more common than for large families of words to arrange themſelves under ſome ſimple root in the Hebrew. Thus the words *fruit*, *fructus*, *fertilis*, *fero* in Latin, φερω in Greek, *Freya* the

Northern goddefs of fertility (whence our *Fryday*) all come from the Hebrew פרה FeRA, to *bear fruit*. Even in the Englifh tongue, where you would little fufpect it, the Hebrew word will account for the Englifh. What is the word *Sweat* but the זעת *Zet* of the Hebrew? *Cypher* in Englifh, is ספר SePheR in Hebrew; *dumb* in Englifh, is דום *to be ftill*: *Shiver* in Englifh is in Hebrew שבר Sheber or Shever, to *break* in pieces: *Hufh*, be ftill, is from השה HaSHaH, to be filent: *Track* is from the Hebrew דרך DRaCH a *way*, which in Arabic is *taracq*: *Earth* is from ארץ AReTZ or EReTZ, a word of the fame fenfe. *Is* in Englifh, and εςι in Greek, and *effe* and *eft* in Latin, are all from the Hebrew יש *Subftance*: *Shed* is from the Hebrew שד, to pour out. In Latin words, which have no affinity with any other word, the like agreement is frequently difcovered with the Hebrew. The word *olim*, hereafter, or long ago, is not a word of a Latin form, but is the fame with עלם Olem *an age, ever*, &c. Thus in Greek the word χιτων, tunica, admits of no Greek derivation, but כתן CheTeN in Hebrew has the fame fenfe.

In multitudes of Greek words, where the Lexicons force an etymology upon them, their deduction from the Hebrew is evident and natural. In their mythology nothing is more common than for the Greeks to ufe terms of which their own language knows nothing. Their religion was more antient than themfelves; and fo has many names which their own language was not antient enough to interpret; though they often

often attempt it in an absurd and ridiculous manner. What can we make of the word Σειρηνες, *Sirens*, first mentioned by Homer, as Nymphs that enchant and destroy men with their *singing?* The Lexicons derive it from σειρα a chain, which is nonsense; but go to the Hebrew, and you find that שיר SYeR is *a Song*, and will therefore very naturally give a name to *Singers.*

Mulciber, one of the names of Vulcan, the god of fire (the same in character with the *Moloch* of the East) which the Latins account for from *mulcendo ferrum*, because they will needs have it from their own language: but it is such Latin as never was used; and besides, *f* never changes into *b*, in the syllable *ber*, but the change is the contrary way. All is plain enough, if we go back to the original Vulcan, which is *Moloch*; for then the word *Mulciber* becomes מלך Melech אביר Abir, the Mighty King, which is Moloch. All the deities, which are many, whose names give them an alliance with Moloch, are from the Hebrew *Melech*, a king; such as *Adramelech*, *Anamelech*, *Milcom*, *Milicus*, &c. *Melicartus*, the Tyrian Hercules, is of no sense in Greek or Latin; but in the Hebrew it resolves itself into מלך ארץ *Melech Aretz*, King of the Earth.

Saturnus, the god Saturn, and the *Satyri* of the woods, are names to which the Latin can give no interpretation: but if *Saturn*, according to his physical character, be taken for that secret *first matter* of Nature, out of which all *forms* arise, and into which they

they are again resolved; and if *Satyrs* are considered as beings hiding themselves in woods and mountains; then they are all accounted for from the Hebrew סתר SaTaR, to hide: and even the discourse called a *Satire*, in which the meaning is always obscure and hidden, is best derived from the same word סתר SaTaR, to hide; as I remember I once mentioned to Dr. Johnson, and he affirmed the derivation to be right. Near of kin to this is the Egyptian *Isis*, the first matter of the world, from the Hebrew יש, *substance*. This first matter is concealed under the *forms* or species of things, and never to be discovered as it is in itself; to signify which the image of Isis had a *veil* on.

They, who have no practice in the pursuit of etymologies, will hardly believe with what reason and certainty a derivation may be hunted down, which at first sight appears very wild and remote.—אש, *Ash*, or *Esh*, in Hebrew signifies *burning fire*. (whence our word *ashes*) Now it seems rash to say that the Latin *Vesta* is from the Hebrew *Ash*; but it is plainly so: for from the original *Ash* is the dialectical Chaldee אשתא *Ashta*, whence the Greek Εςια, and thence (with the soft *F* prefixed, as in *vinum* from οινος) is the Latin *Vesta*.

In accounting for customs which we find in antiquity, we shall often be much at a loss, unless we are prepared to have recourse to the Hebrew. When you read in Xenophon, that the *war-shout* or signal for battle was ελελευ, this word being not Greek, you

 may

may take it for an unmeaning, barbarous outcry, like the *war-whoop* among the American Indians: but it is no other than the antient Hebrew acclamation *Hallelu,* ſo often repeated in ſongs of praiſe. It is alſo written αλαλευ; and was probably the cuſtomary acclamation for mutual encouragement in the wars of the Hebrews with the Heathen nations of Canaan; from whom the later Heathens took it.

The *Phœnicians* ſpoke very nearly the ſame language with the Hebrews; and Virgil acted with judgment in giving Phœnician names to Phœnician people in his poem. The name *Dido* is the *beloved one,* from the ſame root with דוד DUD or *David*; her other name, *Eliza,* is one of the Hebrew names of the New Teſtament; and her ſiſter *Anna,* is the Hebrew *Hannah* of the Scripture. In Salluſt, &c. the famous name of *Hannibal* is Hebrew, and ſignifies *Gracious Lord,* or *my gracious Lord: Hiempſal* is ימשל Imeſhal, *he ſhall reign,* or *be a Ruler*; and there are other like names which can only be interpreted in the ſame way. In one of the plays of Plautus (the *Pœnulus*) a Carthaginian is brought upon the ſtage, as we ſhould bring a Frenchman, to laugh at his broken Engliſh. The language he is there made to ſpeak was taken for unmeaning gibberiſh; till *Bochart* was able, by a moſt happy ſtroke of criticiſm, to interpret it throughout, from the affinity of the Carthaginian to the Hebrew. As the antiquity which is moſt remote brings us nearer to the time when all men ſpoke ſome dialect of the Hebrew, it is impoſſible to interpret the ancient names of perſons and people, but from a familiarity with the Hebrew. The Greeks derived themſelves from a moſt antient anceſtor by the name of *Japetus:* and who can he be, but their real anceſtor *Japhet?* Their *Letters* were derived to them from the Eaſt; and the tradition is preſerved under the fabulous perſon of *Cadmus*; which is from קדום Cadom, the *Eaſt*, or, *a man of the Eaſt*. Every body knows there was ſuch a city as Babylon; but the Hebrew reader only knows it had its original from the word *Babel*, which being interpreted means *in confuſion*, becauſe language was there firſt confounded: and, to this day, a man that talks unintelligibly or nonſenſically, is ſaid in Engliſh to *babble*.

In Divinity it often happens, in particular caſes, that you cannot ſo well judge what is right or what is wrong, nor detect the perverſe gloſſes of wanton or evil minded critics, unleſs you are well enough acquainted with the Hebrew to uſe ſome critical judgment in it: of which Mr. Parkhurſt's pamphlet againſt Prieſtley is a remarkable inſtance, and opens a mine of evidence, which that juggler knows not what to make of. We live in an age fond of novelty; when literary adventurers are rather too free and bold in their experiments upon the Sacred Text. Dr. Kennicott promiſed great things, and raiſed the expectations of the public. His pretenſions were examined and diſputed by ſome perſons who were learned in the Hebrew; and we narrowly eſcaped

 the

the danger of a new text and new verſion. On any future occaſion of the ſame kind, the like danger may not be eſcaped, if the Hebrew language, and its ſcholaſtic hiſtory, ſhould be neglected.

When we conſult Mr. Parkhurſt's Hebrew Lexicon, it is pleaſant to ſee how many paſſages of Scripture are illuſtrated; how many difficulties cleared up by the author: and whoever follows his example, will ſoon diſcover how much his proſpects are enlarged when he ſtudies the Bible in the original. He that ſhould read the New Teſtament in the Greek, and be under the neceſſity of taking all his knowlege of it from the Latin of the Vulgate, would be thought very deficient in his Learning: and the caſe is parallel, if, in the interpretation of the Old Teſtament, we are unable to compare the Greek verſion of the Septuagint with the original Hebrew; which it is often neceſſary to do. Many diſcoveries ariſe, if this compariſon is faithfully made: among other things it appears, from the different manner in which the Greek Tranſlators have pronounced many proper names, that they did not tranſlate from a copy with the preſent Vowel Points *, ſuch as are uſed by the Jews; againſt whom we are to provide ourſelves

* The *Hexapla* of Origen is a work to which I have at preſent no acceſs; but I ſet down what I ſuppoſe to be a faithful account of it. He gives the Hebrew Text in Greek letters: wherein he "uniformly expreſſes what the Maſorites call the quieſcent letters, "the *Aleph*, *He*, *Vau*, and *Jod*, by *Vowels*; but ſo variouſly, that it "is clear he conſidered it to be a matter of indifference by what "vowel,

ourſelves with weapons, as againſt the moſt dangerous enemies of the Goſpel: and who, but a *Hebrew Chriſtian*, can be a match for them in their own way? In the New Teſtament there is a ſort of Greek, which cannot be reconciled with ordinary Greek authors: becauſe there is a frequent uſe of ſuch forms of language (we call them *Idioms*) as are transferred to the Greek from the Hebrew of the Old Teſtament, and which cannot otherwiſe be accounted for.

But now, laſtly, I recommend the Hebrew chiefly on this conſideration; becauſe the language is *in itſelf* inſtructive: its words give us light into *things*, in a manner different from thoſe of any other language in the world: and this, beyond all other arguments, convinces me of its divine original. I will give you ſome examples.—The word *clothe*, in Latin *veſtio*, in Greek ενδυω, gives us no inſtruction; but the Hebrew לבש LeBeSH *to clothe*, comprehends the idea of בש BeSH *Shame*, (whence the Engliſh *baſhful* and *abaſh*) and, with the ל prefixed, it is *for*, or on account of *ſhame*: ſo the *term* not only ſtands for the *thing*, as in other languages, but gives us the *reaſon* of the thing; it refers us to the *moral* hiſtory and origin of clothing; and all this in three letters.

" vowel he ſhould denote them. He always treats the *Ain* and " *Heth* as vowels: and, when two conſonants occur, he ſeems to " have conſidered it optional, what vowel he ſhould admit between " them. All this is diametrically oppoſite to the ſyſtem of the " Maſorites." Horæ Biblicæ, p. 77.

 The

The English word *hail*, in Latin *grando*, in Greek χάλαζα, gives us no information about the nature of the thing: but, if we take the word ברד BeReD in Hebrew, as we took LeBeSH, it resolves itself into רד—ב, which signifies *in descensu*, and so describes to us the physiological formation of hail; which, as philosophers agree, is first formed into drops of rain, and, *as it falls*, is frozen into hail *.

In roots of the Hebrew language, which consist mostly of two letters, some idea is taken from nature; and the word, with some new modification, is carried on, and applied to other objects: and, if there were no other argument, this alone would convince me that the Hebrew, from the simple fabrication of its terms, is not only the first of languages, but of a construction beyond the invention of human wisdom. Thus, for example, the word צלם Tzelem signifies an *image*: but why so? because צל Tzel is a *shadow*, the first of images, such as nature itself makes: the light of the sun forms it naturally, and presents it to the sight of man. In many words, two ideas are comprehended, because they are found together in nature. It is impossible for us, in many cases, from our imperfect knowlege of things, to account for and reconcile the kindred senses of Hebrew words;

* When a Gentleman very learned in the Hebrew saw this account of ברד, he observed upon it that בין an Egg was such another word compounded of ב and יצא; for it is remarkable in the physiology of the egg, that the shell acquires its hardness *in exitu*, as it comes forth.

but

but in many the reaſon of them is too plain to be contradicted. The word ראש RASH ſignifies the *Head*, and it ſignifies *Poiſon*; and the relation appears in nature, which has placed the moſt deadly of *poiſons* in the *head* of the Serpent: a creature of great ſignification in Hebrew doctrine. I do not ſee that this reaſon is aſſigned by the learned Mr. Parkhurſt; but I find it in *Marius—Sunt qui dicunt ſic appellari, eo quod venenum ſit in capite aſpidis.*

The ſame word which ſignifies the *hoar-froſt* ſignifies to *cover*; becauſe the hoar-froſt is a ſudden and univerſal covering ſpread over the face of the ground. The word alſo ſignifies an *atonement*; by which, as it appears from ſeveral paſſages of the Scripture, either the face of the perſon offended is underſtood to be covered, ſo that he no longer looks upon the offence; or the ſin itſelf is ſo covered that it can no longer be ſeen, and even aſſumes a new appearance from the nature and quality of the covering; juſt as the face of the earth becomes white and pure when the hoar-froſt is upon it: which conveys a very beautiful and pleaſant idea of atonement and propitiation. All this is expreſſed by the word כפר CaPHaR; whence is plainly derived our Engliſh word *cover*. This term admits of an accident, which may ſeem to contradict our ſyſtem of *kindred ideas*, but does really confirm it. The word which ſignifies hoar-froſt does alſo ſignify *pitch*; the one as white as ſnow, the other as black as a coal: but the leading idea of *covering* is ſtill preſerved, for pitch is the moſt effectual covering in the world to keep out water and weather. In *Gen.* vi. 14. it is applied to the covering of Noah's ark; and the reader will find that the *pitch* and the *covering* are both expressed by the same word.

גל GaL is a root which, as a verb, signifies to *roll round*, or circulate; and, as a noun, any *round thing*. Hence it signifies to *dance*; because the motions of the dance were circular, to imitate the motions of the heavenly bodies. It signifies also to be *glad*; because gladness is that way expressed. And likewise a *wheel*, from its form and its *revolution*; and particularly the watering wheel of the East, which yields its water by a circulation: Solomon is supposed to have used this term in that famous allegory of Eccles. xii. with an allusion to the circulation of the blood in the human body, which ceases in death: the passage is well worth considering. Hence also we have a name for the human *skull* *, from the roundness of its figure; and also for the *thistle down*, or winged seed, because it is a light round body, and has a rotation as it rolls along before the wind. And I may add, what is as curious as any thing, that the root in question gives us the word גלם GeLeM, which signifies the human fœtus or embryo; and with philosophical propriety, because in that the body is rolled up or folded together. From *Gelem* comes the word *glomus* a ball of thread, and *glomero* to wind about or gather together.

* Hence the word *Golgotha* in the New Testament.

How

How ſimple is the conſtruction of that language, which, beginning with the prepoſition על OL, *upon* or *over*, adds another letter, and turns it into a verb, עלה *OLaH*, to aſcend; which, becoming a noun, ſignifies a *burnt offering*; teaching us to conſider it as an *aſcenſion*, becauſe the ſmoke and flame of it goes up towards heaven, which cannot happen unleſs it is conſumed by fire; on which much might be ſaid! The barbarous people of Madagaſcar have a ſacrifice which they call an *Owley*; retaining the very word of the Moſaic law. From the ſame root we have a word for the *wild goat* of the mountains, from its climbing upwards; alſo for the *leaf of a tree*, from its ſuperior ſituation; whence, with the *f*, or digamma prefixed, we have the Latin *folium*. It furniſhes us alſo with a word for *ſtairs*, becauſe people aſcend by them; and for a *lord* or ruler, becauſe he is *over* others: in alliance with which we have one of the names of God, עליון *Olion*, becauſe he is *over all*; and it is rendered by the word *Altiſſimus* in Latin, in Engliſh the *Moſt High*.

Compare this ſet of words with one another in Latin, and you will find neither root, branch, nor relation among them. *Super* has no alliance with *ſcando*; nor *ſcando* with *gradus*; nor *gradus* with *folium*; nor *folium* with *altus*; nor *altus* with *rupicapra*: every word, when compared with the reſt, is an unrelated individual; and the caſe would be found the ſame in the Greek, or any other language of more modern uſe and invention: ſo that when I

 view

view the Hebrew language, ſuch as I have now repreſented it to you, (in too ſmall a compaſs for the greatneſs of the ſubject) I am perſuaded it muſt either have been originally given to man by his Creator; or framed by men, the powers of whoſe minds were very different from our own.

But give me leave to forewarn you, that caution is to be uſed, and great experience is requiſite, in order to handle the Hebrew with ſafety; otherwiſe you may chance to make that ridiculous, which you intend to magnify. For want of knowing better, we may give *the lead* to a *wrong idea*; that which is not the radical one; and then we ſhall be forced upon ſtrange and unnatural alliances; and, from our imperfect inſight into many things, we may not be able to diſcover that there is any leading idea at all. It is natural to follow with too much aſſurance the alluring purſuits of *etymology*; and, if we are found to do it without temperance or diſcretion, we ſhall find no mercy from thoſe who are not well affected to the originalities of learning and religion; who may therefore treat us with a ſmile, meaning it for the ſmile of ſuperior wiſdom: but folly and ignorance are more given to ſmile than wiſdom and ſcience.

I have ſaid enough to convince you, that the ſtudy of Hebrew, if you uſe it properly, will abundantly repay your labour; that it is even neceſſary and eſſential, if you would be, what I may call (to ſpeak after the Hebrew ſtyle) a *radical* ſcholar, and ſee into the originals of things both ſacred and

profane:

profane: that it is related to itſelf by aſſociations and images, not merely curious, but often very beautiful and inſtructive: in ſhort, that it communicates knowlege of the beſt kind under a ſingular form, no where elſe to be met with. I could have multiplied my examples in abundance; for there was a time of my life when I ſat for half a year together to compare the Hebrew language with itſelf in every word of it (ſo far as it is retained and preſerved) and I have loved and admired it ever ſince. You will do the ſame, if you take half as much pains as I did: and, for your encouragement, you will have an advantage which I had not; later years having produced that excellent work the Lexicon Hebrew and Engliſh of Mr. Parkhurſt; who has made it a magazine of general learning, antiquity, divinity, and natural hiſtory; and has illuſtrated his Hebrew literature from the Greek and Roman claſſics, and from uſeful authors antient and modern, of every denomination.

In the modern Hebrew learning, you have another advantage, and a great one it is; that you are taken out of the hands of the *Jews*; who begin their teaching with the egregious abſurdity of an alphabet without vowels, to make way for their Hebrew points, which are a modern invention, and overburthen you with an inſupportable multiplicity of rules. Their notions of the Hebrew are much of a ſize with their ſenſe of divinity. That noble inſtrument of wiſdom, in their hands, is like an inſtrument of aſtronomy in the hands of a child, or

like

like a telescope with the blind. Trust yourself to Mr. Parkhurst, a good *Christian*, and he will take you by the hand at the first step, and carry you as far as you will wish to go in CHRISTIAN HEBREW. That your success may be such as I augurate from a foreknowlege of your capacity and application is the sincere wish of,

Dear Sir,

Your affectionate friend,

and obedient, humble servant,

W. JONES.

A CHRO-

A

CHRONOLOGICAL CATALOGUE

OF THE

WRITINGS

OF THE

RIGHT REVEREND GEORGE HORNE, D.D.

LATE LORD BISHOP OF NORWICH.

1751. THE Theology and Philosophy in Cicero's *Somnium Scipionis* explained; or, A brief Attempt to demonstrate, that the Newtonian System is perfectly agreeable to the Notions of the wisest Ancients; and that Mathematical Principles are the only sure ones. 8vo. London.

1753. A fair, candid, and impartial State of the Case between Sir Isaac Newton and Mr. Hutchinson; in which is shewn, how far a System of Physics is capable of Mathematical Demonstration; how far Sir Isaac's, as such a System, has that Demonstration; and, consequently, what regard Mr. Hutchinson's Claim may deserve to have paid it. 8vo. Oxford.—Reprinted in 8vo. 1799.

1754. Spicilegium Shuckfordianum; or, A Nosegay for the Critics. Being some choice Flowers of Modern Theology and Criticism, gathered out of Dr. Shuckford's Supplemental Discourse on the Creation and Fall of Man: not forgetting Bishop Garnet's *Vatikra*. Duod. London.

1755. Christ and the Holy Ghost the Supporters of the Spiritual Life, Prov. xx. 27; and Repentance the Forerunner of Faith, Isai. xl, 3, 4, 5;—two Sermons preached before the University of Oxford; the former at St. Mary's, on Sunday, April

April 13; the latter in St. Mary Magdalen College Chapel, on St. John Baptist's Day, 1755. 8vo. Oxford.

1756. The Almighty glorified in Judgment, Rev. xi. 13, 14; —a Sermon preached before the University of Oxford, on Sunday, February 15, 1756. Preached also before the Mayor and Corporation of the City of Oxford, and at several other Places, on Occasion of the late Earthquakes and Public Fast. 8vo. Oxford.

1756. An Apology for certain Gentlemen in the University of Oxford, aspersed in a late anonymous Pamphlet; with a short Postscript concerning another Pamphlet lately published by the Rev. Mr. Heathcote. 8vo. Oxford.—Reprinted in 8vo. 1799, with an introductory Preface.

1760. A View of Mr. Kennicott's Method of correcting the Hebrew Text, with Three Queries formed thereupon, and humbly submitted to the Christian World. 8vo. Oxford.

1761. * The Christian King, 1 Pet. ii. 21; a Sermon preached before the University of Oxford, at St. Mary's, January 30, 1761. 8vo. Oxford.

1761. * Works wrought through Faith, a Condition of our Justification, James ii. 24; preached before the University of Oxford, June 7, 1761. 8vo. Oxford.

1762. * Mercy to those who are of the Household of Faith, Lament. v. 3; preached before the Sons of the Clergy in the Cathedral Church of St. Paul, May 6, 1762. 4to and 8vo. London.

1772. Considerations on the Life and Death of St. John the Baptist. 8vo. Oxford.—A Second Edition in duod. was printed at Oxford in 1777.

1772. Considerations on the projected Reformation of the Church of England. In a Letter to the Right Honourable Lord North. By a Clergyman. 4to. London.

1773. * The influence of Christianity on Civil Society, Tit. ii. 11, 12; preached at St. Mary's in Oxford at the Assizes, March 4, 1773. 8vo. Oxford.

1774. * The Good Steward, Acts xx. 35; preached in the Chapel

Chapel of the Asylum for Female Orphans, at the Anniversary Meeting of the Guardians of that Charity, May 19, 1774. 4to. London.

1775. * Christ the Object of Religious Adoration, and therefore very God, Rom. x. 13; preached before the University of Oxford, at St. Mary's, May 14, 1775. 8vo. Oxford.

1775. * The Providence of God manifested in the Rise and Fall of Empires, 1 Sam. ii. 30; preached at St. Mary's in Oxford, at the Assizes, July 27, 1775. 8vo. Oxford.

1776. A Commentary on the Book of Psalms; in which their literal and historical Sense, as they relate to King David and the People of Israel, is illustrated; and their Application to Messiah, to the Church, and to Individuals as Members thereof, is pointed out; with a View to render the Use of the Psalter pleasing and profitable to all Orders and Degrees of Christians. 2 Vols. 4to. Oxford.——A Second Edition was published at Oxford in 1778, in 2 vols. 8vo.—and three Editions more have since been printed; besides one at Perth in 3 vols. duod.

1777. A Letter to Adam Smith, LL.D. on the Life, Death, and Philosophy of his Friend David Hume, Esq. By one of the People called Christians. Duod. Oxford. Four Editions of this Piece have been printed.

1779. Discourses on several Subjects and Occasions. 2 Vols. 8vo. Oxford.—These Discourses have passed through Five Editions.

1780. * Fast Sermon, Deut. xxiii. 9; preached before the Honourable House of Commons, at the Church of St. Margaret, Westminster, February 4, 1780. 4to. Oxford.

1781. * Fast Sermon, Isai. xxvi. 9; preached before the University of Oxford, at St. Mary's, February 21, 1781. 4to. Oxford.

1783. * The blessed Effects of Perseverance, 2 Thess. iii. 13; preached in the Cathedral Church of St. Paul, before the Society for promoting Christian Knowlege, June 12, 1783. 4to. London.

1784.

1784. * The Antiquity, Uſe, and Excellence of Church Muſic, Pſalm lvii. 8; preached at the opening of a new Organ in the Cathedral Church of Chriſt, Canterbury, July 8, 1784. 4to. Oxford.

1784. * The Character of true Wiſdom, and the Means of attaining it, Prov. iv. 7; preached in the Cathedral Church of Chriſt, Canterbury, before the Society of Gentlemen educated in the King's School, Canterbury, Auguſt 26, 1784. 4to. Oxford.

1784. Letters on Infidelity. Duod. Oxford.—A Second Edition, with the Fifth Edition of the Letter to Dr. Adam Smith, was printed at Oxford, duod. 1786.

1785. * Sunday Schools recommended, Pſalm xxxiv. 11; preached in the Pariſh Church of St. Alphage, Canterbury, December 18, 1785. 4to. Oxford, 1786.

1786. * The Duty of contending for the Faith, Jude, ver. 3; preached at the Primary Viſitation of the moſt Reverend John Lord Archbiſhop of Canterbury, in the Cathedral and Metropolitical Church, July 1, 1786.—To which is ſubjoined a Diſcourſe on the Trinity in Unity, Matt. xxviii. 19; preached in the Cathedral on Trinity Sunday, 1786. 4to. Oxford.

*** Theſe two Sermons were printed together in Duod. 1788, by the Society for promoting Chriſtian Knowlege, and are in the Catalogue of Books diſtributed by that Society.

1787. A Letter to the Rev. Dr. Prieſtley, by an Undergraduate.—A Second Edition was printed in the ſame year.

1788. * Charity recommended on its true Motive, 1 John, iv. 11; preached at St. George's, Bloomſbury, before the Governors of the benevolent Inſtitution for the Delivery of Poor Married Women at their own Habitations, March 30, 1788. 4to. Oxford.

1790. Obſervations on the Caſe of the Proteſtant Diſſenters, with Reference to the Corporation and Teſt Acts. 8vo. Oxford.

1791. A Charge intended to have been delivered to the Clergy of Norwich at the Primary Viſitation.—Two Editions 4to.

1794.

1794. Discourses (Posthumous) on several Subjects and Occasions. Vol. 3d and 4th, 8vo. Oxford.—A Second Edition has been since printed.

The Sixteen Sermons marked * have been collected into one volume 8vo, and were printed at Oxford in the year 1795.

To this Catalogue may be added, the Letters in the Gentleman's Magazine for 1752 and 1753, signed *Ingenuus*, in Reply to the Letters of Candidus, on the Controversy concerning the Cherubim; the greater Part of the Preface to Dr. Dodd's Translation of Callimachus, published in 1755; the Letters in the St. James's Chronicle, commencing January 1, 1767, under the Title of The Miscellany, by Nathanael Freebody; the Republication of Dean Stanhope's Edition of the Translation of Bishop Andrews's Devotions, from the Greek, with a recommendatory Preface by Bishop Horne; the Academy of Abstraction, a Vision, in the General Evening Post, August 31, 1771; Remarks on Voltaire's Pupil of Nature, in the same Paper, September 12, 1771; a Letter on the *Confessional*, signed Clericus, August 17, 1771; another, with the same Signature, and on the same Subject, September 19, 1771; a Modest Proposal, humbly offered to the Consideration of the Legislature, printed on a Folio Sheet without Signature or Date; the Papers signed Z in the Olla Podrida, a periodical Publication, conducted by Mr. Monro, then A. B. and Demy of Magdalen College, and printed at Oxford in 1787, since reprinted (1788) in an 8vo Volume; an Abridgment of the Aurifodina of Drexelius; a short Account of Bishop Andrews, and some other pieces printed in the Second Volume of the Scholar Armed; and the Cautions to the Readers of Mr. Law, together with the Specimens of Poetry, and Thoughts on various Subjects, subjoined to these Memoirs of the Bishop's Life, Studies, and Writings,

This Catalogue is as exact as we can, at present, make it; but we know that the Bishop published several other detached Pieces, of which we cannot yet give an accurate Account.

FINIS.

PRINTED BY J. DAVIS, CHANCERY-LANE.

Lately Publiſhed,

And to be had of the Bookſellers whoſe Names are in the Title Page,

---

1. An APOLOGY for certain Gentlemen in the Univerſity of Oxford, &c. By GEORGE HORNE, D.D. late Lord Biſhop of Norwich, with a new Introductory Preface. Price 1s. 6d. 2d Edit.

2. A Fair, Candid, and Impartial STATE of the CASE between Sir Iſaac Newton and Mr. Hutchinſon. By the ſame Author. 1s. 6d. 2d Edit.

3. A DISCOURSE on the Uſe and Intention of ſome remarkable Paſſages of the Scripture, not commonly underſtood. By WILLIAM JONES, M.A. 1s.

4. A LETTER to Three Converted Jews lately baptized and confirmed in the Church of England. By the ſame Author. 1s.

5. A LETTER to the Church of England, by an old Friend and Servant of the Church. 1s.

6. A TREATISE on the Nature and Conſtitution of the Chriſtian Church; wherein are ſet forth the Form of its Government, the Extent of its Powers, and the Limits of our Obedience. By WILLIAM STEVENS, Eſq. 2d Edit. 1s.

7. THE EXCELLENCY OF THE CHURCH OF ENGLAND, AND THE UNREASONABLENESS OF SEPARATION FROM IT: A Sermon preached in the Pariſh Church of Enford, Wilts, July 29, 1798. By JOHN PRINCE, A. B. Vicar of the Pariſh. To which is prefixed An ADDRESS to the PARISHIONERS. 2d Edit. 1s.

www.ingramcontent.com/pod-product-compliance
Lightning Source LLC
Chambersburg PA
CBHW022007110726
47901CB00006B/1433

* 9 7 8 3 3 3 7 7 2 4 4 5 0 *